# Charlie O

# Charlie O

BY **HERB MICHELSON**

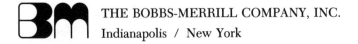 THE BOBBS-MERRILL COMPANY, INC.
Indianapolis / New York

*For Gloria,*
*who gave me a little hell*
*and a lot of love,*
*neither of which hurt at all.*

# Table of Contents

# Prologue

Pious Alvin Dark, fired as manager of the Kansas City Athletics in August, 1967, and hired as manager of the Oakland Athletics in February, 1974, said at the press conference to announce his Finleyesque resurrection that age, experience, and the Bible had finally taught him "how to get along with anyone." Dark was then fifty-two years old and, he said, would be a better man and a better manager. At his first players' meeting with the world champions in the clubhouse of Rendezvous Park in Mesa, Arizona, on March 4, 1974, Dark is reported to have said, in part: "Charlie Finley is the owner and general manager of this team, and he'll be calling me and telling me things he wants me to do. I'll put up with the phone calls as long as I can, and I'll do what he wants."

Outfielder Reggie Jackson, the American League's Most Valuable Player and World Series star in 1973, is reported to have responded, in part: "Fuck Charlie Finley. We'll win it again, anyway."

There were reports of raucous cheering. One player said he caught a hint of a smile by Alvin Dark, who later at the same team meeting asked the players to restrict their obscenities to the clubhouse.

# Introduction

A chain of California newspapers (the *Bees* of Sacramento, Fresno, and Modesto) hired me on a part-time basis to cover all the home games of the Athletics when the team moved from Kansas City to Oakland in 1968. I had not covered sports since college (Indiana University *Daily Student*, 1950–53) but was a devotee of the Chicago Cubs and baseball itself. My last newspaper job before the A's assignment was as a movie-drama critic, which I later learned to value as a prerequisite for observing Charles O. Finley and his baseball team. In subsequent seasons of A's-watching, I met the Owner and General Manager several times in the course of my duties. Not until 1970, when he flew me to Chicago for a five-hour interview and offered me the job of team public relations director, did I ever talk to Mr. Finley at any length. At the time of the job offer, I thought the interview might evolve into a magazine story. My intentions of actually taking the position were minimal. A former vice president of the A's, Bill Cutler, had warned me about Finley's hard, congenial sell. Charlie did not seem to be the kind of man for whom I would want to work. But Cutler had said, "Be careful. He might talk you into it. With Charlie Finley, it's like touching wet paint." I did not touch, and later decided against doing the magazine piece on the perhaps-misguided idea that such a story would be unfair to a man who was sincere in paying my expenses to Chicago for an honest-to-goodness job interview. My next major contact with the Owner came during the planning stages for press services at the 1972 American League playoffs and World Series. As an officer of the Baseball Writers Association local chapter, it was necessary for me to coordinate media seating, feeding, et al with the ball club. The same situation occurred a year later. Each time, I had certain petty beefs with Mr. Finley, but neither year's toil was acrimonious. And so, for a period of six years, I had a casual but not unpleasant relationship with the Owner.

After the publisher of this book contracted with me in early 1974, I wrote to Mr. Finley in Chicago informing him of the project and asking for an interview appointment in Chicago, or Oakland, or at the A's spring training grounds in Mesa, Arizona, wherever and whenever was convenient for him. I sent the letter in mid-February and did not receive an answer.

On February 20, the Owner was in Oakland to unveil his new manager, Alvin Dark, at a press conference. Following the coronation I spoke with Finley and asked if he had received my letter. He said he had not. I explained that I was doing a biography. He said he had no desire to talk to me. He said he had turned down many book involvements through the years. It was nothing personal, he said, but he just simply wouldn't talk about his life.

On March 12 I again wrote to his Chicago insurance company office restating my desire to interview him in connection with the biography. I tried flattery: ". . . would appreciate hearing firsthand the story of your estimable self-made success. The book would not be complete without your comments about your contributions to the game of baseball. . . . I am not taking your refusal to be interviewed personally. You and I have always enjoyed cordial, professional relations. But, in my mind, it is unquestionably to your advantage to discuss your life on your own terms, and with your own perceptive insights. In a month of research, I have amassed some excellent material—much of it quite favorable to you as a person and baseball executive—that begs your commentary."

There was no response.

I saw him next in June in Oakland. He was the defendant in a civil matter (Cutler was trying to recover back wages), and I spent most of four days in the courtroom watching him. He spent a little bit of the four days watching me. Neither of us discussed the book.

Meanwhile, the front office personnel of the Athletics also turned down interview requests. Even one of the team doctors refused. The players, though, had been extremely cooperative, during both spring training and the regular season. Only one of them asked not to be quoted by name. I had also been calling relatives of Finley and not getting much of a response.

On July 8, I watched the A's end the fifteen-game winning streak of Cleveland pitcher Gaylord Perry in a remarkably exciting game. My story for the *Bee* papers noted that a crowd of nearly forty-eight thousand (half-price night) had seen "brilliant, tense, important, fascinating, fun baseball. In the end, what they saw was Charlie Finley baseball. Give the A's Owner his due. Somehow, without even being in the ball park or the state or the West, Charles O. Finley took away the night from Gaylord Perry with a pair of Washingtons—a sprinter named Herb and a hitter named Claudell. . . ." Finley's pinch runner, Herb Washington, had used his speed to tie the game; Finley's recently promoted minor leaguer, Claudell Washington, singled home the winning run in the tenth inning.

At ten the next morning, Finley telephoned. He asked for my home address and zip code. He said he was sending me an order to cease and desist writing the book. He said he had told me once

that he didn't want me to write it. He said that when he was ready
*he* was going to write his story. I told him that he had no right to
tell me what to do, that all he had said to me in our February
conversation was that he would not be interviewed for the book.
He asked again for my zip code. (I gave him the zip code number,
94610, each time he asked.)

He had learned that I was leaving in a few days for a research
trip to Gary, Indiana, where I had an appointment to tour his
former place of employment, an old mill at United States Steel. He
said I had no right to go to the steel mill talking to people, no right
calling his relatives on the phone. He said he was going to put a
stop to it. I asked if the lawyer who was going to send me the
cease-and-desist order was in Chicago or Oakland. He would not
tell me. He said he knew he couldn't tell me what to eat for lunch
but that he could tell me to stop writing the book. When I said
angrily that he had no legal recourse to prevent my writing, he said
I shouldn't get mad, that he was calling me as "a courtesy."

At that point, I thought of using a line I'd picked up in an
interview with an insurance customer of Finley. This man frankly
can't stand Charlie and told me of once having a shouting match
with the Owner. "Charlie shrieked his usual string of obscenities at
me," the man recalled, "and then I yelled back at him. 'I don't let
anyone talk to me like that, and as far as I'm concerned, you're just
anyone.' That seemed to upset him."

I did not use the line, for Charlie quickly changed the subject to
the Gaylord Perry game. He wondered if I didn't think it was as
exciting as, say, a World Series or playoff game. I told him I agreed
and recounted the point of my story—that Charlie had beaten
Gaylord with the Washingtons. He said he knew what I meant.
"Did you really write that?" I told him I did and that I had not
written in mocking tones either. He thanked me, said I was an

honest writer, that he was glad to find an honest writer. He asked once more for my zip code and hung up.

I did not receive a cease-and-desist order. I did go to Gary, Indiana. I talked to another relative while I was there.

Charlie must control, and when he can't he must try intimidation. I am no tough guy, but I do not want to be controlled or intimidated. By anyone. And as far as I'm concerned, Charlie is anyone.

We saw one another at the Oakland Coliseum at two games in late August. I did not speak; he did not speak. I glared; he glared. Then I finished writing the following sort-of biography of Charles O. Finley, Owner and General Manager of the Oakland Athletics.

HERB  MICHELSON

Oakland and San Geronimo, California
March, 1975.

# Charlie O

**1**

# THE FORMULA

The job interview was in its second hour. Charles Oscar Finley had spent most of the time since I arrived in his office early on a Saturday morning talking on the telephone. It was godawful cold in Chicago, and I had come to town without an overcoat, because I didn't own one, and without a belt for my trousers, because I'd forgotten. He was talking contract with Reggie Jackson, one of his stars, and Ron Clark, a fringe infielder. The office of the Charles O. Finley Company, on Chicago's Michigan Avenue, was adorned with baseball memorabilia—uniforms, photos, balls, bats, a piece of elephant statuary symbolizing the old Philadelphia Athletics. Between calls, we would exchange nonsequiturs. I was delighted with the delays, for they gave me a chance to observe the performance. He was being important, it was clear; the functioning executive. The only discomfort I felt was the lack of a belt. The man was charming, informative, interesting. At one point, after a phone conversation, he leaned solemnly forward in his chair, folded his hands on his desk, squinted with utmost sincerity directly into my eyes and in that slow, Messianic manner unveiled the secret of life: "S Plus S Equals S." Then a pause, so that I could blot and not rub. "Sweat . . . Plus Sacrifice . . . Equals Success." I did not answer. He lifted one hand off the desk and began making figures in the air. An apprentice monument carver. "S Plus S Equals S." Then his friend and secretary, Roberta Johnson, brought in more coffee.

> *Bill Dauer* (Chamber of Commerce executive in Kansas City and San Francisco): My god, I've heard the story of all that sweat and sacrifice, of how he made his money, five hundred times.

"Charles O. Finley is as vulgar as spit. I think he's beautiful." Charles McCabe, San Francisco's finest columnist, was getting it on one morning. "If you read the sporting pages, this fellow comes through as a combination of Machiavelli and Billy Graham. In fact, he is merely a routinely offensive business tycoon who is exactly what organized baseball deserves. He is ruthless, insensitive, stingy, callow, and successful. All American, all the way through. Finley is the irrepressible id in the subconscious of baseball. He says right out exactly what other owners think and feel, but would never be caught dead saying in public. In the world of big league baseball, the roughest epithet around is bush. The word isn't strong enough to do justice to Finley. He is pure jungle."

Let us take a short drive with Mr. Finley to a lumber company not far from the Oakland Coliseum, home of his baseball team. The firm, call it Blank Lumber, has complained that sparks from Charlie's fireworks are a nuisance. Charlie enjoys his fireworks; he will deal with Mr. Blank. He bursts, not walks, into the office in the company of an employee, bangs his fist on the counter and loudly demands to see Mr. Blank. He is told that Mr. Blank cannot see anybody. He tells the clerk, with full, abusive fury, that he is Charles O. Finley and that Mr. Blank damn better well see him. And fast. He is told there is no possibility of Mr. Blank seeing him because Mr. Blank is dead. For the past nineteen years. Charles O. Finley removes his hat, places it over his heart, and tells the lumber company clerk that he is remorseful over Mr. Blank's passing, that Mr. Blank was a fine man and a credit to the Oakland community and the lumber industry.

> *Ted Kubiak* (A's infielder): The guy's unique. He seems like he's got two personalities, like two people. There's times he can be great, and then there's times you hate him. I don't think I've ever met anybody like him. I don't think you have either.
> *A Finley relative:* It's important for everybody to be someone. But Charlie's obsessed. As soon as he accomplishes something, it's not enough. He's always acting as if he's trying to prove something.

Let us take a long drive with Mr. Finley after an exhibition baseball game in Tucson, Arizona. He has been given a lift by two sportswriters. They approach two young hitchhikers holding a sign reading "Phoenix." The three men are headed in that direction, and Finley insists that the driver stop and pick up the young people. "We couldn't talk him out of it," says one of the writers. The hitchhikers, just back from a long stay in Mexico, get in the car. Charles O. Finley tells them that he is Charles O. Finley. One of the hitchhikers has never heard of him, the other has a faint recollection. Finley picks up a copy of *Sports Illustrated* magazine, turns to a page featuring his picture and says to the hitchhikers, "That's me, right there."

> *An employee:* He's eccentric, except I think some of his eccentricities are planned.

Let us take a drive with Charles O. Finley to a Chicago hospital, where he will be confined with a reported heart attack. A nursing volunteer is puzzled by "all this confusion and noise and clutter in his room. I mean, here's supposed to be a very sick man and all this busy, busy stuff is going on. Then he makes a big deal about giving gifts to some of us young girls—dime store rings. What a bunch of shit."

>    *Chuck Dobson* (former A's pitcher): His attitude at times seems to be, "Buddy, I got the money, now let's see you bow." He shows that the person with money can do almost anything, that you can buy people, you can buy ideas, you can bring a mule into the lobby of a hotel and not care if it shits all over that lobby.

The Oakland Chamber of Commerce plans a testimonial dinner for Charles O. Finley, who tells the Oakland Chamber of Commerce who will appear on the program, who will sit at the head table. "He controlled that whole party," says a player. "Why do all that at a party somebody else is giving you? You might as well give yourself a party."

Charles O. Finley prefers to think he has.

>    *Finley* (in 1972): I'm a machinist really. I'd still rather work on machines than anything else. I'm more comfortable as a grease monkey than I am doing what I'm doing now.

He may have let more of the truth slip than he wished. The essence of "this big butter and egg man from Chicago," as one writer describes him, is his uncomfortableness with the fulfillment of the great American dream, the blind—albeit loud—march through a half-lived life. People could fathom Charlie Finley, mill worker. Nobody can figure Charles O. Finley, Owner and General Manager; the man who forced baseball to expand beyond its effective capacity when he moved to Oakland in 1968; the man who talked his peers into making the game more interesting, more contemporary; the man who built, bought, psyched, grunted (not to mention sweated and sacrificed) himself a world championship team, all the while being insecure and uncomfortable. Try that angle, and let me know later. And please comfort all those people who know Charlie Finley but cannot explain "what he's really like." Thanks.

"He looks somehow like a man who is trying to escape from a concrete block but doesn't really know what would happen once he got loose," wrote Wells Twombly. "He uses the expression 'self-made' so often, it is as if he either invented the words or as if he were the first self-made man."

*Paul O'Neil* (writing in *Life*, 1968): He has exercised a native inventiveness and industry in the pursuit of his self-made millions. He is a handsome man; he has an erect and jaunty carriage, white hair, a classic profile, heavy dark brows [like Brillo pads, Twombly wrote], and burning brown eyes. Put him in red-tabbed khaki and he would be the image of those stiff-necked British brigadiers who whacked about with riding crops in the heyday of the Empire. . . . His manner is often in startling contrast to his environment. He can be inordinately solemn, even lugubrious. He emits cliches—"a clean mind in a sound body . . . the best things in life are free"—as gravely as if he had just coined them, and uses big words like a cop on a witness stand. He is perfectly capable of saying, "I would prefer to refrain from making statements of that nature," instead of "No." But just behind this façade, a complex, demanding, emotional, even passionate Finley waits with an ego flicking away like the pilot light in a gas oven. . . .

"His voice," wrote *Sports Illustrated*'s Ron Fimrite, "is one of command, deep in texture, measured in pace, an effective instrument." His *most* effective instrument. And one that was cleaned and pressed and tailored for maximum yield. It is the voice of an auctioneer, played at the wrong speed, enamored of itself.

*Frank Lane* (former A's general manager): He's an egomaniac to a degree. He had to be. What he wanted most when he got into baseball in 1961 was recognition. Here's a fella that had worked in the steel mill in Gary, Indiana, and worked like hell. He got this idea about selling a certain kind of insurance to certain people. But nobody really knew about it. And he wanted recognition. There's a lot of people like that. Charlie never would have been known if he hadn't bought the ball club.

*Chuck Dobson:* I think when he was sick with tuberculosis in the forties and laying in that hospital bed all that time he made a resolution that if he ever got out of that situation he would let people know that he was alive, that he wouldn't ever let opportunity fail him. And he hasn't burned that up yet. I don't think he's found out that all this success is not that important. Who cares besides him? I don't even think he cares that he might be killing himself, except he's not ready to die yet without satisfying his ego more. He'll never satisfy it enough, but he keeps trying and keeps fighting a losing battle.

The Sweat: Door-to-door selling as a kid in Birmingham, Alabama. Odd jobs after high school in Gary, Indiana. The steel mill in the late thirties: long hours, low pay. An ordnance plant during the war and insurance moonlighting. Insurance full time: sixteen, eighteen, twenty hours a day. Thousands of clients. Thousands. Then baseball and hockey, and basketball. Productivity around the clock, around the country.

The Sacrifice: Health (perforated ulcer, pneumonic tuberculosis, reported heart attacks). Family (living part of the time in a hotel near his Chicago office while wife Shirley and the seven children were at the farm in LaPorte, Indiana). Friends, real friends.

The Success: Millions. National publicity (not always positive). Access to celebrities. A baseball team he calls "the best in the history of the game, and this includes the great New York Yankees of Babe Ruth's day."

The side effect of S Plus S Equals S is the man's relationship with his fellows. "No regard for human beings whatsoever," says one writer. "It's impossible for anybody around him to have dignity."

"You don't know how terrible it is to have somebody think he owns you," says a man who has known Charlie many, many years.

> *Mike Epstein* (former A's first baseman): He has a lust to intimidate people. He once asked me why I never said hello to him. I told him, "Personally, I'd rather not." He said, "You're an independent son of a bitch. I've never seen anybody like you before." In Finley, I see a man who tries to generate so much hate against himself by the ballplayers that they'll play better. A team with a common enemy has better unity. He wants to get them so ticked off that they'll say to him, in effect, "No matter what you do to us, we'll show you. We'll win." So they give him just exactly what he wants.
>
> *Alvin Dark* (after being fired by Finley as manager in 1967): I tried not to argue with him, but after a while I got the idea that Charlie *likes* shouting matches.

Gene Tenace is a decent young man raised in the Finley baseball organization. A briefly hot bat made him the hero of the 1972 World Series. Tenace is not a brilliant fellow. But he does care about the game, he does seek to understand what is happening on the field and off, as far as the Athletics are concerned. And he cannot understand. He is the fallout: "I've often thought about what Mr. Finley wants out of life, and I don't really know. I just don't know how a man can be in the position of Mr. Finley—you know, all the money that he could ever want—and still not treat his players right. We've won world championships, and you can't tell we've won anything. It's kind of a sad situation. It's kind of puzzled me, and I don't think anybody on the ball club can pinpoint why he does it. I have no idea if it's selfishness or what it is."

"I don't ask to be loved," Charlie once said.

"He's very easily hurt and very, very sensitive," a relative said. "He needs approval, particularly from women, very badly. A lot of the crust and hard stuff is a coverup for his soft side."

The coverup has prevailed. The façade, whatever its discomfort, has worked. "Ours is the only sports franchise I know that has people talking more about the owner than the players," says one of them, Joe Rudi. Another fellow mused about the effects of Henry Aaron playing for the A's and suggested that Charlie could divert attention from Aaron, too—while making certain that Henry helped the club win.

That's what it all came down to in 1972. Winning everything. Jimmy Piersall, the emotionally erratic former major league outfielder, once worked for Finley in group sales. After he left the A's, Piersall said, "I had no trouble working for Charlie. I'm even flakier than he is." Piersall also said, "Nobody knows what Charlie put into that 1972 season. I saw it. I lived with him. I know what he went through. Up until 4:00 A.M. trying to make deals to help the club. Up again at eight. On the phone all the time. Talking to a million people. Trying to do whatever he could. Nobody will ever know. Nobody."

After winning—with Gene Tenace—the 1972 World Series, Finley said, "I sweated blood for twelve years. I lost sleep. I lost hair. My family suffered. All for this. I'm damn proud of my team. And frankly, I'm damn proud of myself."

"We showed 'em," he shouted in the clubhouse. "We showed 'em all."

Here is how. . . .

# II

## HUCKLEBERRY FINLEY

*The Saturday Evening Post* reported in 1964 that life for Charles Oscar Finley "began on a small farm" and that he played baseball "between farm chores." United Press International reported in 1972 that Charlie traced his business acumen to his enterprising work around his parents' farm. In February, 1959, the Gary *Post-Tribune* reported that Charlie said he lived on a fifteen-acre farm as a boy. It is possible that in the early days of Charlie's notoriety some writer erroneously reported that the Owner and General Manager ascended, Alger-like, from the soil and from then on other publications and other writers simply continued reporting this tidbit. That can happen in the writing biz. But it is more likely that Charlie himself fostered this impression, complete with descriptions of living on a dirt floor. There is no question that Charles O. Finley made it the hard way, but from his point of view it has always seemed more heroic to embellish.

An uncle, Tom Finley, who lived in Birmingham, Alabama, when Charles, as the family calls him, was going through his purported dirt floor and farm days, says, "At no time in Alabama did Charles live on a farm. He did not. And he didn't live in a house that had a dirt floor. No, no. He's exaggeratin'."

One asks why, and Tom Finley says, "I don't know. I've read that crap in the paper myself. It's hogwash. I laugh at it. I can't figure out why he'd say those things. My daddy lived on a farm. Charles didn't."

Both Uncle Tom and one of Charles' aunts, Mrs. Clara Holdcroft, say that the Owner grew up in two "nice" frame houses in "nice" residential neighborhoods in the Shadyside and Hueytown sections of Birmingham, where he was born in 1918 on George Washington's birthday. "Probably had a couple hens back of the house," says Uncle Tom, "but those places weren't farms."

The area is now incorporated as Ensley, Alabama. It was a mill town in the twenties. "A wonderful, wonderful place," as Tom Finley recalls it. Tom worked in the mill, as did his older brother Oscar, Charles' father; the Finleys were steelmen. Their father, Randolph, had come to Tuscaloosa, Alabama, from Londonderry, Ireland, as a boy, worked in the blast furnaces in Tuscaloosa and thence to the machine shop in the mills at Ensley-Birmingham. Solid, industrious, responsible Irish Protestants. Randolph and Emma Caroline Finley had eleven children (seven still living in 1974) and a transient stock of horses.

*Tom Finley:* When my daddy retired from the mills, he became a horse raiser and trader. He knew horses. He was a great trader. He'd ride down the road and see another man ridin' along and they'd stop and go to jabbin'. Daddy'd get out and raise the man's horse's lips up and look at the teeth and fool around and punch the horse in the side and say, "How you swap?" And he would always come out on top. He brought the bacon home. They had this big livery stable in Birmingham—just like a used car lot is now. They would just run those horses right through that place. Put halters on 'em and run 'em right through, and my daddy'd go down and bid on 'em and then take 'em out and sell 'em to some farmer. Why, some of the horses he sold, the farmers couldn't even get any work out of after they bought 'em. But my daddy was respected and liked. (Laughs.) People respect a good horse trader—to a certain extent.

Charles was four years old when his grandfather Randolph died. Uncle Tom says Charles spent very, very little time with his grandfather. Uncle Tom says Charles' younger brother Fred "looks more like my daddy than Charles does. But I think that Charles is a lot like his grandfather. I've seen that. He's after that dollar, that's it. And his grandfather was a hard man with a buck—always tryin' to get that little extra difference in horse tradin'. He always wanted the caboodle."

Charles' mother, Burmah, attended the same grade school as Tom, who recalls that "her people came from Georgia. We used to play baseball on the dirt road in front of her house right down the street from us. Her people, the Fields, lived in the same kind of house as we did. I think Oscar met Burmah while he was still an apprentice in the machine shop at the mill. Her father died young and her mother married a streetcar motorman."

Nearly everyone who knew Charles' parents suggests that Burmah was the stronger personality of the two. Oscar is generally described as "a very quiet man." One relative said, "Oscar would usually shut up rather than fight. But when he'd lose his temper, he'd let them all have it." Uncle Tom says neither Oscar nor Burmah "pushed Charlie all that much. They just wanted him to be a good religious boy. Both of them were very good church workers. Burmah was very big in the Pike Avenue Baptist Church."

Charles says his mother was church organist and his dad Sunday school superintendent. He told a reporter that "when the preacher got up to preach," he would sleep in his mother's lap. The Owner one day would donate nineteen thousand dollars to that church.

> *Question:* Was Charles a good religious boy?
> *Tom Finley:* Aw, no, you know that.
> *Aunt Clara Holdcroft:* As a child, Charles was real obedient. Just as nice as he could be. I used to take care of him sometimes when Burmah went to church meetings. She was a good churchgoer.

And Charles was a good worker. "Always what you call a go-getter," said Aunt Clara.

"Always a kid who would never sit still. Always trying to prove he's good enough for somebody. For everybody," said another relative.

"Nice boy," said Uncle Tom. "But a very bold boy. Very bold. He never was shy."

The middle child, too. Sister Thelma just a few years older; brother Fred one year back of him in school. The simplistic notion that the middle child is by nature rebellious (otherwise how will he be noticed?) and craves affection-attention is—if you're seeking answers about the Owner—too pat perhaps. Yet, the applicability in this case should not be ignored totally.

Charlie has said he took his first job at the age of twelve. He mowed lawns six days a week, he said, making from $1.50 to $3.00 a day. There was so much business, he said, that he organized a crew of grass cutters and increased his income.

He has spoken also of being a newsboy and a magazine salesman. He has said he was awarded a bronze medal of Benjamin Franklin for being a supersalesman of Curtis Publishing Company magazines. He sold so many magazines, he said, that he earned a bicycle.

Charlie said he was a youthful hit as an egg salesman. He said business was so good that he couldn't get enough eggs from his own chickens to serve the customers. So, he said, he found an egg candling plant and bought the eggs that didn't pass the candling tests for five cents a dozen. He would then sell them to office workers in Birmingham, he said, for fifteen cents a dozen. "The only disadvantage," he told a reporter in 1959, "was that I could never go back for a resale."

Aunt Clara says Charles was a "brilliant little" businessman. "He wasn't satisfied selling magazines just around where he lived, so he had his mother take him to the apartment buildings on the south side of town, where people had a little more money."

Charlie has said he and his friends used to pick small grapes and make them into wine and sell the wine in those dry days. "He worked hard," says a relative. "But he worked hard his way. His father was a regulated person, but Charles was always unregulated, not the kind of person who could handle a routine."

Two relatives remember that Charlie had a speech impediment quite early. One of them insists that the Owner was so embarrassed by "being a little tongue-tied, having difficulty pronouncing some words" that he began developing that painfully slow manner of speaking that became one of his trademarks, what one later business associate describes as "that monotonic walrus voice."

"Remember," says one relative, "Charlie does not like to be laughed at. He doesn't want to be embarrassed."

An employee of many years said that Charlie "would never admit making a mistake. Never." And a relative adds, "But he's always looking for something to catch *you* on."

In 1974, Jim Finley was seriously ill with emphysema in Texas. He was only eight years older than nephew Charles. There may even have been a sort of brotherly relationship between the two for a time. Tom says Jim never amounted to much and that

Charles in later years tried to be helpful. In 1959 Jim was staying on Charles' farm in LaPorte, Indiana. The Owner had not yet taken up full-time residence on the farm. One evening, Tom and Jim had themselves a little party. "Just a few drinks of Charles' good whiskey," says Tom. "Plainly speakin', Jim got drunk, but he hadn't done anythin' wrong. Somebody else on the place called Charles. What I should have done was took Jim and brought him back to Gary with me. That's what I should have done. Charles just came and called the police and told them to get Jim off the farm. He stayed in jail a couple days until Charles got him out."

Sergeant Roger Zimmerman of the LaPorte County Police Department said the records showed that one James Finley was jailed on June 4, 1959, and released on June 9.

"After that," says Tom, "Jim worked for Charles in the insurance office in Chicago. Charles bought him a couple suits of clothes. But he lasted at the job only a month or so."

Tom Finley, a retired mill worker who moved to Gary from Birmingham a few years after Oscar in the thirties and continues to live there, says he is not certain how deeply "the family rates" with Charles. "I know I don't," he says. "For a while, my brother Harry did. He and his wife used to come up here to visit Charles on the farm."

Harry Finley, nine years Charles' senior, still lives in the Birmingham area. When I phoned him, he said, "There's nothing I wouldn't hesitate to tell you in a minute, but I'd have to see how Charles feels about it first. I'd have to talk to Charles."

Inadvertently, Charlie found himself talking to me about Birmingham in April, 1974, in the clubhouse of the Oakland A's. The Owner was sitting in the office of Manager Alvin Dark as the press walked in to glean postgame comments. The Owner had been quoted a few days earlier as calling his team the best in baseball history. And the name of Babe Ruth entered the conversation.

"I was a bat boy in Birmingham when the Yankees came through for an exhibition game. Imagine, a twelve-year-old kid, and bat boy for Babe Ruth. After the game the Yankees left behind a box of baseballs. All of them were autographed by Ruth. And I found them."

I asked if he kept them all. Charles smiled and said, "Of course. Imagine, twelve years old." Then a pause, as he saw me taking notes. "Well, I got only three of those balls. I returned the box to them and they gave me three balls for being so honorable." He again paused to watch me scribble. "And that's a true story," he concluded.

Aunt Clara Holdcroft says Charles got the bat boy's job with the Birmingham Barons (a minor league club he would someday purchase) without any trouble. "He just went over and asked for it. When he wanted something, he just went out and got it," she says. "I'm very proud of him. Real proud of him."

According to various accounts, Charlie's pay as a bat boy was either fifty cents a game or one used baseball and all the broken bats he could carry. He has said that he "dreamed more than anything" of being a big league ballplayer, but that "I wasn't blessed with the talent." The ambition would have to manifest itself in another way, in another time, in another place.

The mill at Ensley was cutting back the work week of its hands in 1933. As Tom remembers it, Oscar was "slacked off" to only a day or two each week. "Our brother Bill was up in Gary at that time and he wrote Oscar a letter and said to come up and work at the mill there. And Oscar did."

Burmah and the kids followed in an old Whippet—a mattress tied to the top of the car and furniture crammed inside. Charlie would later tell a friend that the only food they ate on the way was peanuts. He will, some have said, drop southern anecdotes at odd moments. Yet at times he has not wished to be identified as a southerner. Uncle Tom is not certain about the reasons for this ambivalence.

"Charles just wants to be looked up to, I guess. But I'm proud of him. I am really. I can't help but to be. I can't help it. He's family. I like Charles. He's never given me a dime but he's never done me no harm either. Not a bit of harm in the world. But I wouldn't ask him for nothin'. I wouldn't want him to turn me down. I'm plainly speakin'," says spare, seventy-two year old Tom Finley.

The blackness is pervasive in Gary, above and below. The belching energies of the steel world fill the skies, providing an ersatz cloud cover for the inner city, for the abundant black population. In a back-wetting, steamy July week in 1974 in Gary, a visitor has never been more convinced of his whiteness. A Finley hunter is warned not to go to a certain address, for that place is smack in the middle of a black drug battleground, the locale of "The Family," homey but ominous. White strangers as far east as Michigan City, Indiana, are amazed that one has survived a week in Gary. But there has been no trouble, save the reticence of a few Finley friends to talk to the hunter.

Charlie's people are still there. With the passage of forty years, they are on the outskirts. But still there. The steel mills, and the town, have been good to them.

You can walk into the bar of the Holiday Inn across from Gary City Hall and lightly ask the black barmaid if the black mayor ever drops in for a drink. You can talk astrology with others in the bar, all black, and live to drink another day. Possibly the white strangers down the pike in Michigan City have not been to Gary for some time. But Charlie still pops by, as well he should. The memories must be marvelous, and his people care. Most of Charlie's people are fiercely loyal. They drip with admiration and

respect; they will not bad rap. You don't knock people from the
old neighborhood. You just don't. And good for them. "If I was to
see a fella like him again today, I would know that this fella was
going to be a millionaire," says Sam Joseph, who saw Charlie
almost before anyone else in Gary when the Finleys came north in
1933.

Most probably, in his own way, Charlie cares for the people and
for Gary. There were rumors in 1963, after a local political
scandal, that Charlie might run for mayor. But no. He said then,
"If I had the time, there is nothing I would love to do more than
get into that race and clean up the mess and clear the name of the
good people of Gary. I love Gary. There are some wonderful
people in Gary. . . ."

Sam Joseph must have been one of the best. He is a bricklayer,
as was his father, who owned an apartment building in which the
Finleys first lived when they got to Gary. The Joseph family was in
the middle flat, Finleys upstairs. There were five Josephs in a
two-bedroom and six Finleys in the same-sized place: the parents;
Charlie and Fred; and Thelma and husband Calvin (Buster) Smith,
who would become the man in charge of Charlie's Los Angeles
insurance office.

"I learned quite a bit off Charlie," says Sam. "When I look back
at it now, I wish my children were like him. He was a striver. A
worker and a striver."

One of Sam's children answers the phone when I call the Joseph
home in Hobart, just outside of Gary. The youngster says Sam will
be home from work at 5:00 and out of the shower at 5:30. By 5:35,
Sam is relaxing on his sofa and talking about the days at Emerson
High School with Charlie from 1933 to 1935. The days the kids
called Charlie "Alabama."

*Sam Joseph:* Boy, when he first came to Gary he had that thick,
syrupy southern accent. He really had it. And a popular song then

was "Stars Fell on Alabama," so everybody went overboard for Charlie and Fred. Everybody got a kick out of the accents, and I think he strived to lose the accent. He couldn't pronounce my name. He'd say Saaalmm. He'd get the "l" in there. Every once in a while, he'd say, "Saaalmm, do you think I've lost my accent?" (Laughs). But I don't think he was embarrassed by it.

As a kid, he would try to run things, sort of be the boss if he could—even in the little jobs we used to get. He always wanted to be the leader. This guy never stopped. He was always looking for work, always looking for money, always looking for advancement. He'd go out and get a job—washing windows, busboy, anything— and he'd drag his brother Fred and me along. He'd get a job and we'd all work. Then he'd quit and look for something better. We wanted to keep what we had, but not him. He was going, always on the go. When he was out of work, he would go to this stationery store down on Sixth and Washington streets and buy this cheap stationery. Then he'd gather the three of us, and we would go through all the bank buildings and office buildings selling stationery to the secretaries. Any way to make a dollar. Once we all got jobs at the Kalamazoo Stove Company. We moved stoves around on Saturday. Jobs that kids would do but an adult wouldn't ask for. We always had money in our pocket because of him. I don't know what he did with the money he made; he may even have been supporting himself.

Sam Joseph remembers Charlie "always in softball. He was a good player and played all positions."

Roz Corwin, another Emerson High classmate, recalls the summer that Finley managed a ball team and got sponsorship money from a local sports shop. "One day the sports shop owner came out to the field to see his team. And Charlie had furnished the kids with sweatshirts only. Nothing else. I think the sports shop man expected to see his store's name on full uniforms. Even then, Charlie was a salesman."

"He wanted to play football at Emerson," says Joseph, "but he had a little conflict with the coach because Charlie thought he should have gone right in and played with the varsity and the coach didn't think he was good enough to. The coach thought he should work his way up. But Charlie wanted to be number one right away. So he didn't play at Emerson, not even on the jayvees."

After his junior year at Emerson, Charles O. Finley transferred to Horace Mann High School. He did not move to the Mann district. "I don't know how he worked it," says Joseph, "because it was impossible to do it. But he did it. He walked to Mann and it was a couple of miles, a long walk. We were only two blocks from Emerson. Maybe he left Emerson because there was a bunch of roughneck kids who wouldn't accept his leadership. I remember that some of them started making fun of him because of his accent."

One Emerson friend of Finley who wishes to remain anonymous suggested that Charlie transferred schools for another reason. "He told me he wanted to go to Mann because the rich people went there and he wanted to get acquainted with the rich people. He was hustling all the time, and he wanted to marry a rich girl. Which he did. I remember that before he met Shirley, though, he did get acquainted with some rich girls and started dating them. They would pick him up in their cars. I think I remember that because I might have been a little jealous of him."

*Roz Corwin:* He was a man's man, a handsome kid with red curls, and all the girls at Emerson were kind of oohing and ahing over him. He always had that devilish kind of smart aleck grin. Just devilish. He always seemed to be maybe smiling at something other than what he seemed to be smiling at. His mind was definitely always working.

Sam Joseph says, "A lot of us at Emerson got sort of down on Charlie for going to Mann. We were sore at him for leaving."

At Mann, his arrival was apparently less than triumphant—even though the school was seeing a new Finley. For what is fascinating is that between the end of his junior year at Emerson and the start of his senior year at Mann, in the space of one summer vacation, "Alabama" Finley became Chuck Finley. In three months he had lost his southern accent. Mann classmates do not remember him having that accent.

One of them, Joe Goffiney, who lives only a few blocks from Sam Joseph in Hobart but more affluently because he is supervisor of the Gary works of U.S. Steel, has a sports-related memory of Finley at Mann. "Chuck came out for football. The school had been on some sort of athletic probation, and when the coach found out that Chuck was living out of the district, he didn't want to risk ineligibility. So Chuck did not make the Mann team—and he would have given his right arm to play football."

> *Frances Helmerick McBride* (a senior at Mann with Finley and Goffiney): I don't really remember too much about Chuck. He really was an average nondescript type of high school student. I'm surprised he did as well as he did. I really didn't realize he had that potential. I can still see him walking down the hall with his hands in his pockets and the books tucked under an arm, not caring whether he made it to class or he didn't. Things just seemed to roll off his back. He was content to go along and ride with the current.

Mrs. McBride, a widowed librarian in Crown Point, Indiana, and an amazing fount of Garyology, has great pride in the Horace Mann High School of her day. "It used to be known as the Five Hundred," she says. "The select. We've had some quietly successful people come out of the class of '36. Although Chuck was not one of the *quietly* successful ones."

Jack Morfee apparently was. He is senior vice president of the Gary National Bank and a man several people in Gary told me was "Chuck's closest friend." On the first visit I made to the bank, Jack Morfee asked if this book was being written with Charlie's authorization. I told him it wasn't. He asked me to check back with him in a day or two. On the second visit to the bank, Morfee said he would not be interviewed for the book. He would not tell me why.

The senior picture of Charles Finley appears on page 24 of the Horace Manual, the school's yearbook in 1936. His curly hair is cut short. He is wearing a striped tie and dark suit and has a meek, almost frightened look. On page 115 the senior description for Chuck reads: "He who mischief hatcheth, mischief catcheth." Also in the back of the book, in the individual credits section, Finley is reported as having been involved in football in 1933, '34, '35; track in '33 and '34, and Golden Gloves in '33, '34, '35. He had attended Emerson those three years, but Sam Joseph says Finley was not on the Emerson track team, nor, as Sam mentioned earlier, on the Emerson football team.

"We always had boxing but it was more intramural," Sam says. "We had sort of a carnival every year and part of it was a boxing program. I remember that Charlie did box in the carnivals. But it wasn't Golden Gloves."

Goffiney, however, does recall that Chuck "was in the Golden Gloves competition that was connected" with the sports program at Mann. "That's the type of person he was," says Goffiney. "Aggressive, very aggressive. That was his nature then. He'd just go all out. Whatever it took to do something, he did that and more."

The credit information for the 1936 Horace Manual "was turned in by the students themselves," says Frances McBride.

The senior prom for Mann's class of '36 (326 strong) was on June

9 in Gary's Masonic Temple. One month later, as Charlie has recalled it, he was unloading box cars at the Gary works of U.S. Steel. He called the job hard labor "but a blessing in disguise. I'm thankful for having had that opportunity to learn the facts of life." Frequently, Finley has said that he became a machinist at U.S. Steel. Harold Murphy, the zone foreman during most of Charlie's days at the old west mill, also known as the Merchant mill, does not recall Finley working as a machinist. Murphy, still a resident of Gary but in 1974 an employee of Bethlehem Steel, said he did not know if I'd want to talk to him "because I've got nothing but good things to say about Charlie." I told him that was just fine.

> *Harold Murphy:* I remember that Charlie was hired in the labor gang and would work all shifts. He'd been a laborer only a few months—making under four dollars a day—and then was put into the tool room working straight days. He was a clean-cut young man, and after being assigned to the tool room he built his job up to be quite a thing. He was the finishing-in checker making sure all the tools that had been passed out were properly taken care of. He had good organizational ability and he really set up an organized tool room. His job was like being a blue collar accountant. His good work in the tool room got him a raise to over six dollars a day. We had about two thousand men working in that zone. The old mill itself was about a mile and a half long and had fourteen rolling mills in it. There are thousands of tools that you have to use in the process of finishing steel, and Charlie impressed everybody with his ability to get at the root of any problem. He was definitely a good leader, and everybody respected him for it. I said *respected* him. I'm not saying everybody *liked* him. At first in the tool room he was quiet, cooperative, and courteous. But he was always a pusher, and he was always pushing Charlie. Everybody at the mill kept saying to me about Finley, "He'll be your next foreman." But people are just jealous of success. Finley and I understood what we were fighting: resentful people. I liked him then. Always have and always will.

The mills had their share of Finleys, and just about everybody else in Gary, in the late thirties. Charlie was one of thousands, but not for long. He would find his way out of the masses.

Years later Charlie told a Gary reporter that his job at U.S. Steel "ended suddenly in 1941," altogether a hectic year for the Owner. He has said that he was classified 4-F because of a perforated ulcer and that he left the mills to work for the duration of the war at the Kingsbury Ordnance Plant, east of Gary in LaPorte. And in May, 1941, he married Shirley.

The same high school yearbook in which Finley was heralded as a mischief hatcher describes Shirley M. McCartney, who was in the graduating class just ahead of the Owner, as "the quiet kind whose nature never varies."

"All I remember about her in high school was that she was a very pretty girl. And quiet," says Frances Helmerick McBride.

"In high school, Shirley was very attractive and very happy-go-lucky. Full of fun," says Mavis Goffiney.

"Real easygoing," says Mavis' husband Joe. "Everybody liked Shirley."

One liners fall on Shirley McCartney Finley. Always one liners.

"She smiles good," says Chuck Dobson, a former A's pitcher.

"She's such a gracious person, she makes you feel like she's known you for years," says Roz Corwin.

One liners, and the appraisals generally stop right there. If Charlie indeed strived for a rich girl, he could not have done much better—at least in terms of looks and character—than Shirley McCartney. The accruable wealth is open to speculation, however. Shirley's father, Red, was a prominent plumbing contractor in Gary. "A nice Irish family," says Janet Burton, who knew Shirley at Horace Mann High School and would later work with her at the Gary *Post-Tribune*. "Red acted like Irishmen were supposed to act in those days."

He had been born in San Francisco, reared in the wine country just north of the Bay. A brother was credited with the development of propane gasoline. Nice credentials, the McCartneys.

None of the Mann graduates with whom I spoke recalls Charlie dating Shirley in high school. One story is that the two met on a blind date in 1940, one year before their marriage. Another report has them meeting in an Indiana University extension class. Mavis Goffiney says Shirley was working in Red McCartney's business. "I think the family had the Seven-Up bottling plant in Gary then, too," says Mrs. Goffiney. "They belonged to the country club and lived in Morningside."

Joe Goffiney added, "That was the exclusive section of Gary at that time." After Charlie and Shirley married, the Goffineys said, they lived not far from the McCartneys in a basement apartment in Morningside. Soon the Finleys moved to LaPorte because of Charlie's work at the ordnance plant.

"They were a logical couple," says Joe Goffiney. "The type that hit it off together, I thought."

"I don't think money ever changed either Charlie or Shirley," says Mavis Goffiney. "They're the same people to us as we knew when they were young."

> *Beryl Brownell* (women's editor of the Gary *Post-Tribune*): The McCartneys weren't tycoons, but they were well-known in the county. Shirley is one of the nicest persons I ever knew—very, very attractive as a young girl. She had bright red hair when she was young and it seemed to turn white in the days she was working here. I never heard a complaint from her. She was always herself. Phonies hated her and real people enjoyed her. She'd call me about parties they would have on the farm in LaPorte and say, "If you want to come to the farm for a story, fine. If not, just come and be a guest." And he was just as nice to me as Shirley. Very cooperative.

Finley recalled that after being at the ordnance plant a month, he was one of twenty-eight employees sent to a special training center in New Jersey and that after returning to LaPorte was promoted to assistant general foreman and later superintendent of one of the plant's five divisions. His old U.S. Steel foreman, Harold Murphy, corroborates Finley's success at Kingsbury. Murphy worked there, too, although, he said, not in Finley's division.

By the time Charlie left the ordnance plant, apparently in 1946, he had dipped a more than tentative toe into the insurance business. Moonlighting policy sales reaped such promising results that he decided to catch on full-time with an agent in Gary. The postwar boom would not be detonated without a few decibels from Charles O. Finley. Except that almost before he could get started with his twenty-hour-a-day strivings in the insurance world, his budding ascendancy was dealt a nearly fatal blow. He would now need his family to hang on, his parents and his Shirley.

"In those days," someone in Gary says, "having tuberculosis was almost like having leprosy." Tuberculars would need help.


J. O. Parramore Hospital is a rambling, two-story, red-bricked structure just north of Crown Point, Indiana. For many years Parramore Hospital had served its county's tuberculosis victims, but in the summer of 1974 the place was nearly empty. Soon, the adjacent Lake County Convalescent Hospital would be using Parramore, too, for its good works. In the busy days at Parramore, four wards housing some four hundred patients were operative. Patient Charles O. Finley, who entered the hospital in December, 1946, the victim of a body rebelling against overwork, is remembered by one nurse as occupying Room 127 in Ward F1, on the ground floor.

Charlie says he had driven himself so hard in insurance sales

that he had contracted an immensely debilitating case of pneumonic tuberculosis. The only road to physical restoration, he has
said, was rest and courage.

> *Finley:* I was determined not to die. I'd lose my food, and I'd push
> that button and get that nurse back with another tray. I found that
> anytime you toss your cookies, if you go ahead and force food down
> you don't toss 'em a second time. I'd gone down from 160 to 97
> pounds during my illness, but I walked out of that hospital weighing
> 209 pounds. Today [he is quoted in a January, 1973, issue of *Parade*]
> I keep my weight around 180.

Charlie told a *Life* writer that he tangled with this dehydration
devil for twenty-four days until he could force himself to stop
tossing all his cookies. *Life* quotes him as muttering after
thirty-two days, "I've got it whipped." He hung on for his
twenty-ninth birthday—and for nearly two more years beyond
that.

Shirley and their first two children were living with Charlie's
parents in a modest home owned by the elder Finleys in Gary's
Glen Park district. Shirley got a job as a proofreader at the Gary
*Post-Tribune*; her father knew the newspaper's publisher. She may
have made as much as thirty-five dollars a week on that job. On
Wednesday evenings and Sunday afternoons, visiting days at
Parramore, Shirley would get a ride down to Crown Point to see
her husband, whose only physical ally was time.

A friend, who prefers anonymity, would often drive Shirley to
the hospital and recalls, "Shirley was a very congenial person and
easy to cope with. She was young then and made the best of
things. But Charlie used to give her a rough time when she visited
him. She would be distraught on the way home. He always was a
difficult man."

A nurse who worked Finley's ward at Parramore in those days—and who also asked anonymity—backs up Shirley's friend. "He would yell at his wife, slap her face, throw things at her. She'd come out holding her face, with the imprint of his hand on her face. Many of the times I saw her, she was leaving his room crying. She'd bring him flowers, too. I don't know, maybe he didn't want her to spend money."

Another nurse, Mrs. Jenn Carija, now director of nursing at the Lake County Convalescent Hospital, was a student nurse next door at Parramore in Finley's final months of recuperation, and she remembers him as "a very congenial man—he was friendly and talkative and well-mannered with the student nurses."

But our first nurse, whose comments are corroborated by a colleague, says that Charlie's conduct toward the regular nurses was different. "He was restless and impatient and would bark at the regular nurses. He was generally complaining."

The other adds, "I think maybe that was the sign of a typical patient on his way to recovery and anxious to get out. But if he hadn't become famous, I wouldn't have remembered him. He wasn't that distinctive."

> *Anonymous Parramore nurse:* He was highly hypertensive. He was fairly cooperative as long as he got his own way. When I would be taking rounds to make sure each patient was breathing, I would creak his door a little bit and he'd say, "Boo!" He was a kidder, at least I think he was kidding when he tried to make time with a lot of the nurses. Because he did bring up a real good family, didn't he? He seemed to want to be popular. He was very vain; he thought he was just about *it*. And he was very good looking then. He wasn't satisfied with the food, and he wouldn't want a bed bath if he was busy studying. His wife would bring him books—insurance study courses, I think. His room was full of insurance books and insurance forms. There usually is something outstanding about a patient that you

remember. And I remember Charlie Finley's temper. I'd say he had a violent temper and it was hard for him to control it. The staff would bend over backwards for him. They'd cater to him just to keep away from trouble.

Also bending over backwards for Charlie was the corner grocer-butcher, George Marks, whose IGA market was only a couple of doors away from the elder Finleys' home in Glen Park. Millie Marks recalls that her brother George gave Charlie food on credit in the Parramore days. A brother-in-law of Marks would take magazines to Charlie at Parramore. "He's always treated us nice," says Millie Marks. "To me, he's never changed." A friend says that Finley ordered meat from George Marks once over the telephone. Charlie was calling from Oakland at that time, needed meat, wanted to buy from a man who had been kind in the old days. I wanted to ask George Marks about his relationship with Charlie, but he flatly refused to talk. A shame, because Marks seems to be one of the few nonfamily links with Charlie during those dark days. Friends from Emerson and Mann generally report they lost contact with Finley in his tubercular days, that they didn't realize his condition until they read about it years later.

**III**

# THE INSURANCE MAN

Before his stroll through the valley of the shadow, Charlie was becoming a crackerjack insurance peddler for The Travelers. While still working at the ordnance plant, he had met an insurance salesman from Gary, Louis Duke. Charlie says he was so impressed with Duke's pitch for life insurance that he asked Duke for job advice. He has said that part-time sales for the Equitable Life Insurance Company of Iowa eventually led, by early 1946, to full-time sales with The Travelers. The Owner also was taking correspondence courses in the field and moved briskly along. In one two-week period in April, 1946, he wrote a dozen policies. His existing file at The Travelers in Hartford, Connecticut, is slim, but what's there bespeaks his sales energy and results. In 1946, despite the late-year illness, he established an all-time Travelers high sales record by writing $15,450 in accident premiums, plus $2,412 in health policy premiums. Some life coverage, too.

Alan R. Fletcher, supervisor of press relations with The Travelers, said that Charlie began peddling for them as early as 1943 and in three separate years in the mid-forties was their leading agent in selling newly purchased accident and health insurance. Finley's sales totals for those big years are not available, but, says Fletcher, Charlie did set a sales record that "stood for a number of years. It is a moot point if he still holds any Travelers' records because agents have added so many other lines to the accident and health field." But Fletcher says that Finley's record did hold up at least through the early sixties. Fletcher sent memos in March, 1974, "seeking someone familiar with Finley's career with The Travelers" and told me "no one remembers him from that time."

Charlie kind of forgot about what he was doing for The Travelers himself. The long confinement at Parramore reminded him.

> *Finley* (to a writer from *Life*): Here I was selling health insurance and I didn't have any myself. I'd told myself I'd buy some when I was forty. But I was only twenty-nine. I was the living proof that professional men needed it. My kids were the living victims. I couldn't wait to get out and preach the gospel.

As one insurance expert told me, "The only thing worse than dying is to be alive when you're dead—emotionally or financially dead." For a time at Parramore, that's the way it must have been for the Owner.

American history texts will not tarry over the saga of disability income insurance. You may have disability coverage on your job and not know it. You may know you have disability coverage and not understand it. The word disability sounds so frightening, you don't want to think about it. Charlie had to think about it: disabled all those months, in the care of the county, no disability income. A supreme irony of his life, to be sure.

> *Edward J. Mitchell* (San Francisco insurance broker): Before World War II, very little disability income insurance was being

written. Companies weren't pushing it. People were just not ready for it yet. The few companies that were writing those policies before the war really took it in the ear when the depression came along, because there's a strange thing about disability insurance: when the economy is good, the claims are low. When things are bad, claims are high. So during the depression, there was a tremendous increase in claims. I know of one company that wasn't able to pay off its debts from the depression until almost 1970. But then with the prosperity of the war years, a big demand was being built up for this type of insurance. And nobody was there to cover that demand.

*A Finley client:* Charlie arrived in the infancy of what was a fledgling industry. People now had jobs and money. There was now a higher regard for insurance, and a growing public awareness of the need for insurance because of an educational campaign by the insurance industry. Group insurance benefits were starting, medical technology was improving, and people saw a need to protect their families.

As Charlie perceived during his excruciatingly long hospital stay, doctors were a whole new field within this whole new field. Doctors weren't employed by giant corporations. A doctor wanted a fringe benefit, a doctor paid for a fringe benefit. Sure, medical associations existed then, as now, but not for the purpose of selling their members group insurance coverage. Not until Charlie persuaded them. Not until he sold them Finley.

*Ed Mitchell:* This kind of thing is fraught with politics—this business of selling insurance to professional associations. You've got to rub elbows, you've got to get to know people who know the right people. It takes not only an enterprising agent, but also a guy who has the ability to pull it off. You don't have to be a salesman as much as a promoter, because you're not really selling—you're promoting an idea. You have to spend a lot of time, and that can be very dangerous. If you devote all your time and energy and resources to one project and it loses, then you're out of business. Unless of course you have an outside income. Or nothing to lose.

Charlie had the time, the energy, the enterprise, the promotional flair. And nothing to lose.

The way several people recall it, Charlie was less than dapper those first few insurance-peddling years after Parramore. Plainly, he was surviving on talk and not appearance. He talked his way from doctor to doctor and finally to the county medical association level. He was fondling the medical group mailing lists and, finally, selling. The Lake County Medical Society was his first group: $100 a week in disability income plus other benefits for an annual premium rate of $176.60. Administered, via the Provident Life and Accident Insurance Company, by Charles O. Finley and Company, Inc., up there in a little cubbyhole on the tenth floor of the Gary National Bank Building. Two other Indiana county groups, LaPorte and St. Joseph, followed. Thence to districts (five to twelve counties) and states.

His sales pitch must have been based, in great part, on his personal disability. Other selling points to doctors? Well, in April, 1974, the folks at Minnesota Mutual Life argued the case thus in a mailer: ". . . a professional man [should] use noncancellable disability income as the foundation for his disability insurance program. Determine the minimum amount of monthly income needed to sustain basic needs—i.e., food, clothing, and shelter. . . . Marginal needs such as country club dues, auto payments, savings for various travel and educational purposes, etc., can be protected through association group disability plans. . . ."

As a Finley client puts it: "At the time Charlie came along, doctors, like everyone else, didn't know that this kind of coverage was available. But they did recognize what the loss of income would mean to their families." And to their country club memberships.

It would not be fair to say that doctors are hypochondriacs. So I will be unfair and present the opinion of a man who believes he understands doctors because he does business with so many of them, a man who says: "When a doctor feels a pain, the first thing he does is self-diagnose. And what he instantly discovers is that he is suffering from the most serious thing possible. If he gets a little pain, immediately it's cancer of the colon—not just passing gas. He's so afraid of the consequences, he doesn't want to go and have this pain checked out by a specialist. He feels that's the end."

Trouble is, these ever-dying medical men had little time to see insurance salesmen. Once Charlie could sit them down and present Finley live and in color, he had a deal. Sitting them down was the trick.

I know one insurance salesman who would hang around medical schools or hover in hospital cafeterias. "They're receptive if you can get their time and confidence," he said. "And you gain their confidence with sincerity and—name-dropping. Other doctors' names. As far as doctors are concerned, the only people who have any intelligence are other doctors. So you tell them the names of other doctors who are your clients—even if you sold this other doctor only an hour ago. The new doctor figures that if all those other doctors are buying from you, then the policy has to be good for him, too. Doctors have almost no knowledge of anything outside of medicine. And an insurance salesman can't use flattery as a major technique with doctors. They can't be fooled by flattery because doctors are flattered constantly. I mean, patients fall in love with them, nurses think they're great, most people think that doctors come directly from God. Once you get the routine in how to sell them, they're more easily sold than others. And when information comes out of a medical association about a group insurance program, it's like the Good Housekeeping Seal of Approval. Because, after all, doctors take care of doctors, and the impression the individual doctor has is that leading doctors are looking over all of the available policies and saying what is best for all doctors."

Okay, but how do you sell him on protecting that country club membership?

"A doctor," says my insurance salesman friend, "wants to project a great, successful image—an image that helps his practice. He's got to have status symbols. His wife suffered through the interne days and can't wait to belong to the country club and have a yacht and a hundred thousand dollar home and the whole bit. So a doctor has a tendency to spend everything he makes, and more. He's a poor money manager. He's mortgaged to the hilt. I mean, who wants to go to a doctor who drives a Volkswagen? So because of all these debts, he sees the need for disability insurance. He needs that cash if he's unable to practice."

DISCLAIMER: My friend is not referring to every single physician in the United States. Surely not to his family doctor, or mine, or yours. Or, for that matter, Charlie's. Surely not.

> *A Finley client:* Finley likes doctors because they represent something to him he's not.

If his principal clients were big image-weavers, so was Charlie. Many Gary acquaintances remember that the Owner drove a Cadillac even before making his first big insurance score.

> *Tom Finley:* Back in those days he'd park it out in front of the bank building. Right in the "No Parking" zone. People'd pass and say, "Whose car is it?" And somebody'd say, "Belongs to Finley." Charles would say, "Pays to advertise." You know. If he'd get a ticket, he'd mail it right in and park right in the same place again the next day. Finley's car.

John Mihelic, a neighbor of Charlie in the Glen Park district and later the Owner's farm caretaker, remembers Finley telling him: "You got to put up a front in insurance. You got to look prosperous."

Mihelic's son, Ron, later to work in the A's front office in Oakland for Charlie, says, "My dad used to tell me the story about when Charlie would take clients out to lunch or something and would drive them past an exclusive part of Gary and point out a big, fancy house and say, 'We can't go in there. The decorators have the place in a mess.' But he'd never drive them past the place he really lived."

The man could be charming, could sell doctors, could domino the county medical societies, could aim higher. But regional and national groups could not be enrolled without help. He needed financial backing to go with his charm. He needed "carriers," insurance giants to venture into this new field, and that couldn't have been easy, for the carrier would have to be willing to take a multimillion dollar risk. A man who has dealt with many major carriers says, "The insurance business is very strange in that the decision you make today you have to pay for ten years down the road. And it may break you. You just don't know. Executives in the home offices of carriers are very cautious men. They want to move up the ladder and not have a ten-year-old decision haunt them. They're very protective of their jobs. I would guess that the big hunk of premium money Finley was going to get from medical associations appealed to some of these insurance company executives back then. They figured this new business would make them look good, that they'd get raises. And because there was no real precedent for this type of business, the carrier could set almost any premium rate he wanted to. Plus, because Finley was going to bring in all these new policy holders at once, the carrier eliminated the high cost of merchandising."

Charlie had all the mailing lists.

> *L. P. (Bud) Gillespie* (vice president, group sales, for Fireman's Fund American Life Insurance Company, a man who has known Finley, the Insurance Man, for twenty years): Carriers don't necessarily welcome or search out the association kind of business. It's a special deal. You can't devise an arbitrary rate for that kind of deal, and you usually end up with a compromise. It takes time—anywhere from six months to a year—to put that kind of program [i.e., a medical association coverage plan] together, and it's expensive. Even if you get all that business, it's instantly a target for competitors because of the great amount of money involved. And should you lose the program, it's a big chunk out of your business all at once. That's why some carriers are cautious about taking it in the first place. But it does have the advantage of being a good, money-making piece of business, and covering doctors is prestigious, with advertising spinoff benefits.

Charlie negotiated nearly two years to interest Chicago's Continental Casualty Company into underwriting a big national plan—a package for the massive American College of Surgeons with a total premium potential of perhaps six million dollars. But to get the contract, Charlie had to borrow five hundred dollars from a businessman friend in Hammond, Indiana. He needed a suit of clothes and a plane ticket to the College's convention in San Francisco. Plus a fountain pen, which he borrowed from a secretary in Gary. And never gave back.

The big contract was so lucrative ($441,563 in commissions in 1952, according to the U.S. Tax Court) that Charlie was able to move his offices from the tenth floor to larger space on the fifth floor of the bank building.

An early employee recalls that Charlie "hollered a lot" in the office. "He screamed because, I think, he was shy. If you looked him straight in the eye, he'd shut up. He'd shut up quick if you yelled back. Maybe he was shy because of his poor beginnings. He always used to talk about growing up in a house with a dirt floor. I noticed that he hollered the loudest when he wasn't sure about something. Once he told me to shut up when I wasn't even talking. What a horrible temper."

By 1952, Gary was too small for the temper and the business. He maintained his home in the mill town but opened a second office in a building on Chicago's Michigan Boulevard. Downtown. The Gary office remained operative to process the Indiana accounts.

"Didn't surprise me, his success," says an old acquaintance. "I knew that after he sold the small group policies, he could sell the large ones."

And, of course, himself.

He bought a large home in one of Gary's better neighborhoods, hired John Mihelic for odd jobs, took old friends for fast rides in the Caddy, employed a maid.

> *John Mihelic:* He was always good to me. He seemed to like me a lot. He took me to ball games. I felt like his friend, and I thought he was my friend. He was a nice man then.
>
> *Sam Joseph:* I'd lost contact with him for years. Then one day I was walking down the street downtown in Gary and he drove by in his Cadillac and honked and pulled over and we talked awhile. He had just sold that first big contract. We were happy to see each other, but the first thing I told him was, "Charlie, please don't sell me any insurance." Seemed that everybody and his brother was in the insurance business at that time.

At that time it also seemed as if Charlie had *sold* insurance to everybody and his brother. In 1953 he picked up the Southern

Medical Association, a group with member doctors in seventeen states and an eventual premium yield of more than three million dollars annually. To think that not too many months earlier a secretary had to remind him to change socks regularly and "drink your coffee without slurping." Once he mastered those facets of life, he was able to hit big casino—the American Medical Association, a deal wrapped up in 1961. Again, Continental Casualty (now CNA) was Charlie's carrier, although by 1967 the Owner and the company would bump heads over the AMA account. But by then Charlie was dealing with other carriers and had developed immense clout within the industry and, to an extent, the medical profession. Bud Gillespie recalls that at one point in the early sixties, Finley "was covering about fifty-three different associations—all of them professional and almost all of them medical. He always kept on the good, clean side of the association [group insurance] business, dealing with professional men, people who had money and were able to pay for things."

Not every member of every medical association bought a Finley policy, so in that sense the word group is a misnomer. Take, for example, his disability income coverage for members of the California Medical Association. By 1974, with Lumberman's as the carrier, Finley may have enrolled as many as seven thousand of the California Medical Association's twenty-five thousand members in his program. The doctors who don't sign up with Charlie can, as one expert in the field says, "get as good or better coverage at the same premium rate from somebody else."

But Charlie could survive without insuring *every* doctor in the United States. And did—survive very nicely, that is.

*A Finley client:* Charlie succeeded because he was first, because he's tenacious and smart, because there was nobody more aggressive in the association and group insurance business. He could have been far wealthier with a far less aggressive attitude and a mediative approach to his clients. But he probably reached the point where there was no difference in making another million bucks. He was able to get the cash flow and obtain what he wanted with the business he had.

*Bud Gillespie:* He once said to me—it was in 1967 during his fight to hold on to the AMA—that he didn't know why he stayed in the insurance field. He said, "I could retire on $250,000 a year right now." I kiddingly said to him, "My heart bleeds for you." I think he really loves the insurance business just like he does baseball. He's not in it just for the money. He's interested in getting the right policies to the people who need them. He knows his business in depth. His success in insurance was no fluke. He's a tough competitor.

*A Finley client:* In business, Charlie Finley is the ultimate street fighter.

By 1967, Finley and Continental Casualty were covering forty thousand members of the American Medical Association for disability income insurance. The annual premium total was eight million dollars, eight million out of his total premium writing of about forty million dollars, the latter his figure. Twenty percent of his gross came from the AMA. There is no way, without sending my own plumbers' unit to the Internal Revenue Service, to determine what percentage of the AMA premium money accrued personally to Charlie, although one source put the figure at seven percent. The men who sell policies work on a variety of commission structures. A life insurance salesman can get as high as ninety percent commission on the premium. On automobile and homeowner policies, the commission averages about twenty percent, because this kind of insurance is easier to sell. And the commission on disability income coverage for groups and associations?

*Ed Mitchell:* Premiums were high in the 1950s, and I would think that the commission then might have run as high as fifty percent.

But if I were to sell you a disability income policy today, I would make anywhere from forty to fifty percent off the first year's premium payment. Then it would go down in succeeding years as you renew your policy.

The insurance companies had special deals with Charlie, were paying him to "administer" the programs, a payment that was included in his commission percentage. Charlie handled all the mailings out of his Chicago office. "It took anywhere from three to twenty mailings to enroll a new medical group, and then he had to keep track of individual enrollees after starting a program," says Bud Gillespie.

"All Charlie does," says the client who describes himself as "Finley's worst enemy in the insurance business," "is collect the premiums and solicit new accounts."

But he is certainly better rewarded than your basic mail order house. It would not be unrealistic to presume that the AMA account yielded Charles O. Finley at least half a million dollars a year. At least. One would not hesitate to become an ultimate street fighter to preserve a half a million dollar account, would one? One certainly wouldn't.

> *John Ahlers* (a senior vice president of Fireman's Fund): Finley would be more likely to alienate the executives of an association in terms of wanting to help the individual members. He cared for the members.

As Fireman's Fund vice presidents Ahlers and Gillespie recount the situation, the board of trustees of the AMA was prepared to dump Finley as the broker of their disability income insurance program in 1967. Continental Casualty was to be retained as the carrier with slight changes in the nature of the benefits and/or premium costs. Finley could not fight the AMA board alone. He needed another carrier. Enter Fireman's Fund.

> *John Ahlers:* Charlie went into a vigorous letter-writing campaign to almost every one of the forty thousand doctors he covered. He said he had a carrier who would continue the same coverage for them. There was eight million dollars in premiums at stake. He's a good salesman. To be a good salesman, you've got to understand people. And he does. He's more people-related than anything else. You have to have an ego to be a good salesman.

The lobbying must have been intense and acrimonious. The client who doesn't like Charlie says that Finley had doctors fighting doctors during the AMA war of 1967. The board's move to shelve Charlie was taken to a House of Delegates vote, and all that letter writing paid off. "After an awful lot of discussion and dissension," says Ahlers, "Charlie won."

He cited this victory more than a year later in a letter to the chairman of the insurance committee of the Southern Medical Association. The letter was necessary because the seventeen-state SMA, with some seven thousand members paying more than three million dollars annually in premiums for the Finley coverage, was on the verge of saying bye-bye to Charlie. Early in 1969 he again was forced into a letter-writing campaign that well may have been patterned after his AMA-saving correspondence. He had landed the big Southern group in 1953 and watched its membership more than double; he didn't want to lose it now.

His key tactics, evidenced by the available correspondence sent to the SMA membership, involved lauding his work and denouncing the prospective competition, the World Service Life Insurance Company of Fort Worth, Texas, and Connecticut General. He appealed to the Southern doctors for "fair play" and said he was "shocked and chagrined" to think that the SMA "would be so quick to forget the help we had given them over the years."

The transfer of the coverage, he said in the letter, "is uncalled for, ruthless, and deplorable. . . . I can assure you that your insurance programs can very easily be led into a state of chaos and ruination within one year. . . ."

One source says that Charlie was getting at least half a million dollars of SMA's annual premium payment. Five hundred grand was sufficient to induce Charlie's further written articulation. In other words, he fought like hell to hang on to all that dough. Even if the executives of the SMA did not seem to be ecstatic over his retention, Charlie figured the membership would rise and back him, à la the AMA.

In a letter to doctor-members, SMA insurance committee chairman Dr. Joe T. Nelson said, on January 28, 1969, that the switch was being made to save about half a million dollars a year. Ousting Finley, he said, would "obtain for you the best possible insurance at the lowest cost to the group." Charlie fired back a letter warning the membership against buying "a pig in a poke." He added, "It doesn't make good sense for a doctor to rely on a doctor for insurance advice."

Meanwhile, he was soliciting SMA members to continue their insurance with him outside the aegis of the association. He had built an operation called Medical Arts Insurance Trust, described by his nonfriend client as "a euphemism that enables him to write a franchise [quasi-group] plan for doctors, gives him an entré to doctors, and preserves his status as an agent for doctors should he lose any one medical group."

Charlie predicted he would hang on to ninety percent of his SMA enrollees under the Medical Arts Trust blanket. In late March, 1969, he told the doctors that their renewal had reached seventy-two percent. He apologized to the doctors for bombarding them with correspondence but told them he felt obligated to give them "the complete story."

In another letter to SMA doctors, he quoted Lincoln's "all of the people all of the time" admonition, and added, "Charles O. Finley says: 'We present all of the true facts, to all of the people, all of the time.'"

Lincoln notwithstanding, Finley could not reverse the decision of Dr. Nelson's committee or the SMA executives. Charlie had lost an entire region of the country. Five years later, the country itself, at least as represented by the AMA, was seceding from the Finley union.

> *Dr. Ernest B. Howard* (executive vice president of the AMA in a letter to members dated March 21, 1974): On January 11, 1974, the American Medical Association was officially notified by Fireman's Fund that it will not renew beyond its September 1, 1974, expiration date your AMA members' disability insurance program with its *present* rate and benefit structures. Accordingly, your AMA Committee on Insurance engaged in an extensive review of the present program aimed at developing the best possible insurance program with emphasis on stability. . . . The AMA Board of Trustees . . . selected a *new* broker and administrator. . . .

The underlining of "new" was Dr. Howard's.

> *A Finley client:* He's losing the AMA because his carrier's programs are not particularly competitive. What Charlie offered was a policy with average benefits. But he was there first and so tenacious that he had the ability for longevity.

The men at Fireman's Fund would not discuss the firm's imminent departure from the AMA account. There was a hint, however, that claims were on the increase, that the company no longer looked with delight on the advertising spinoff benefits of covering forty thousand doctors for disability income insurance. The economic distress in this nation in 1973 and 1974 was not the depression all over again. Yet. But, as the man said earlier, when times are bad, claims are high. One source said Fireman's Fund "has dropped millions—a lot of millions" on this AMA coverage.

The timing that was so right for Charles O. Finley in the early fifties had started its counterclockwise movement after more than two decades of remarkably lavish ticking. There would be fewer filing cabinets with fewer names and addresses to show visitors on Michigan Avenue now. And fewer mailing lists. The impression was, on the brink of the AMA's departure, that Charlie's street-fighting instincts were lagging.

> *A veteran Finley insurance employee:* Maybe it's just that he sometimes gets bored with things. The AMA. Even, once in a while, baseball. I think the AMA loss came just because he doesn't anticipate things. And you know, the total insurance concept is not that important to him. Just the selling. One of his people used to nag him about expanding life insurance sales, and Mr. Finley would say, "Stop reading those goddamn books."

The money came so abundantly and speedily to Charlie after he contracted with the American College of Surgeons in 1951 that he appeared to many friends and business associates in succeeding years as a man walking on nails, through fire and under water, but never getting cut, burned, or drowned. The instant, or at least relatively instant, success must have terribly confused the man. His education had been limited (two years at Gary College, he has said) and he certainly was no authority on the principles of sound management. The Owner had to play tycoonism by ear; there was no choice, no time. The premium money and his "administrative fees" were torrential. His gut reactions, his instincts, would have to serve him in the conduct of this colossal commerce. The only way to get anything done at the beginning was to do it his way, and only his way, not through "conferences" or "meetings" or "brainstorming sessions" or "memos" or any other time-depriving practice of large, leisurely corporations. His best weapons would be his abundant energy, his guile, his fierce guardianship of a dollar's value. An ingenuous millionaire to be sure, but one guided as much by the fear of losing as by the lust of gaining.

> *Tom Corwin* (former A's traveling secretary and son of Emerson High classmates of Charlie): His philosophy is, take care of the little things and the big things will take care of themselves. Hence, he's gonna watch pennies. He'll pay more attention to an unpaid twenty-five-cent phone call on a player's hotel bill than he will to a two or three thousand dollar loan to a player. The loan will be paid back. But the quarter he'll never get. Somebody's *taken* him for a quarter. He's almost paranoid that somebody's gonna take money off him—take money out of his pocket, as he's fond of saying. It's *his* money. He makes that very clear. Like Scarlett O'Hara, I guess he just never wants to be poor again.

Charlie fancies himself as an economic genius. There can be no legitimate argument with that appraisal in terms of quantity. And yet . . .

Well, any of us can quibble with procedures; any of us can always deduce a "better" way to do things if we've worked at a job any length of time. We all have these standards, right? Not being an intellectual snob, Charlie had no standards laid upon him. There was never a commanding need for him to be consistent or practical or even contemporary. One relative says that Charlie "always wants to do whatever is popular at the moment." More accurately, Charlie wants to do whatever he *thinks* is popular at the time. He will tell a prospective employee, as he once told me, that he wants "you to work with me and not for me." He likes the sound, the compassion, of the phrase. He does not for a moment mean what he is saying. Not for a moment.

Ron Mihelic, son of Charlie's farm caretaker, worked in group sales for the Oakland A's. Ron says Charlie would tell him, "I don't want you sitting in this office. I can hire an order taker or clerk for seventy-five dollars a week to answer the phone." So Ron would hit the street, knock on doors, try to sell tickets. "And then the first time Charlie would call the office and I wasn't there, he'd scream at me later for half an hour because I wasn't available when he wanted to talk to me. His cousin Carl Finley used to say to me, 'The most consistent thing about Charlie is inconsistency.' "

Jim Piersall told a writer that, as Finley's group sales peddler in 1972, he sold two hundred thousand dollars worth of tickets. The next year, Piersall said, he was told he couldn't leave his desk, and he departed the Oakland organization. On the surface it would appear that to Charlie an employee's availability is of more value than the employee's productivity.

> *Ex-A's announcer Harry Caray:* If you're independent, Charlie is the greatest guy in the world to work for. If you need a job, and if the money you make out of your job is of vital importance to you, he's the worst guy in the world to work for because he senses that and he'll kick you around.

"At the start," says a veteran employee, "he succeeded because he had some good people. But everybody leaves. A lot of them just got an ulcer from all of his screaming."

Two vice presidents of Fireman's Fund, both of whom speak with a measure of respect and affection for Charlie after many years of dealing with him in the insurance world, suggest that he has limited his capacity for success by personnel practices. "One of his weaknesses is his staff operation," says Bud Gillespie. "He doesn't have enough backup people."

Gillespie's colleague John Ahlers says, "Usually in business there are many captains that are that way. They don't want other captains around them. Charlie's method of operation is being involved in everything and not delegating authority. But if you're trying to perpetuate a business, then you've got a problem. He started with a one-man involvement and he never got out of that habit."

A former A's announcer, Bob Elson, put it more bluntly. "Charlie butts into everything," he said. "He'd sell tickets, hawk programs, sweep out the ball park, anything. He's the hardest-working man in baseball, but Charlie Finley feels that if Charlie Finley should drop dead, the world would just stop turning around."

> *Tom Corwin:* I think he has an overwhelming strength and desire to succeed, to work, to do things that nobody has done because they didn't want to drive themselves. He enjoys driving himself. He enjoys working eighteen, twenty hours a day. And this is part of the reason, the problem, that employees don't get along with him in a lot of cases. Because he expects them to do it, too. He just has an awesome capacity for work. One of the reasons I quit [as A's traveling secretary] was it seemed to me that working eighteen to twenty hours a day to make money for somebody else didn't make much sense. At thirty years old I felt there was more to life than working all those hours every single day. I minded not being able to have a picnic in the park on a Saturday afternoon.

Bob Bestor, once Finley's hockey publicity man in Oakland, said he never knew "what it was like being a common laborer until I worked for Charlie. He is a straw boss on a construction job. He's from a whole different world." Bestor had previously worked for one of the celebrated geniuses of the professional football world, the Raiders' Al Davis, whose capacity for work is as awesome as Finley's. Bestor compares: "Davis is like the CIA, but Charlie is like the Fourth Marine Division. He just rolls over you. The thing that finally got me out of there [the Seals] was when he took a full hour explaining to me how to address an envelope."

In 1972 Charlie told UPI that he had to have a majority interest in anything he owned. "If I can't control something and run it the way I want to run it, then I don't want any part of it," he said.

> *A Finley employee:* He wants to know everything—and has to. I don't mean that I have to ask him if I can go out and buy stationery. But he has turned down the purchase of small items just because he doesn't want to spend money on that particular thing or that particular person. I think it depends on what the return might be. And his priorities sometimes are unbelievable. Right after the last game of the 1973 World Series he went to Francesco's restaurant in Oakland and bought drinks for the house, including employees there. The bill was over six hundred bucks. But then you'll ask him to spend about twenty bucks for some pictures of a ballplayer and he'll say, "Hell, no." See? It's a question of priorities. A standard joke around the A's office when he does something like that—something we think should have been done from a public relations standpoint—is, "Well, that guy will never be a success doing business like that. He'll never make any money."

In 1959, Charlie told the Gary *Post-Tribune* that he attributed his success to "people helping me along the way and hard work."

There is no demeaning the man's industry. Because he is that way, he expects everyone who works for him to be that way. And a few have been. They survive. Most have not been, and they either quit or get fired, thus the transient nature of his "staff." If he had found this massive employee turnover hurting business, he would have stopped turning the people over. But business thrived, no matter who was on the other end of the phone, so who could tell him he was running his enterprises the wrong way? An old high school friend, Joe Goffiney, says, "The way he does things is his own business. Oh, I've given him advice—but not about business. Just little things. But he'd never listen to me, anyway. I doubt if he listens to anybody."

Several people who have worked for him are convinced Charlie often knows when he's ignoring good advice, but that he goes ahead and makes the wrong decision anyway. Masochism? "He loves controversy," says Tom Corwin. "He likes to create problems to solve. As a challenge, I guess. He'll tackle a seemingly impossible task. He won't shy away from anything. He doesn't worry about taking a personal risk. He's a man of courage. Absolutely."

He expects the same gutsiness and pugnaciousness from all who surround him. He wants the people who work for Charles O. Finley to be just like Charles O. Finley but at the same time to recognize that there is only one Charles O. Finley. And he has a total insistence on loyalty, which has often led to divisiveness among employees who are constantly trying to outloyal each other. Whatever the resultant schisms, Charlie always finds out what he wants to know. Although once in a while he must be surprised at the extent of the loyalty.

Vern Hoscheit was a coach for the Oakland Athletics from 1969 to mid-1974. One of his major assignments during that period was to guard the bag of practice baseballs. No one was more fiercely protective of old baseballs than Vern Hoscheit. The impression was that he had orders not to let those balls get away. Balls cost money. Charlie once casually reached into the ball bag to grab a couple, and Hoscheit gave the Owner hell. As Tom Corwin recalls it, Finley said, "You can't talk to the Owner like that." Hoscheit responded that he didn't care who Finley was—"I've got fifty balls here that I've got to turn in at the end of the season, so put 'em back in the bag until I get a written notice from you. In your own handwriting."

"Charlie appreciates this kind of loyalty and honesty," says Corwin. "It builds trust."

The Owner must have been amazed that someone really cared about protecting his money. One of his former employees has the notion that "because Charlie had to claw and scratch and cut corners on his way up, he knows every trick in the book as far as getting money out of someone else. And because he knows that, he's not gonna let his employees get away with it with him."

Over the years—or at least until the market thrashed itself mercilessly in 1973–74—Charlie apparently enjoyed great success in stock investments. The ballplayers for whom he invested swore by his stock selections, and one Oakland man said Finley once told him he had made more profit on the stock market than in the insurance business. There is every reason to believe that the Owner's brokers received as many telephone calls daily as his baseball managers.

Finley without a telephone would be like an octopus without a tentacle. The telephone is his life. When he calls, you know he cares. When he does not call (as he did not call A's manager Bob Kennedy in the final several weeks of the 1968 season), you know he no longer cares.

One employee told me that Finley used to spend at least fifty thousand dollars a year in outgoing calls from his Chicago office before discovering he could purchase a WATS line that would give him a cheaper monthly long distance rate. "And when the telephone man came to the office to install the new equipment, Charlie showed him every socket."

Some people are convinced that when the Owner has nothing else to do, he picks up the phone. With a call, he can reward, or punish, or buy, or sell, or merely advise another human being that "this is Finley." Indeed, it is.

CHAPTER **IV**

# "SO YOU WANNA WORK
# FOR CHARLIE FINLEY?"

Jim Bank did, and because of that yearning he and I were forced
to leave Yom Kippur services in Baltimore, Maryland, in October,
1973, in a police car. But that's another story.

Jim Bank didn't know if he *really* wanted to work for Charlie
Finley, but it sure was worth a try. It was July, 1972, and Jim felt
the University of Alabama had no more minutiae with which to fill
his mind, so why not go to work. He read about Finley buying the
Memphis Tams basketball club and thought he'd apply for some
sort of job, despite lack of experience and total unfamiliarity with
Charlie. Bank did, however, know two fellows who had toiled for
the man: Paul Bryant, Jr., son of Paul (Bear) Bryant, and a man
who once handled Kansas City baseball tickets. Bank spoke with
the two a day apart. Bryant, who'd been an executive in the A's
farm system, told him, "You don't want to work for Finley. He's
very demanding. He'll tell you one thing one day and change his
mind the next." And the former Kansas City ticket man told him,
"You don't want to work for Finley. He's very demanding. He'll

tell you one thing one day and change his mind the next." Not wishing to press his luck, Jim stopped talking right there to former Finley employees and fired off a letter and résumé to the Tam owner. Despite his youth, Bank had a refreshing view of the business world. "I figured that Mr. Finley could do whatever he wanted to with his money and his organization."

Using Bryant's name as reference (Paul, Jr. had mentioned Bank to Charlie in a conversation), young Jim shakily telephoned Chicago for an interview and was stunned when Finley told him to fly on up. Two days later, Bank did. He was excited and scared and insecure and awed and had to wait two hours until Charlie arrived at the Michigan Avenue office.

> *Jim Bank:* The reception room door just booms open, and there he is. He's wearing a seersucker jacket and a little short-sleeved knit shirt and white loafers—not what you'd expect your everyday millionaire to be wearing—and he asked me to come into his office. I didn't leave until five hours later. It was really an experience. Out of that five hours, he must have talked to me personally a total of about thirty minutes. The rest of the time mostly he was on the phone. He offered me lunch, but I didn't eat because he had his secretary make him a mixture of chopped beefsteak, navy beans, and ketchup. You see, he'd recently lost his false teeth in a motel and had to gum everything. I couldn't take that kind of meal. He'd make a phone call, do some paperwork, and then maybe look at me and ask me one question. He even asked me to go with him to the A's game in Milwaukee that night, but I said no because I thought I might be imposing. I was awestruck by the fact he was even seeing me, and this was my first business experience outside of college jobs. My true love was hockey; I'd already tried to get a job with the Atlanta Flames of the NHL, so I asked him if he had any openings on his hockey team. He goes, "Hockey! You don't know what a fucking hockey stick is." I had to laugh and tell him I sure did, but he just changed the subject.

Earlier, said Jim, Finley had told him there were no front office jobs open with the Tams. But after several hours, Charlie offered him an assistantship in the public relations department in Memphis. Then came salary negotiations: Charlie against the kid. The veteran, shrewd bargainer against a novice.

> *Jim Bank:* He remembered that I'd told him on the phone—he has a phenomenal memory when he wants to—that I just wanted to make living expenses. He asked me how much I wanted. Now, I had been warned ahead of time by my friends that he's the kind of guy who asks *you* what you want. He never offers. I told him I had two other job possibilities: one selling advertising at my father's radio station and the other as assistant sports information director at the University of Alabama. I told him both jobs were paying four hundred dollars a month, which to me at that time was a helluva lot of money. And Mr. Finley started laughing. I mean literally out loud. He said, "Four hundred, huh?" I said, "I'll need a little more to live in a big city like Memphis." And he said, "All right, let's start you off at six hundred." I just couldn't believe it. That's what I was making a year in college.

Nine months later, after the American Basketball Association season ended, Finley dispatched Jim to the A's, telling him, "We'll start you off in the public relations department and see what develops." Bank started driving to Oakland the next morning and upon arrival—after his car broke down in the desert—phoned Charlie to see if the new job might be worth more than six hundred dollars a month.

> *Jim Bank:* I knew that Mr. Finley would ask me how much I wanted, so I made up my mind to ask him for another hundred fifty or two hundred a month plus a car, just to see what he'd say. He gives cars to people a lot of times. He asked how much I was

making, and right away he offered me a hundred fifty dollar raise a month. I wasn't going to argue with that at all. I wasn't going to press my luck, so I didn't ask for the car.

His first six weeks in Oakland, Jim worked in the concessions department. He would start at the A's office in the morning and not leave the ball park until midnight on game evenings. He would unload shipments of novelties, he would check out the salesmen. He was not a very happy young man.

But then A's public relations director Art Popham, also in his twenties, quit, and Jim was named interim p.r. director. "I was a little nervous," he says. "Starting on top like this with the world champions of baseball?" He was told that, with Finley, an interim job could last for years, but in his case the job ended in a few weeks when Charlie brought his Memphis publicity man, Bob Fulton, to Oakland. Once again, Jim's morale suffered, although he blamed fate and not Charlie.

Four months after he came to Oakland, and thirteen months after he began working for Finley in Memphis, Jim Bank was appointed traveling secretary of the A's when Tom Corwin abruptly resigned. Jim couldn't believe his good fortune; Corwin's job had seemed to him to be paradise for a single young man. On the first road trip, Finley phoned Bank in Anaheim.

*Jim Bank:* He asked me how much I was making, and I told him. He asked me how much I made in Memphis, and I told him. He probably knew, but couldn't think of it right then. But he's going to know if I'm telling the truth or not. And he upped me a thousand dollars a year, making it retroactive to the day I started the traveling secretary's job, which was only about a week. I thought that was very nice of him.

The photographic blowup of the contract between the Owner and one William Cutler was tacked and taped to a large, legged slab of beaverboard standing inches away from juror number one, a twentyish fellow with styled hair and uncaring eyes. It is unlikely he ever looked at the oversized contract, for during these four days in late June, 1974—despite the overwhelming presence in an Oakland courtroom of the Owner—juror number one stared impassively forward. He did not appear to see Finley, or Judge Robert Barber, or Bill Cutler, or flamboyant attorney Robert Burnstein. Or the contract clause that had been underlined in red by Finley's attorney, John Wells, who early on referred to the trial as "a very simple case"—words that seemed also to be underlined in red when he said them.

> *The contract clause:* Finley agrees to employ Cutler, and Cutler agrees to serve, as vice president of the baseball division of the Charles O. Finley Company, with such authority and responsibility as may be assigned to Cutler from time to time by the president of the company.

Cutler signed the contract in November, 1967, and was fired by the president of the company some six months later. Now—six years later—Bill Cutler was asking juror number one and eleven other folks who weren't impassive to award him $57,500 in back wages. Give to Cutler, take from Finley . . . A very simple case.

> *Bill Cutler:* It's always been my feeling that if Charlie hadn't met me and other people through meeting me, he never would have gotten into baseball.

Bill always wanted to get involved in baseball. He knew it never could be as a player. Back in Grand Rapids, Michigan, as a kid, he tried. "But I was humpty-dumpty. I couldn't throw, I couldn't run, I couldn't hit. I loved the game, though." And in 1945, a rainstorm in Washington, D.C., spread sunshine over the ambitions of Bill Cutler. Life is not supposed to happen the way it happened to Cutler. American League president Will Harridge was not supposed to come along in his car when an Army Air Corps staff sergeant from Grand Rapids was thumbing a ride home in the rain outside Griffith Stadium. Harridge was not supposed to tell the young man to "look me up if you get to Chicago." Cutler was not supposed to visit Harridge two or three times in the next few years. Harridge was not supposed to give Cutler a job in the American League office in 1948. The American League office was not supposed to be located in a large building in Chicago at 310 South Michigan Avenue. The Charles O. Finley Company was not supposed to have its offices at 310 South Michigan Avenue.

It happens.

Bill is not certain when he first saw Charles O. Finley in the building's coffee shop. "You couldn't have missed noticing him," Cutler says. "And from the way he looked and talked you didn't figure him for a rich man. In those days Charles was the kind of guy I'd call a jock sniffer. A jock sniffer with a lot of money. He followed Notre Dame in football. I remember once he brought Rocky Marciano into my office. He kept keeping contact with us in the league office. If I had had any sense, I would have remembered what he was like in the building."

Soon after Finley landed the Kansas City franchise, Cutler was offered a job. Bill says he saw no role for himself then with the A's and turned down Charlie. Six years later, when the A's were moving to Oakland, Finley courted Cutler again. Bill admits that Charlie may have sought him for quasi-political reasons. Cutler, by then an American League executive for twenty years, could keep things cool for Charlie with league president Joe Cronin.

Cutler wanted to be a general manager. Finley had been his own general manager for several seasons and wanted Cutler to handle public relations duties. Cutler told Charlie he knew nothing about p.r. As they talked in the coffee shop of Oakland's Edgewater Inn in the fall of 1967, Charlie made notes on a paper place mat. Cutler said Finley agreed to name him "vice president with the duties of a general manager." Charlie has maintained that the contract meant what it said: Cutler would do whatever Finley told him to do.

In the next few months, Finley told Cutler to handle public relations. Cutler again said no. Finley told Cutler to sell advertising space for the new scoreboard at the Oakland ball park, and Cutler again said no, that he'd been hired to perform the duties of a general manager, not a space salesman. Finley told Cutler to run the farm system, and Cutler said no. Take the farm system job or you're through, said Finley. Cutler said no and was canned—with three and a half years remaining of his four-year contract. He said he was so incensed when Finley tried to prevent him from receiving unemployment compensation that he hired an attorney. Bill Cutler, on behalf of himself, his twelve children, wife, two cats, and a dog, gave Bob Burnstein two grand and a projected settlement percentage to sue the Owner for breach of contract.

The case finally was heard in Oakland before Alameda County Superior Judge Leonard Dieden in 1972. An eight-man jury found in favor of Cutler and awarded him $13,500, a half year's salary. But the judge in effect overruled the jury and withheld the finding. Bob Burnstein appealed successfully before the California State Supreme Court on grounds of the abuse of discretion by the judge in the face of evidence. The retrial began on June 25, 1974. The only change in the cast of principals was the judge—Barber instead of Dieden.

*Day One.*

Cutler was saying that Finley "is fine until you work for him. Then everything changes. His eyes. His voice. Everything." Cutler was fifty-four, two years Finley's junior. In his blue knit corduroy suit, his red tie, his white loafers, his rosy cheeks, his whitening hair, Bill Cutler could have been a young Uncle Sam. He introduced me to Burnstein, his attorney; together they answered questions about the background of the retrial. Burnstein, also mid-fiftyish, was quick, glib, modish, a happy bassett.

"The nub of the case," he said, "is what Cutler was hired to do."

Cutler reminded me of a story he'd told me shortly after Charlie fired him in 1968. Bill said he wanted to see his family in December, 1967. He asked Charlie to let him go home; after all, Cutler said he told Charlie, his contract with the A's didn't start until January 1 and he wanted time to move his family to Oakland from Boston (where the American League headquarters had been transferred). And, Bill said, he missed his wife.

> *Bill Cutler:* Charlie told me, "Draw fifty dollars out of petty cash and go out and get laid. Then you won't be so lonesome." I told him to shove the job up his ass, and I packed to go home. But on the way, I stopped in Chicago to talk to Charlie and he asked me not to quit, that it would look bad for his image.

Cutler was telling me that Finley once offered to settle the suit for "five thousand dollars and a pitcher named George Lauzerique" at a time Cutler was running a minor league team in Portland, Oregon. Just then Charlie and his son Paul passed us. Finley was most cordial, and we all walked in to watch Burnstein and Charlie's man, John Wells, pick a jury.

Charlie was in the lightweight glen plaid suit he'd worn to the ball park the previous evening after flying in from Chicago. I had been sitting in the A's dugout listening to the Owner give batting tips to first baseman Pat Bourque.

Into the wood-paneled, air-conditioned courtroom filed three dozen prospective jurors. They were plopped in their box, and Judge Barber introduced the principals to them. Charlie smiled broadly when his name was called. A little lady juror, a part-time ticket seller at the Oakland Coliseum, smiled back. They were strangers, but Burnstein would bump her with one of his challenges.

As each juror recited personal statistics, Charlie took notes on a piece of lined yellow legal paper he'd cadged from his attorney, a handsome Burt Reynolds type with a Fu Manchu mustache, a member of one of Oakland's most prestigious law firms. Wells lacked the aggressiveness of opponent Burnstein. He was less frenetic, less articulate. He had—and needed—the necessary patience.

A pleasant man in the box, a carpenter, told Judge Barber that he had been a juror in a criminal trial. "Pimpin' and prostitutin'," he giggled. Charlie giggled back. When a middle-aged hippie with a headband said he'd once heard on television "about Mr. Finley firing some people," Charlie shot him a stern glance. Wells later challenged him off the panel.

During a morning break, twenty-one-year-old Paul Finley and I chatted about Indiana University, my alma mater and Paul's college for a year. Paul had transferred to Arizona State, was working for his dad in Chicago now but living in LaPorte with his mother. Without mentioning her divorce action, I asked Paul how she was getting along and he said just fine. I wondered if she would be vacationing this summer—without telling him I hoped to speak to her in LaPorte within the month. He said she frequently went to Europe with the wife of Chicago sportswriter Dave Condon, but that he didn't know her current plans. "I don't know what she likes about Europe so much," Paul said. "I've got no interest in the place." In all, a pleasant, curly-haired, open young man.

After lunch, Finley was speaking to an older man just outside the courtroom doors as we all waited for jury selection to resume. Wells walked up to his client and asked to speak to him. "Don't bother me," Charlie said, rather loudly. "This man asked me a question. Now get away and don't bother me." Heads turned. Later, Burnstein told me that Wells was concerned about Finley speaking to a prospective juror and had simply wanted to caution him.

Back in court, Wells wondered if any of the prospective jurors were A's fans, and if so, had they any particular feelings about the Owner. Or had they even heard of him?

"If you live in Oakland, I guess you'd have to have heard of Charlie Finley," said one woman in the box.

A man from the Southern Pacific said he'd read about the A's in the newspapers and that "it sounds like, to phrase it, a screwball operation." Wells had that fellow excused.

"I guess I blame Finley when the team loses," said a male fan/juror. "But I was sure happy when they won the World Series."

Burnstein suggested while questioning a juror that "the vicissitudes and problems of the Oakland A's don't concern you" in this trial. He said he hoped the jury would not be influenced by the fact that "an unimportant man" like Bill Cutler was taking on "a prominent man" like Charlie Finley.

Finley kept peering back at the prospective jurors who had not yet been summoned to the box. Looking for a businessman type? His people? If so, there were not many who seemed to fit that assumptive bill.

Burnstein challenged four, Wells five. Judge Barber excused

two. The twenty-third juror in the box was an insurance salesman. Wells and Burnstein were satisfied with the seven men and five women in the box. Burnstein said he wanted an all-male jury in the first trial on the assumption the men would empathize with Cutler. This time around, he said, he didn't feel the jury's sexual composition mattered.

And, in a voice reminiscent of Shelley Berman, Bob Burnstein told the jury how good old Bill Cutler thought he was going to work for good old Charlie Finley as a vice president with the duties of general manager. As Burnstein spoke to the jury, Finley alternately scowled and made notes in firm, large strokes.

Cutler had been making about twenty-six thousand dollars handling player matters for the American League. That figure included extra compensation for performing duties on behalf of the commissioner's office at World Series time.

Under the terms of his deal with Charlie, Cutler would be paid twenty-seven thousand in 1968 and a thousand dollars more each year for the next three years. Instead, Cutler worked in 1969 as an eight thousand dollar a year scout for the Montreal Expos and in 1970 and 1971 as general manager of the Portland club of the Pacific Coast League at seventeen thousand annually. His earnings in six months from Finley had been $13,500. Burnstein scrawled all these figures on a board and informed the jury that Cutler wanted the difference in what he earned elsewhere and what he would have been paid by Charlie—$57,500. And Shelley Berman Burnstein sat down.

Wells' opening statement began with a brilliant synthesis. He tacked up the contract and told the jury that Cutler was hired to carry out whatever assignments Finley chose to give him and not as a general manager. "It was clearly Mr. Cutler's choice" to do what Charlie asked or to leave, said Wells.

My notion was that Wells had made an excellent, telling point and would now sit down. "That's what he should have done," Burnstein said to me later. But Wells continued at length, while Charlie made some more notes—at one point passing a scrawled message to his working attorney.

Cutler was Burnstein's first witness and told of his first few days "on the job" with Charlie. In November, 1967, Cutler attended the major league meetings in Mexico City. He had agreed to work for Finley but technically was still an employee of the American League. Cutler testified that when he arrived in Mexico City he learned the press had been told he was "vice president in charge of public relations" for the A's. Bill said he told Finley immediately that he had never wanted to be the club's p.r. man. He testified that Finley said to him, "You've already quit your job with the league, so you'll do whatever I tell you."

After court, Charlie and I went to the ball park, separately, and watched the A's take their second straight from the California Angels, whose manager, Bobby Winkles, was in deep trouble.

Finley had changed suits—now he was in dark blue—but I was still in my respectably cruddy blue cords and Levi shirt. It was unfair that he looked fresher.

*Day Two.*

Cutler continued his testimony, Charlie his note taking. Bill said he kept turning down Finley's p.r., advertising sales, and farm system assignments because those were not included in a general manager's domain. "I was hired as a vice president with the duties of general manager," he reiterated.

He recalled that at one point Finley told him, "You've got to start doing something." I glanced at the jury for signs of reaction. None.

Documents indicated that after Cutler turned down the farm system directorship, Charlie gave him five days to reconsider or be terminated. Cutler still refused and was canned on May 28, 1968.

The only other significant moment in Cutler's direct examination came when a young lady juror asked somebody to define the meaning of farm system. At that moment, I wondered why nobody yet had defined the duties of a general manager of a major league baseball club.

Wells began his cross-examination of Cutler as if he were dealing with a child who refused to eat his supper and was sent off to bed summarily. "All you had to do to get that fifty-seven thousand five hundred dollars was to do what Finley told you to do, right?"

Only, Cutler said, if his orders involved general managership duties.

Wells mentioned that Charlie had given Bill a five grand bonus to sign the contract and had forked over some sixty-six hundred dollars so Bill could move his wife, twelve children, two cats, and a dog from Boston to California.

The place mat, treated as gingerly as if the Magna Carta had been penned thereon, was introduced. There was no notation on it about a general managership or p.r. directorship. All that Finley had scrawled over coffee seven years earlier in connection with Cutler's assignment were the words "duties . . . all duties."

Charlie fingered a ruler, wrote notes to Wells, stared solemnly at Cutler on the stand, watched the jury. Busy, busy, busy.

During a short recess, Cutler said to me, "Looks like Charlie's handling his own case." Burnstein, standing nearby, heard and smiled.

Wells had Cutler retrace his career. Bill told about getting that ride from Will Harridge outside Griffith Stadium. He recalled

Harridge saying to him, "You seem like a clean-cut boy in the service. When you get out, come and see me." Wells was attempting to establish that Cutler came to the A's with limited business experience.

Cutler talked about some of his early duties in Oakland, about laying out the Coliseum for baseball. "Charlie wanted to put the foul poles inside the park," Cutler testified. "Everybody knows they go outside."

Lunch time, and just outside the courtroom Finley runs into the judge at his first trial, Leonard Dieden, still on the Alameda County bench. There's a cheery greeting, and Dieden says, "You're not drawing enough fans. What you need is me as general manager." Both laugh heartily.

Finley himself is due on the stand in the afternoon, and I am due at the ball park for another game between the A's and Angels. Frustration at missing Charlie's testimony. But maybe Burnstein won't finish with him until tomorrow. Help me, Burnstein, help me.

Dave Hamilton stops the Angels on two hits. The word out of Anaheim is that California Angel board chairman Gene Autry, president Bob Reynolds, and general manager Harry Dalton had been meeting in the morning to parry the dismissal of manager Bobby Winkles. In the clubhouse after the game Winkles tells us, "I don't know what came out of that meeting but I guess I'll find out tomorrow. I've really enjoyed being in major league baseball." One of his players shouts at us inquiring reporters, "Why don't you fuckers leave the poor man alone?"

What us poor fuckers failed to realize was that within the hour Charlie Finley would be meeting in a hotel two miles from the ball park with Autry and Reynolds to discuss Winkles' successor. Man named Dick Williams.

*Day Three.*

I was lucky. Burnstein had not finished his examination of Charlie. I frankly was surprised that Finley had been called as the plaintiff's witness. "Why not?" said Burnstein.

Paul Finley again was in court with his father, as was Charlie's Oakland secretary, supremely loyal Carolyn Coffin, whom I had asked many weeks earlier for an interview in connection with this book. I told her I sincerely wanted the appraisal of Charlie's loyalists and suggested she might wish to call him to get his approval. She said she did not have to ask his approval. She turned me down on her own.

Miss Coffin and Paul sat in the spectator seats directly behind the defense table. Since the beginning of the trial I had been seated to the rear of Burnstein and Cutler, not out of a sense of partisanship, although I'm sure it appeared that way to Charlie, but because it gave me a better angle to view Finley at the defense table. He would often turn and glare or wink or simply stare without expression. In the first two days our only conversations consisted of "good mornings" and my questions about possible baseball deals. I saw no reason to impose, being I'm (1) somewhat shy, and (2) accepting of his earlier refusal to talk about himself for the book. There was no point in pushing anything, especially not in court. I doubt if my presence made him uncomfortable. Mere mortals cannot wreak that havoc upon a Charles O. Finley. Not so it would show, I mean. And there is no hostility in the above.

"Boy, you really missed it yesterday," Burnstein said. "I couldn't get him to answer a question directly." Apparently, from reports I'd received, Charlie had circled the bases whenever Burnstein asked him to throw down to second. An Oakland *Tribune* writer who'd covered Finley's testimony of the day before showed me one interesting quote from Charlie: "Vice presidents are a dime a dozen." I don't think that was in answer to one of Burnstein's direct questions.

Charlie was wearing his third suit in three days—an interesting, plaid-like striped affair of several dark hues. But for the third straight day he was shod in black boots, which crept out as he sat on the stand, arms folded, rigid for combat with that slow, sure, syllabizing Joe McCarthy voice. The surrealism of the late senator from Wisconsin answering the questions of Shelley Berman. I wanted to listen with my eyes closed, but I knew it was more important to see Charlie.

There were times during Finley's testimony one could have sworn that Charlie, not Barber, was the judge. Even unrobed. Charlie would rock in the swivel chair, or lean forward, or pensively reflect with right index finger probing right cheek, or judiciously consider with chin cupped in left hand.

And, my god, juror number one never looked at him once.

Charlie continued being playful with Burnstein, talking around the corner and up the block. Burnstein kept complaining about "all of these rhetorical responses . . . I can't get a yes or no. What did you say, Mr. Finley? . . . Just a simple yes or no, please."

Charlie answered one question by saying, "Yes and no."

When giving some long answers, particularly in matters related to technical elements of running a baseball team, Charlie would turn to the jury, a professor of the national pastime lecturing to a freshman class. Several jurors seemed mesmerized by the voice.

He suggested that Cutler had agreed to be his p.r. vice president at the beginning, that Bill told him, "I'll do the best I can," and that he told Bill, "If you don't find that kind of work enjoyable, we'll find something else."

He said he believed Cutler could handle the public relations assignment because all a p.r. man had to be was "a good-looking fellow . . . with an average amount of intelligence . . . who could get along with people." Cutler, testified Charlie, fit this bill. Charlie was sure because back in Chicago, he said, he had known

Bill socially. "I'd say public relations is very important in any field," said Charlie. "I didn't need a p.r. expert but a baseball expert. I could go and hire a p.r. man from a meat-packing firm, but he couldn't do a p.r. job in baseball until I trained him for a couple of years."

He was enjoying sparring with Burnstein. Nothing big, just a little jabbing. Before returning to the stand after the first recess, Charlie borrowed a ruler from clerk Louise Keturi. He fingered it, palmed it, and slapped his boot and knee with it for the next hour. Judge Barber suggested that Charlie be more direct with his answers, so Finley responded—briefly—with quick bursts.

A young lady juror wove a ponytail out of her long, dark hair as Charlie continued testifying. And unwove it. And wove it. I found the ponytail more fetching, frankly.

When Burnstein handed Charlie a piece of evidence, Charlie would read more of it than Burnstein asked. Bob would try to cut him short, and Charlie would smile. The dark brows would unknit; a little boy would be giving the jury a cutesy-poo grin.

Charlie says he would have assigned Cutler any job within reason—"with dignity to it." He says he was willing to train Cutler in advertising sales work, train him as a farm director.

Burnstein passed the witness another document, asked Charlie to read. "It's already been read," said Wells. "Lemme read it," Charlie told his own attorney. Wells told his client to go ahead and read. Once Burnstein reached for a document when Charlie finished reading. Finley held tight, wouldn't let it go. Bob grabbed again, and this time Charlie handed it back. Then he smiled impishly at the jury.

The next day, while waiting for the jury to come back with its verdict, I asked Cutler's attorney about that moment.

> *Bob Burnstein:* If Charles is put in a position to be subservient— and that's what being on the witness stand can become—he will do

certain things to show he doesn't feel totally subservient. He had to do something to take away the play from me.

During the lunch break of the third day, veteran Oakland *Tribune* courthouse reporter Havelock Hunter, who had watched the morning's testimony, said to me, "The jury seems to be giving Finley tolerant laughter, like they're just watching him play the big shot. But I don't think that attitude will mitigate their verdict."

Before the afternoon session began, clerk Keturi asked Charlie to autograph a snapshot of her eight-year-old son David, in an A's cap. Charlie obliged, read aloud what he wrote on the back of the snapshot: "The A's will win again in '74."

Burnstein was ready for his final witness, which was a notebook. Former Finley attorney John Stevens had testified in the first trial. Stevens had become a federal appellate judge in Chicago, and now his testimony was coming from his earlier statements. Judge Stevens had said that while preparing Cutler's contract with the A's, he told Bill, "You and I both know that Charlie is a difficult man to work for. Before you take the job, you have to commit yourself . . . Bill knew he had to be prepared to get along with Charlie. . . . Cutler was not clear in his own mind what his duties would be with the A's."

The jury was growing weary as Burnstein read further from Stevens' testimony. But by 2:00 P.M. Bob had finished and rested his case. Again, here came Charlie.

He was the witness for his own side this time. He folded his arms and stared sinisterly at John Wells. At the beginning he gave Wells short, direct answers—five "rights" in a row at one point.

Then Wells asked a question that required a much, much longer answer. He asked Charlie about his educational and business background. In jumped Burnstein. Bob did not want a recitation of the life of Charlie Finley *by* Charlie Finley. Bob did not know what effect such Horatio Algerizing would have on the jury. "I will stipulate," Bob said, "that Mr. Finley has become a very substantial man, whether by formal education or not."

I wanted Finley to talk. I wanted his autobiography on record. The judge obliged me and permitted Charlie to emcee his own version of "This Is Your Life."

He studied "mechanical engineering at school." Thence to U.S. Steel in Gary in 1936. "I like to think I'm younger than I look." (A woman whose insight and judgment I value suggested to me that Charlie refused to tell the world he was fifty-six "because now that he's on the brink of being 'single,' he doesn't want the ladies to know his age." Accepted.)

Charlie said he was in "the mechanical end" at U.S. Steel. In the machine shop, he said. In 1941, he said, he and his brother (Fred) "decided to leave the mills to go in the service." Fred was in, Charlie said, but he was judged physically unfit. Thence to the Kingsbury ordnance plant. After five years, Charlie said, "I have five thousand employees under my supervision. I was divisional superintendent at the age of twenty-seven." (Any juror mathematically inclined would then have doped Charlie's age.)

"I then decided I wanted to go into the insurance business . . . I took to insurance like a duck to water . . . I enjoyed it. I got lucky." He discussed his record-setting sales performance for The Travelers. "I worked twelve, fourteen, eighteen hours a day, seven days a week, I enjoyed it so much . . . I'm an insurance peddler . . . I write every type of insurance."

Wells jumped in to ask his client to move along to baseball and to the A's. Charlie was in no rush. "Let me finish," he admonished Wells, who let him finish.

"I got lucky my first year [in business] and made a potful of money. But I started coughing up a storm." Finley related his twenty-seven-month invalidism with pneumonic tuberculosis.

"But the TB sanitarium was a blessing in disguise," he said. "I had plenty of time to do a lot of thinking about insurance and came up with a *tremendous idea*." The jury was absorbed, totally. Enraptured, almost. Even juror number one seemed to be looking straight ahead with more conviction than usual.

Finley traced his idea of group coverage for doctors. "I couldn't wait to get out and get started, it was such a tremendous idea." He cited all the medical associations that began subscribing to his group programs. He said he once covered associations in seventeen states. Then came the American Medical Association.

"Today," Charlie said, "all the doctors in America are insured under programs originated and administered by Charles O. Finley."

Charlie discussed his "overnight wealth" from the group coverage business. "I made so much I didn't know what to do with it."

There was no special reaction from the insurance salesman/juror, nor from Burnstein. Bob had no intention of cross-examining Finley on his résumé. I only half-kiddingly suggested he pump Finley on the early days in Birmingham. "I could sure use that stuff," I giggled, not meaning the giggle. But Bob repeated that he did not want any more of Finley's life to reach the jury, that he did not want them to fall in love with this success story.

"This is so long and rambling," said Burnstein, "we could be here for hours."

Charlie smiled. "I decided I wanted more happiness. So instead of investing my money in myself, I bought me a baseball team . . . Yes, I have had many hectic years. But I have enjoyed the fruits of my labor." He reminded everyone of the Athletics' two world championships and concluded, "I hope to do it once more in '74. Thank you, Mr. Burnstein."

Court was briefly recessed. Apparently Finley had to make an urgent telephone call. During the break, Burnstein asked Wells if Charlie ordered himself questioned on his life. Wells would only smile in answer. I asked Wells the same question later. "I refuse to answer on the grounds I might incriminate myself," he said.

Wells was courteously curt to me. I understood, and accepted.

Soon after Charlie returned to the stand, Wells asked him if general manager's duties had been promised to Cutler. "Absolutely no," said Finley. Maybe someday, said Finley, Cutler might possibly be g.m. material.

Burnstein began objecting to some of Finley's answers on various grounds. Even as Bob was reciting his objections, Charlie kept right on talking. Lovely Mary, the court reporter, was clearly not able to record two conversations at once, and Judge Barber suggested Charlie stop his comments whenever Burnstein objected. "Thank you," said Charlie. "I'll govern myself accordingly."

"You'll just have to restrain yourself," said Wells soberly. Now there was a request.

Off and on, Finley kept calling Cutler's attorney "Mr. Burnstein." No longer—to my ears—was Charlie Joe McCarthy. Now he was Charles Foster Kane talking to Everett Sloane. (Any objection to the irrelevance will be upheld.)

Burnstein now had an opportunity to cross-examine Finley and wondered why Charlie didn't list himself as general manager in all the pertinent baseball publications. "Out of modesty," said Finley. Updating his status as Owner and G.M., Finley then said, "It's very questionable as to how much longer my doctors will permit me to continue as general manager. I felt that eventually I would turn over the general manager's job to my eldest son (Charlie, Jr.) after he got the experience, or employ someone."

Finley soon was finished, and again a recess. I remember seeing the insurance salesman/juror talking warmly and handing his business card to the carpenter/juror. Out in the corridor I asked a young associate of Burnstein who had watched the trial since its start (there never were more than six or seven spectators in the courtroom at any one time) what effect he thought Finley's testimony had on the jury. Rather, what effect Charlie himself had. The young attorney's only answer was, "What impact did he have on you?"

A good question, one I didn't feel I knew the answer to. I ducked by saying, "I've watched and heard Charlie for too many years to be objective." Well, maybe I wasn't ducking. The Owner's ego was evident, his theatrics obtrusive. To me. The jurors? I just didn't know.

Judge John Stevens' old testimony (deposition) was now recalled to the witness stand by John Wells. He read some sections Burnstein hadn't.

> *Judge Stevens:* Cutler was not sure what his duties were going to be [when the two of them talked about preparing an A's contract for Cutler]. I told Bill that Finley was an executive who some people had difficulty getting along with, and that he had to be prepared to accept whatever assignments Charlie gave him . . .

Stevens said that at the time of Cutler's termination in May, 1968, "It really wasn't clear to me what Cutler wanted to do with the club."

When Wells finished reading Stevens' deposition, Charlie asked his attorney to recall him to the stand to discuss one subject—the comparative salaries of public relations men in the American League. Finley was attempting to show that although Cutler's salary of twenty-seven thousand was a new high for an A's p.r. man, it was in line with the salaries of a few other team flacks.

"I have here in my hand this American League Red Book . . ."

said Charlie. Ah, Joe McCarthy was back and Charles Foster Kane restored to the body of Orson Welles. (Objection overruled.)

The defense rested and the session was recessed. On my way out of the courtroom, I heard Mary the court reporter saying to Burnstein and Wells: "This is one of the most enjoyable cases we've had in a long time. Not because of the subject matter, but because of the cast of characters."

*Day Four.*

I'd been babysitting with my five year old (Molly) and four year old (uh, Charlie) and missed the first forty minutes of Burnstein's final argument to the jury. He told me later that he had dazzled the jury with a shaggy dog story. I asked him the relevance. He said the punch line concerned "the tail wagging the dog." He said the jury loved it. I was too embarrassed to ask for further explanation.

I did catch Bob's final fifteen minutes, however. Quick, bell-clear Shelley Berman. Burnstein often caught himself speaking too quickly, aware that his excellent mind was outracing his larynx. Charlie, handsome in a dark blue suit (tainted, however, by a white belt), grinned frequently as Burnstein lauded Cutler's baseball background. When he wasn't grinning, Charlie was whispering rebuttal fodder to Wells.

Carolyn Coffin and Paul Finley were on hand again. Paul was in a suit. It was Friday, and he and his dad would be leaving by day's end to weekend with the A's in Kansas City.

Burnstein was saying that Cutler had performed his originally anointed tasks and that Charlie had breached their agreement. "You have to decide who's telling the truth," Burnstein told the jury. As his summation ended, the ponytail-weaving juror dozed. She did not hear Burnstein say, "You don't play with people's lives—move them around, send them here and there. . . . Charles O. Finley is a hard-headed businessman and he is successful. That's clear. And he is even gracious sometimes, as we all are."

Burnstein wanted to attack Finley without attacking Finley.

At the first recess, I intended to ask Charlie about an interesting little event that had occurred early the previous evening. The California Angels had fired Bobby Winkles and replaced him as manager with Dick Williams. Angel general manager Harry Dalton said that on Wednesday (day two of the trial) Charlie had had lifted a court injunction against Dick—an injunction that prevented Williams from managing for anyone but the A's. Angel board chairman Gene Autry said Finley did not ask the Angels for compensation and had let them hire Williams "on a friendship basis."

I remembered the phone call interruption in court on Thursday and was curious if that call was from Autry or involved the court injunction against Dick or had *anything* to do with the Angel managerial shift. A silly little curiosity, but I get that way sometimes.

Charlie appeared too wrapped up in the case to be bothered, however, so I asked Carolyn Coffin if her boss had spoken with Autry yesterday. "Why don't you ask Mr. Finley?" she said. Quite properly.

I waited a few feet away while she whispered something to Charlie. He then walked toward me and said, rather angrily, "If you have any questions about my personal phone calls, ask me and not my family." I felt like a scolded child. Asking Carolyn had been impolite, I guess. I told Charlie in a surprisingly strong voice, I thought, "I'm sorry, you're right." Ten minutes later he smiled and winked at me.

In the corridor, Burnstein's young associate said, "This is really a case of Bob against Finley. They're almost the same kind of man. Sure, Bob could have been rougher on Finley, but you can't go too far in fear of antagonizing the jury."

Charlie was munching an ice cream bar and reading a newspaper account of Williams' signing with the Angels. It was only eleven in the morning, and he was making a nonbreakfast eater like me hungry. But before lunch, John Wells' summation.

"We have spent too much time on matters that don't have much to do with the case," he began. "Why are we even in court? The contract seems so clear." He said that Cutler wasn't qualified "to come in and take over as general manager" and that quite obviously Charlie wouldn't give Bill the duties of g.m.

The insurance man/juror was making notes on small cards. A likely foreman, I thought.

"Memories may fade," said Wells, after suggesting that Cutler "may have stretched the truth." But, Charlie's lawyer continued, "the place mat and the contract are unchanged."

Wells called his client "a strong, aggressive leader. A dominant individual in his own organization. Do you think for one minute that Charles O. Finley would undertake to hire Bill Cutler to take his place as general manager? Charles O. Finley was and is his own general manager, and a highly successful one, I might say." As Wells continued, Charlie glared at Cutler, who spent the entire trial seated a few feet behind his attorney, just in front of the spectator section. Depending on what Wells was saying about Cutler, Charlie would glance over at Bill with alternating scorn, pity, regret, pained betrayal. In the thirty-seventh minute of Wells' summation, Charlie slipped a note atop his counsel's attaché case and grew impatient because Wells didn't see it immediately. When he could finally catch Wells' eye, he pointed to the message, which concerned the fact that Cutler had failed to testify he was warned about working for Charlie by Judge Stevens. Of course, Cutler was not asked about his conversation with Stevens. Still, Charlie/Wells had made a good point, I thought.

Yet, as he continued, Wells was beginning to confuse me, to dissipate his earlier lucidity. I wondered if the jury was equally mystified by the clutter that had shrouded the blowup of the contract. Burnstein was certainly a master at maximizing, and Wells seemed to be sucked into Bob's planned whirlpool.

Wrapping up at last, Wells told the jury that Cutler's "refusal to carry out Charlie's assignments was a breach of contract." Wells said that Cutler "is counting on your sympathy and the fact that Finley is a rich man and has a deep pocket. If you give Cutler anything, it would be solely a gift. Cutler is trying to get something for nothing. The fact Cutler has gotten as far as he has with this case is due to the ingenuity and resourcefulness of his counsel," said John Wells in tribute to Bob Burnstein.

"We're not asking for a rich man to be punished," Bob said. "I've never heard of a 'deep pocket' theory. This case is just a question of the truth. We never said that Cutler was an audacious man who was trying to take over from a man as strong and vigorous as Charles O. Finley. You know that no one will ever do that." Charlie smiled at Bob.

"Of course, Cutler was never certain of his duties. What do you do in the loom of a powerhouse? What *are* your duties? You've seen Mr. Finley pass notes back and forth to his own counsel. I thought he was going to make his own closing argument. With him, he does all the work." Charlie laughed; the jury—save for number one—smiled.

Burnstein discussed premises and beginnings and ends. "What

we have here," he said, "is the error of the undistributed middle."
The insurance salesman/juror nodded in understanding. I won-
dered if the undistributed middle had anything to do with
Burnstein's dog-wagging tail.

"If you cull through the magic and articulateness of Mr.
Finley—and even my inability to interrupt him—you'll see
that all the testimony supports Mr. Cutler." Burnstein was
through.

Judge Barber was about to instruct the jury when the carpen-
ter/juror pleaded to take a leak. When he finished, Barber decided
to delay his charge to the jury until after lunch. Good idea. I had
to take a leak, too.

Cutler told me he turned down Charlie's invitation to lunch.
Instead, Bill joined me at McDonald's. I insisted on buying our Big
Macs with the stipulation that if Cutler won his $57,500 from the
jury before sundown, I would get a McDonald's franchise in
return. He demurred. As we chomped, Bill talked about his
present job, running the Spokane Indians of the Pacific Coast
League. Six of his kids worked for him at the ball park. On busy
nights, he said, his wife manned a box office. But there weren't
that many busy nights. He enjoyed Spokane, he said. He'd hated to
leave the Bay area, but life in the Northwest seemed tamer and
less hurried. It would be difficult coming back, he said.

Bill said his second oldest daughter, Carol, was married to major
league infielder Jack Heidemann, who started spring training with
the A's in 1974 but was waived before the season opened.
Heidemann had fought Charlie in salary arbitration proceedings
after Finley cut him thirty-one hundred dollars, said Cutler.
Heidemann lost in the arbitration. Cutler said that of course Finley
knew Jack was his son-in-law. Bill didn't want any of McDonald's
little cookies, so we went back to court.

I rode the elevator to Barber's courtroom with one of the jurors. She yawned all the way up. "Boy, am I tired," she said.

The judge's instructions stretched nearly twenty-five minutes, and the jury strolled next door to begin deliberations at about 2:00 P.M. "The first jury was out about three and a half hours," Burnstein said. "But I'm looking for a verdict today about 4:30." I was ready to bet that the insurance salesman would be elected foreman. He was busy taking notes while Judge Barber instructed.

I asked Burnstein if the hope of beating Finley was a big deal to him. He said no, "it's just a case. I believe Bill's story. The delight if we do win is because Charles told me I couldn't win."

What did he think of Finley?

"I think," Burnstein said, "this is the greatest superego I've ever met in my life. It's almost parasitic. His technique in this courtroom has been very affected and obvious. Almost amateurish. He could impress only people who are impressed by personalities. I think he did impress the jury tremendously. He was on stage all of the time. No question he comes across beautifully. Would I handle a case for him? Sure, if there was a legitimate reason to take the case. You know, a few minutes ago Charles said to me, 'You're my kind of guy, Burnstein. You're a tiger. You're the only attorney who could have kept this case going this long.' "

Word came from the jury room that a fellow named Meyer had been elected foreman. Meyer? Who was Meyer? What was his occupation? Charlie asked around, but nobody knew. Finally, the clerk told him Meyer was a tool and die foreman. Finley threw me your basic sidelong glance. "That's good," he said. "That's okay. We'll be all right." Maybe Meyer would remember Charlie's days at U.S. Steel.

The talk switched to baseball. "Did you know that the Giants just got rid of Charlie Fox as manager?" Finley asked. No, none of us had heard. "Just got the word," said Charlie, pleased with passing the information.

He seemed relaxed, so I asked what he would have done had the Giants sought to hire Dick Williams. Finley said he would not have permitted it. He did not explain why. All he added was, "Dick and I always had real good rapport."

At five minutes to four, the jury asked for information and was brought into the courtroom. Foreman Meyer wondered about Cutler's earnings in 1969–71. Judge Barber told him, and the deliberations resumed. What did the question portend? I figured the jury simply wanted to do some quick arithmetic. Perhaps they'd forgotten what Cutler was seeking.

"That often happens," Burnstein said. "The monetary figure isn't listed on the verdict forms the jury gets. They just forget. If that's why they asked the question, they should be back in here in no more than five or ten minutes. Which means we've won."

Finley asked Wells, son Paul, and secretary Carolyn to step outside with him. "Maybe he's going to chew out Wells and wants an audience," said Cutler. In a few moments, Burnstein checked the enemy's conversation and discovered that Charlie was doing nothing more than theorizing with his supporters.

"They figure the jury wanted that salary information to remind themselves that Bill didn't make as much away from the A's as he was being paid with them. Which means that Bill didn't have the experience to handle general manager's duties. That's their theory. Who knows?"

When ten minutes passed and the jury still hadn't returned, Burnstein thought that Charlie's hunch might have been correct. Finley was bantering with Bob now. "You said so many nice words about me and inflated my ego so much that it took me half an hour to get back down to earth," Charlie said. Burnstein thanked him, and the jury buzzed that it was ready with a verdict. It was sixteen minutes past four.

Finley rested his chin on his right hand and stuffed his left hand in his suit jacket pocket. He was ready.

He didn't budge when Louise Keturi informed the courtroom that Cutler had won. What he had won, the clerk read, was fifty thousand dollars. Charlie still did not budge. Wells asked for a poll of the jurors. One young man said he agreed with the finding but not the settlement. The blonde girl who wondered what a farm system was said the final verdict was not hers. Cutler had won the ball game 10–2.

Foreman Meyer would not tell me what the jury thought of Charlie. But later one of the jurors, a young man, responded to my question by saying, "I thought he was an ass. A hard-nosed, successful businessman, yeh. I was impressed with him because he is very successful at what he does. But the way he handles people rubbed me wrong. I saw him chew out his own attorney in the hall and I didn't like that." He said Finley's personality was not discussed during deliberations.

One other juror, a woman, appraised Charlie for me. "I thought," she said, "he was very impulsive."

Burnstein made a motion to add extra interest payments to the settlement. Charlie continued to sit with one hand on his chin, the other in his pocket. An appeal was still possible.

I was in a hurry to pick up my date and ran past the courthouse concession stand, manned by a young fellow wearing an Oakland A's T-shirt, and outside to my car. I nearly bumped into John Wells.

"Guess you have another chapter for your book," he said.

Cutler missed his flight back to Spokane and spent the evening at the Los Angeles Dodger–San Francisco Giant baseball game in

Candlestick Park. During the game a scoreboard message told the fans: "Welcome to Bill Cutler, general manager of the Spokane Indians, who is here celebrating a great victory." The scoreboard did not elaborate on the nature of the victory.

# V

# IN SEARCH
# OF A FRANCHISE

One major league executive in 1964 told a *Saturday Evening Post* writer: "I never saw anybody who wanted to get into baseball so badly [as Finley]. He'd have bought anything. Why? I guess he wanted to wear a cap with a big league team's name on it."

One can revel in having played first base for the Gary Merchants or the Ensweiler Printers of the Gary Twilight League only so long. Memories of being a bat boy in Birmingham can stretch only so far. Until the money came, all Charlie could do was go to the games, see the White Sox in Chicago. After the money, well, a man should be able to have a game of his own. But it took Finley six years to crack the baseball Establishment; he did not seem to be their kind of man. He once told American League owners he'd give them a five-million-dollar check to prove he could handle the purchase and operation of a franchise. And multimillionaire Tom Yawkey, owner of the Boston Red Sox, is reported to have said, "The only thing that bothers me about this guy is that he thinks five million is a lot of money."

*Frank Lane* (Finley's first general manager in Kansas City): For a long time, the owners of the American League clubs didn't give him much attention or time. Charlie was always just an applicant.

Two years before he bought his beloved farm in LaPorte, Indiana, Charlie tried to buy a major league baseball team. That was in 1954; the insurance business that had taken off with the policy sale to the American College of Surgeons in late 1951 was already drowning Charlie in money, and the cash torrent was only beginning. To him, an obvious investment was a baseball team. Never mind the money-draining potential of a sports franchise; for Charlie there was an emotional commitment to baseball—and quite probably a need for a little write-off. Sam Battistone, who made millions with a restaurant chain called Sambo's, organized a sort of sports-franchise-buying conglomerate in 1973 and says he discovered that normally prudent businessmen flipped at the chance to own *any* kind of ball club. "You talk about business standards and depreciation and so forth," he said, "but there is a glamorous part of sports that just has no relationship to whether you're going to make money, no basis in economic analysis. There's glamor in associating with people who excel in areas you would have liked to excel in."

First surgeons. Then shortstops.

*Bill Veeck* (former major league owner): Finley had first appeared on the baseball scene during the bidding for the Philadelphia A's, waving a check for something like $250,000, and offering to permit innocent bystanders—like me—into his syndicate.

*Calvin Griffith* (owner of the Minnesota Twins): I remember Charlie coming to Philadelphia with that big certified check. He was the only one to bring a certified check to that meeting. I remember Charlie saying that the Internal Revenue had told him to spend some of that money that he had hoarded up, or else declare a dividend. And of course if he declared a dividend, he'd just be declaring it for his wife and all his kids. So I got the impression that the IRS gave him two or three years to go out and buy something.

He was ready to buy the depressing Philadelphia Athletics from legendary Connie Mack and his sons for three million dollars. There is a story, doubtless apocryphal, that Charlie was one hour too late in making his bid. The reality of the situation, however, was that Charlie had no clout with the people who counted in the American League, people named Del Webb and Dan Topping, owners of the New York Yankees. A fellow who did was Arnold Johnson, an associate of Topping in a nonbaseball business. Arnold Johnson was awarded the Athletic franchise and moved it to Kansas City. Johnson had the bad manners to die six years later, and Charlie would still be waiting, still an applicant.

> *Calvin Griffith:* I was very impressed with Charlie at the meeting in Philadelphia. He was the only franchise seeker who followed the ground rules at that meeting. We had to take Topping's word on Arnold Johnson. But you had to admire Finley for how he had become a millionaire. That was the most impressive thing. And at that meeting, Charlie said everything that you would want to hear—that he himself did not know anything about baseball, that he would go out and get the greatest general manager, that he would go out and get the best manager, that he would allow these people to run his ball club for him.

Although he lost the franchise fight in 1954, Charlie always held onto that speech. One can gather that the American League owners next heard the speech in 1956, when Charlie bid to purchase the Detroit Tigers. He told the Gary *Post-Tribune* that he had the financial support of such prominent Midwest business names as Storer, Goldblatt, and Armour. According to Veeck,

Finley's bid for the Tigers was exceeded by four others. A fellow named Fred Knorr landed the Detroit franchise, which at least would have been closer driving distance to Gary-LaPorte than the Philadelphia/Kansas City Athletics.

In 1958, however, an athletic Eden beckoned to Charlie: the Comiskey family was selling the Chicago White Sox. This time Charlie might have a chance because his chief competition was coming from Veeck. Now Bill Veeck was a known gadfly to the Establishment because of his marvelously irreverent success with both minor and major league franchises previously. The Establishment did not trust Veeck; he had a sense of humor. To them, Finley was an unknown gadfly. If Charlie could put together a deal with the Comiskey family, he could own a team in his own back yard.

> *Jerry Holtzman* (Chicago *Sun-Times* baseball writer): Late in 1958, I had written some stories about Veeck being in town putting together a syndicate to buy the White Sox. He had taken an option to buy the majority interest from Dorothy Comiskey Rigney. A couple days after I wrote the story, I got a phone call from a guy who says to me, "I'll tell you why Veeck isn't going to buy Dorothy's interest. You just get a pencil and paper and listen." And this guy gave me all kinds of figures. It was the first time I'd ever heard of the possibility of depreciating ballplayers. Well, this conversation went on about forty-five minutes, and I asked the guy his name. He wouldn't tell me. I kept pushing and he finally told me. It was Finley. First time I'd ever talked to the man. I checked out his information and thought that maybe he was put onto me by Chuck Comiskey, who was feuding with Dorothy, his sister, about selling the club. I asked Chuck. He said he wasn't working with Finley but that he'd heard of him. Chuck said, "He's an insurance man around town."

Veeck wrote in *Veeck—as in Wreck* that he had given Dorothy Rigney one hundred dollars for his option. Veeck says he was going to include Finley in his syndicate to purchase the White Sox. Then he learned that Charlie put up half a million to deal with Dorothy on the chance that Veeck eventually lacked funds to exercise the option.

> *Bill Veeck:* Being rather narrow-minded about having people in my own syndicate working the other side of the street, I informed Finley that he had disqualified himself [from being part of the Veeck group]. One thing you have to say for Finley, he's not a man to nurse a grudge; he promptly offered to buy my hundred dollar option for $250,000.

Veeck finally put together sufficient funding to buy the White Sox. Charlie and his earnest money were once more dangling fantasies to the baseball Establishment. But Finley was starting to become something of a national nonfigure.

> *A relative:* He loved the fact that his name was on the radio when he tried to buy the A's from the Macks. And when he was trying to buy the White Sox, he started getting really wild on the phone, calling to see if there was anything in the paper about him.

If he could not buy a baseball team, he at least could pick up other property. In the spring of 1956, Charlie purchased 240 acres of LaPorte farm property from a Chicago industrialist for what one friend estimates as more than $120,000. Finley eventually acquired more acreage around the place and added to the size of the main house on the farm. He brought in three carloads of Georgia marble for construction of a cabana and other additions. The incursion of the Indiana Toll Road lopped some fifteen acres off his property in 1957, but Charlie later did take advantage of all that traffic by emblazoning his barn, which overlooks the toll road, with a massive ball, bat, and A's insignia. All, for some reason, in red.

His old Glen Park neighborhood friend, John Mihelic, was hired as caretaker on the farm after tending to handyman chores at Charlie's large home near downtown Gary. Finley trusted Mihelic with many expenditures on the farm. "I think he might have trusted my dad more than anyone I can think of," says Mihelic's son, Ron. "He could relax around my dad. He'd know that my dad wouldn't stab him in the back."

John Mihelic would often chauffeur Charlie from LaPorte to Chicago. John looked upon the relationship more as a friendship than as a job. "Charlie really cared about the farm, I think," says John Mihelic. "He spent a lot of money fixing it up, but he didn't spend that much time there. It's confusing. And when he was home on the farm, he'd spend lots of time on the telephone."

Charlie bought a liquid fertilizer company, New Plant Life, and moved the operation from Chicago to LaPorte. By 1974, Charlie had nearly 430 bucolic acres on his farm. But in the memory of sportswriter Jerry Holtzman, Charlie was less a farmer than "a big butter-and-egg man from Chicago."

After the collapse of the White Sox negotiations, Charlie next surfaced in the baseball world at the winter meetings in 1960. Once again he was an applicant. The American League was about to expand. There would be new franchises in Los Angeles and Washington, D.C. Maybe this time. Maybe some ball club someplace.

*Jerry Holtzman:* At that meeting in 1960, Bill Veeck was trying to control about five franchises in the American League. His friend Hank Greenberg had the best shot at the new Los Angeles franchise. Veeck was going to hold onto the White Sox. A friend of his from St. Louis Browns days, Elliot Stein, was going to buy the Kansas City

A's from Arnold Johnson's probate. And Veeck had Edward Bennett
Williams lined up for the Washington expansion club. And of course
his old trusted friend Nate Dolin was at Cleveland.

Slowly, and predictably, Veeck's jigsaw fell apart. After Commissioner Ford Frick ruled that owners of the American League's
new Los Angeles franchise would have to indemnify L.A. Dodger
owner Walter O'Malley, Hank Greenberg dropped out.

> *Jerry Holtzman:* And so Finley is sitting in Chicago reading about
> all this in the papers. He'd been anticipating that Greenberg would
> get L.A. and that Veeck would go with him. And that would leave
> the White Sox for sale. So he flew to New York to the baseball
> meetings. But when he realizes that Greenberg and Veeck aren't
> going to L.A., he comes in and makes a bid for the L.A. franchise
> himself. There were several other bidders already, but Charlie tells
> the owners he's also interested. Webb and Topping go up to him and
> pat him on the back and tell him they're impressed with his
> presentation. They suggest he go out to L.A. and get some local
> backers there to join him.

Veeck says Finley could have bought the White Sox from him at
that point. If he'd only asked. "But Charlie was hot for the
franchise that was available at the moment," wrote Veeck, "and
for that I couldn't blame him." Veeck said he told Finley at the
time that the Kansas City club also was available but that Charlie
now had his heart set on Los Angeles, that he thought he had the
blessing of Del Webb.

From the looks of things, about a dozen wealthy gentlemen
thought they had the blessing of Del Webb. The coowner of the
Yankees was also in the ball park construction business and
doubtless wanted to be assured that expansion teams would have
their parks built by him. While Charlie ferreted about the coast

looking for local backing—and for Casey Stengel as his prospective manager—the Los Angeles Angels of the American League were about to be granted to a southern California group headed by movie cowboy Gene Autry and his partner in a radio chain, Bob Reynolds.

> *Jerry Holtzman:* When Charlie heard that Autry was in a group bidding against him, he stopped off in Scottsdale, Arizona, to try and find Roy Rogers and get him in *his* syndicate. He was going to match the opposition cowboy for cowboy.

Autry and Reynolds got the Angels, whose eventual new stadium in Anaheim, California, would be built by—Del Webb.

As a consolation prize, Charlie got the Kansas City Athletics from the estate of Arnold Johnson. His late 1960 bid of just under two million dollars to a Chicago probate court turned out to be a winner. He also agreed to pick up two hundred thousand dollars in back bills. And on December 19, 1960, he owned fifty-two percent of a major league baseball team. By the time he purchased the remaining forty-eight percent from local groups in Kansas City in February, 1961, Charlie had forked over nearly four million dollars for the opportunity to have complete control of an awfully bad baseball team, a club that had finished in eighth (last) place in 1960 and clearly had nowhere to go in 1961 but down. Which it would, because of the addition of the two expansion teams to the American League.

He might have been better off restoring the Ensweiler Printers of the Gary Twilight League.

Everything that happened in Kansas City baseball in 1961 presaged the future conduct in the game of the Athletics' new forty-two-year-old owner. There were gadgets and gimmickry in the ball park. A manager was fired in midseason. A general manager was fired in late season. Attendance was weak. The Owner dabbled in on-field matters. For administrative purposes, the insurance business and team business often overlapped; in that first year Charlie named his top aide at the Chicago insurance office, Pat Friday, as vice president and treasurer of the A's. There were promises never to leave town. There were promises to move the family into town. The only element about the A's that would ever change was the nature of the team itself. The team, ultimately, would be the best in baseball, but by then the team would no longer be playing its home games in Kansas City.

After acquiring the Arnold Johnson stock in December, 1960, Charlie said, "My intentions are to keep the A's permanently in Kansas City and build a winning club . . . I am not interested in capital gains nor am I a fast-buck man. I have bought controlling interest to stay in baseball, to stay in Kansas City."

As evidence of good faith, Charlie now called the semipro and Little League teams he sponsored back in Indiana the Gary Athletics, LaPorte Athletics, and Little Athletics.

On radio in Kansas City, he said, "When I was chasing the Detroit Tigers, I wasn't going to move the Tigers out of Detroit. When I was chasing the White Sox, I wasn't going to move the White Sox out of Chicago. And when I got a place to roost in Kansas City—brother, I mean to tell you I'm here to stay."

Within the next seventeen months Charlie twice considered the prospect of moving the team to Dallas, Texas.

Finley's first manager at Kansas City was Joe Gordon, who in August, 1960, had been the first major league manager ever traded for another major league manager. Gordon was swapped by the Cleveland Indians for Detroit Tiger manager Jimmy Dykes. The man who pulled the deal was Cleveland general manager Frank

Lane. And Finley's first general manager at Kansas City was Frank Lane. Tantamount to reuniting Stalin and Trotsky.

> *Frank Lane* (by 1974 seventy-five years old and a superscout with the Texas Rangers): Charlie always wanted to be the great white father. Even from the beginning, he thrived on controversy. He would have enjoyed it if Gordon and I had been warring, with him, Charlie, the great white father, in the middle. But Joe and I got along fine.

True to his prediction, the Owner had hired one of the finest general managers in baseball. Lane knew talent, understood how to put together an appealing, interesting, competitive ball club. He also knew how to get lots of ink for Frank Lane. There was bound to be friction between the Owner and his general manager.

> *Frank Lane:* Stoop that I was, I thought I was the g.m. But I found out quickly that I wasn't. I hadn't been working for Charlie more than a week when I told him, "I can't understand why you hired a general manager. You don't need one." And he said, "You found that out, did you?" I told him, "I wish to hell I'd found that out a week sooner, I wouldn't have been here."

Lane says he signed a four-year contract as g.m., with a four-year extension as an "advisor." At the beginning, says Frank, the Owner gave him use of a Cadillac. "But then he told me he had a Mercedes that he didn't like. He said it was too damned fast. So he offered that to me instead, and I took it. Must have been worth more than thirteen thousand bucks." Frank probably could have tooled around in the Mercedes for eight years. Instead, he drove the car in Kansas City for "eight months, twenty-two days, about eight hours, twenty-two minutes, and thirteen seconds." Charlie fired him in late August, and it look Lane nearly four more years to recover the wages due him in the contract: he sought $144,000, was granted $113,000 at a settlement in federal district court in Chicago. The disposition of the Mercedes was another matter.

> *Frank Lane:* After I got fired, I drove down to Acapulco. But at the end of 1961, when I'd need new license plates, I had to have the bill of sale. And I couldn't get it. Charlie had it. As a consequence I put the car in my brother-in-law's garage in St. Petersburg, Florida. About three years later, Joe Brown [Pittsburgh Pirates executive] said to me at a baseball convention that he heard I had a car as good as new. I told him that I could sell him the key, but that Finley had the title—and Charlie was sitting right next to us. So Charlie helped me sell the Mercedes to Brown. Finley got a thousand for the title, and I got two thousand for the key.

The dismissal of Gordon was not accompanied with as much exotica. The manager had inherited a last place team that had lost ninety-six games and was, at best, lackadaisical. The 1960 attendance in Kansas City was 774,944—the lowest since the club had moved from Philadelphia in 1955.

But never—not once in his seven years in Kansas City—was Finley's team able to attract more fans than that lowest figure of the pre-Finley years. He came within a thousand or so in 1966 but could never outdraw his Kansas City predecessor. There are those who contend the Owner truly didn't want to attract great numbers, a theory to be propounded further into this exercise.

> *Frank Lane:* Charlie was liked immediately in Kansas City. They'd applaud whatever the hell he said.

He was, of course, saying all the right things, charming the right people, evincing concern for the comfort of the fans, vowing there would be "no more deals" with the New York Yankees. (Johnson had made many trades with friend Topping. A former Athletic named Roger Maris would have a particularly big year as a Yankee in 1961.) And Charlie displayed no reluctance to spend money to improve the ball park and the ball club. It was much easier pouring money into the stadium; the club itself would take years of bankrolling and tampering.

The 1961 Kansas City Athletics went through twenty-two pitchers including forty-year-old Gerry Staley and eighteen-year-old Lew Krausse. Another pitcher that season was Ken Johnson, whom both Gordon and Lane wanted to send to the minors. Finley told them he thought Johnson deserved another start, so Johnson did get that start, and lasted less than an inning. "If we're going to continue spring training into the summer," said Lane, "we'll drop so many games it won't be funny." Charlie said he wanted to "give our ballplayers every possible chance to make the team." Johnson finally was sent down.

Charlie prevailed, though, when his manager and general manager wanted to farm out pitcher Norm Bass, who was to become the best K.C. hurler of 1961 with an 11–11 record.

"Well," said Lane, "if this team can't experiment, who the hell can? Finley has sunk four and a half million dollars into the club. If he thinks he's protecting his investment by disregarding the advice of experts, I can't argue."

Manager Gordon couldn't argue either. He could, however, before one game hand the umpire a lineup card upon which was written: "Approved by C.O.F." And he could complain to the press about Finley's dabbling in player moves. And he could scratch his head in wonderment when on June 15 Charlie made a deal with—oh, my goodness—the New York Yankees. Pitcher Bud Daley was traded to New York for pitcher Art Ditmar and young outfielder Deron Johnson.

*Deron Johnson:* I played for Joe Gordon one day. I joined the club in Minnesota and he got fired the next day. The public address announcer called Hank Bauer out of right field, and he was the manager the rest of the year. It was a surprise to everybody, and Hank had kept quiet about it. I had known him from spring training camps with the Yankees, but he never said anything to me. It sure was a surprise to Joe Gordon, too.

*Frank Lane:* Charlie had told me he was gonna fire Gordon. And he did it right after we had had our best road trip. We were something like 6–2, which was unheard of because we'd had a bad ball club. But Joe had done a few things to upset Charlie, like the lineup card thing, and you just don't do that. So I made no real strong fight to keep Joe. Bauer hadn't been my choice to replace Gordon. I told Hank he was foolish for taking the job because it was a bad ball club. But Finley said to Bauer, "Are you afraid to take this job?" And Hank says, "I'm not afraid of anything." Which he isn't. Hank wasn't the greatest manager in the world, but he was a hard-working guy and a hero in Kansas City because he lived around there. He was a hero to me because he was such a great ballplayer.

Gordon had managed the club to a 26–43 record. Bauer would finish the season 35–57, or three percentage points better than Gordon. Hank would stay at the helm for all of 1962 and lead the A's to a ninth place finish—improving on their overall record of 1961 (when they tied for ninth—not to mention tenth). In his full year Hank was 72–90, and gone. But the ex-Marine and ex-Yankee World Series star would be back with Charlie in Oakland in 1969.

According to Lane, Bauer barely made it through 1961. "About four or five days before I got fired," says Frank, "Charlie wanted to fire Bauer. I said, 'Charlie, you can't do that. You just got through firing Gordon a couple months ago. And this is Bauer's backyard. It would be a horrible thing.' "

Finley concurred, and fired Lane instead.

*Frank Lane:* I was making a speech in a hotel in Kansas City, telling the audience that Mr. Finley was a good operator and a great fan and that we'd have a great ball club. When I came out to get a cab to go to the ball park, the cab starter said, "Gee, that's tough luck, Mr. Lane." I asked him what happened—was a ballplayer hurt? He said, "No, you got fired. Didn't you know that?"

*Deron Johnson:* Charlie treated all the guys on the club just great those first couple years. But we just had a bad ball club and there was nothing we could do about it. It was a happy club but not a winning club. There was no talent. And there really wasn't that much potential. A few young kids coming, sure, but pretty green.

By the time Finley left Kansas City at the end of the 1967 season, the only remnant from his first club still on the A's roster was pitcher Lew Krausse. Gone were the Jungle Jim Riveras and Marvelous Marv Throneberrys, the Joe Nuxhalls and Don Larsens and Mickey McDermotts and Paul Giels. Great names had passed through the Finley payroll: Gino Cimoli, Granny Hamner, Moe Drabowsky, Jim Gentile, Rocky Colavito, Don Mossi, Ralph Terry. Not to mention Joe Grzenda, Ossie Chavarria, Aurelio Montea-gudo, Jess Hickman, Santiago Rosario, George Alusik, Charlie Shoemaker, Chuck Essegian, Sammy Esposito, Dan Pfister, Jay Hankins, Billy Consolo, Gordie Windhorn, Marlan Coughtry, Rupe Toppin, Bob Giggie, Leo Posada, and Ted Bowsfield, who in the years 1963 and 1964 had a pitching record of 9–14 for the Kansas City Athletics. By 1974 Bowsfield, a handsome southpaw, was an executive with the California Angels.

*Ted Bowsfield:* Ed Lopat was the manager when I got there in 1963, and the general manager was Pat Friday [Finley's insurance aide]. I was treated quite well. They were all good to me, and I never had any problems with Charlie. But I had some doubts as to whether Charlie gave any importance to winning in those days rather than to showmanship. I wasn't sure what he was doing sometimes, because some of the things that happened definitely did not point toward trying to win every ball game. For example, at Farmer's Day in 1963 Charlie asked me to drive a hay wagon with that day's pitcher, Diego Segui, aboard. I was to stick hay under my hat and under my uniform and drive Diego to the mound, pat him on the back, and then get the horses back out to Charlie. We were playing the Washington ball club, and they razzed me, called me a showboat. Next day they beat my brains out. Then another time he hired a taxicab and left it out in center field with the meter running. Lopat said before the game that if he needed a relief pitcher, the man should wait in the bullpen until the taxicab came to pick him up. Well, we're playing the Yankees and leading 2–1. I'm trying to heat up in the bullpen because two left-handed hitters are due up. I'm called into the game and forget all about the taxicab; I walk all the way to the mound. When I get there, Lopat says, "My god, you forgot the taxicab." Sure enough, it was still out there with the meter running—maybe up to thirty, forty dollars. Well, I get the two guys out, we win 2–1 and I come into the clubhouse and am told that Finley wants to talk to me on the phone right away. And he ripped me up and down one side and the other: Why didn't I ride the taxicab? That left some doubt in my mind about the importance he put on winning. But we were a bad ball club. No pitching. No defense. It was the worst team I ever played with in the major leagues.

Under Lopat the 1963 Athletics were 73–89, losing one less than with Bauer in 1962 and moving up to eighth place. There seemed to be some hope for improvement, even though, as Bowsfield commented, general manager Friday "didn't know much about baseball. Pat was just a figurehead. But fortunately they had Hank Peters in the front office."

Peters may not have been Frank Lane, but he quietly knew how to spot and procure talent. The bodies were beginning to fall in line; the hard core that would carry Charlie to the top was being signed and groomed. Dick Green already was wearing a Kansas City uniform by 1963. Bert Campaneris would join him in 1964, and Jim Hunter and Paul Lindblad a year later. In 1965 the A's system was signing people named Bando, Fingers, Tenace, and Rick Monday, to whom Charlie would pay a bonus of over one hundred thousand dollars but who would finally be sacrificed in a deal for a pitcher, Ken Holtzman. Pitchers John Odom and Chuck Dobson were Athletics by 1966, the same year a college athlete named Reggie Jackson was signed for a big bonus and en route to joining a young Californian named Joe Rudi in the A's farm system.

Yes, unspectacular progress was being made. Charlie was not skimping. Lane was right—the Owner did care.

> *Frank Cashen* (executive vice president of the Baltimore Orioles): Sure, the A's had a lot of high draft choices because they kept finishing so low in the standings. But you have to remember that there are other teams that have been at the bottom of the league for a number of years and had a similar drafting opportunity as Charlie's and never did cash in on it. Some of the guys who worked in his farm system in Kansas City, guys like Hank Peters, for instance, have to come in for some of the credit for the A's success. I think some people may labor under the illusion that Charlie went out to the highways and byways and found people like Vida Blue and Catfish Hunter himself. But he had to have somebody at the top to identify the personnel. He did have the imagination and the pocketbook to sign them. Somewhat flamboyantly at times, perhaps.

In the interim, Charlie was giving the folks in Kansas City sheep beyond the outfield and a zoo beyond belief, seeing that it contained rather lethargic monkeys. "Catfish Hunter and I would go out to the ball park early and feed the monkeys grasshoppers. Then sometimes we'd give them cough medicine and sleeping pills," said pitcher Lew Krausse. Bowsfield recalled that the sheepherder once failed to ring a bell, as he was ordered, following an Athletic homer and was thus sent out to another pasture. "Guy kept falling asleep," said Bowsfield.

> *Dick Green:* The whole thing was a zoo, a circus. The whole purpose then was to entertain the crowds and not to win games. Most of us in those early years were lucky to be in the major leagues. I knew that I was a fringe ballplayer on a bad team. We all knew our place, so we'd go along with anything that Charlie was doing.
>
> *Paul Lindblad:* Some of the players used to say that the reason Finley had all the sheep out there was to keep everybody loose. I guess you can read between the lines.

I guess.

In June, 1964, pitcher Bowsfield was able to read between the lines, and what he observed was the imminent departure of manager Lopat. Ted said he probably was the catalyst for Lopat's dumping.

> *Ted Bowsfield:* Charlie wanted Jose Santiago to start a game instead of me in Washington just before the roster cutdown deadline, and I needed just a few more days on a major league roster to get five years in, for pension purposes. And Lopat says, "I'm supposed to pitch Santiago but I'm going ahead with you." Eddie stuck by me, and I won. Three days later, Lopat was fired. And the new manager, Mel McGaha, came right out and told me I'd get one more start but that it was "do or die." Fortunately I shut out the Tigers and I was kept around long enough to get my five years.

Lopat went out with a 17–35 record; McGaha finished 40–70.

And in 1964 the Kansas City A's were dead last (tenth) in the American League, losers of 105 games. The drudgery was similar in 1965, as McGaha and successor Haywood Sullivan combined to keep the A's in last place but reduced their total losses to 103. McGaha lasted all of twenty-six games as manager that season— winning five of them. Sullivan became the first exclusion to Charlie's manager overlap system: Haywood was not retained for the 1966 season. The new Kansas City manager was Alvin Dark. Maybe he would start putting it all together for Charlie; Alvin had managed San Francisco to a National League pennant in 1962. And he would guide the A's all the way up to seventh place in 1966. They would win seventy-four games, more than any Athletic team since 1952. You could see the light at the end of the tunnel. You could also see who was holding the on-off button.

"That next year, 1967, was interesting," says pitcher Chuck Dobson. "Very interesting."

Lew Krausse cost Charlie Finley $125,000. That was in 1961, when Lew was barely eighteen and the Owner was not yet fed up with Kansas City and the lack of artistic productivity. Lewis Bernard Krausse, Jr., was Charlie's first big bonus baby, a redhead with a strong right arm and a father who had pitched for the old Philadelphia Athletics thirty years earlier and now was a signif-icant member of the scouting staff of the transplanted A's. The position of the father did not make Kansas City's signing of the son a lock. Lew, Sr., told the A's that Lew, Jr., would go to the highest bidder, which seemed fair. And Charlie was the highest bidder, which seemed nice. Before pressing that much money on that ingenuous flesh, however, Charlie brought Lew to Washington to throw a little batting practice. Pat Friday watched the lad fling and then said to Lew, "I don't know much about baseball, but you look like you throw the ball pretty hard." Then Friday and young Krausse went to wrap up the deal with Finley at the Shoreham Hotel. Six years later Krausse would pick up a phone in a room at the Shoreham and be told by Finley that he was suspended indefinitely from pitching for the Kansas City A's.

The time, and the money, go quickly; the limited notoriety that comes from being a quasi-bad boy is more ephemeral. Lew Krausse does not use the word "squandered," but comes wistfully close. He is now thirty-one years old on a bright 1974 spring day in San Francisco, fragilely on the pitching staff of the Atlanta Braves, rooming on the road with a pitcher named Jack Aker. Circles within circles.

> *Lew Krausse, Jr.:* Back in those Kansas City days, I was young and single and immature. And I had some money. I don't know if I did some of that shit just for fun or because I was drunk. I really believe that if I hadn't screwed around as much as I did early in my career, I would have been a different pitcher. When you get released from your original club, nobody seems to give a shit about you. My father never talked to me about some of those things I did back in Kansas City. He figured he'd let me learn for myself, and it cost me a lot of money to learn. I went through more of my bonus than I have left. When I'd be having trouble, Charlie would always say to me, "You know, your dad wouldn't be very proud of you." He'd always seem to mention my dad's name. Finley is a really intelligent man, and I think he feels that maybe you'll catch a hint if he throws out little tips here and there. You know, trying to make me feel guilty. And I did. I always felt bad afterwards.

The bad came unexpectedly for the pitcher they called "Lulu." In 1966 he won fourteen games as the A's finally seemed to be showing promise. But at the end of the season, Lew's mother died, and in 1967 nothing seemed to go right for him. Finley probably expected him to win twenty games that year. Instead, Lulu nearly lost twenty. "I guess," he says, "Charlie was disgusted with me."

Early in the 1967 season Krausse said he kicked down a hotel room door in Anaheim. On June 6, he was pounded by the Detroit Tigers 11–1 in the first game of a double header in Kansas City and left the ball park for his room at the Bellerive Hotel—stopping en route for a drink. Or two.

> *Lew Krausse:* I just got wasted. I really did. I was discouraged, depressed, everything. I tied one on. From the bar I went back to the hotel. Now the day before my room was on the backside of the Bellerive, and there was nothing out my window but trees and a park. But for some reason that day, they had changed my room. I went up there and still really felt pissed off. I guess I reach a point when I have too many drinks where I get pissed off as hell. I get crazy. I didn't want to beat up on the wall and hurt myself, so I just raised a window and got my gun, an old police thirty-eight special an uncle had given me. I stuck the pistol out the window and shot it off twice, just maybe to get something out of my system—maybe hearing the noise or whatever. Then I put the window down and went to sleep.

Lulu next heard from the world at seven the following morning. It was Finley on the telephone. Krausse reels off the specifics of the conversation. He says Charlie asked him if he had a gun. He says he told the Owner he did. He says Finley asked him if he'd shot the gun the night before. Krausse told him that, as a matter of fact, he had. Twice.

> *Lew Krausse:* I said to myself, "Holy Christ, what did I do now?" I thought I'd killed somebody. Shit, now I'm scared to death. I put on a raincoat so I can carry the gun under it, and it's about a

hundred degrees outside. I go to the train station, put the gun in a little locker, and then come back to the Bellerive. And there's all kinds of detectives in my room. Must have been five of them in there. They had different kinds of measuring devices—angle type things—trying to check the trajectory of a bullet. They were dusting the ledge of the windowsill with powder. By now I'm sure that I killed the president or something. The police told me there were reports from the room next door that gunfire had come last night from my room. They said that the shots went into an office building, the Phillips Petroleum building, across the way, but that no one was injured. They had to know that the shots came from my room, but they never told me I was going to jail or anything. When the police left, I called Finley back. And he just raised hell with me. But outside of just chewing my ass out, he didn't fine me or reprimand me. All he said was, "This is it. This is your last chance." I don't know how he found out about it, probably from somebody in the hotel. When he talks about the shooting, he says I came close to hitting a cleaning woman. He says the bullet went in the Phillips building and ricocheted around and the cleaning lady was diving on the floor, and then she gets back up and BANG, here comes another shot and she's diving some more. That's what he says happened. When I think about it now, I guess you can say he was really protecting me at the Bellerive, although he didn't put it that way when I called him back from my room that day. And after that call, I didn't hear from him again until a month or so later in Washington.

That call concerned not the shooting but the activities aboard TWA Flight 85 from Boston to Baltimore to St. Louis to Kansas City on August 3, 1967, the plane trip that made Ken Harrelson some money, cost Alvin Dark his job, got Jack Aker tipsy, sidelined Lew Krausse for a few days and put Charlie Finley in the headlines. Flight 85 wasn't "The High and the Mighty," but it sure must have been fun. Or must it have been?

*Ted Kubiak:* I was sitting up in front, so I don't know what the hell happened in back. All I know is that nothing was going on up front. So how bad could it have been?

*Alvin Dark:* I had a policy to stay up front on team plane trips and not rubberneck. The players knew how I felt about drinking, but I'm not about to tell a man he can't drink. He has to make that decision for himself.

*Chuck Dobson:* I'm sitting in the middle of the plane, reading or sleeping or something. Very relaxed. The plane wasn't crowded at all. Just a routine flight, and nothing happened.

Not in the front. Not in the middle. And in the back?

*Paul Lindblad* (A's pitcher): I was back there—right amongst it all, or whatever it was Mr. Finley accused everyone of. The stewardesses came back there and we did the usual thing with stewardesses. You know, talk and joke with them. But outside of that, to my knowledge nothing else happened. Oh, yeah. Lulu and I were playing five-point Missouri Mule Pitch. Just the regular Pitch game we played all the time. And nothing happened. Nothing. We just had our usual amount of drinks. Three or four. Right in there somewhere. I thought it was a very down-to-earth trip.

*Lew Krausse:* The whole back of the plane was ours almost because there were hardly any regular passengers. I remember there was a crew change in, I guess, Baltimore. And the new crew of stewardesses were based in Kansas City. Ken Harrelson and I and a couple other players who were single knew these girls. And when the girls got on, they asked if we wanted drinks. We said we did, but that we'd rather not pay for them. So they just handed us a tray of drinks, and everybody had a couple. Nobody got rowdy.

*Jack Aker:* I was sitting in the back with Krausse and Lindblad, but I wasn't playing cards. I remember that the stews parked the little drink cart right in the aisle between our seats and told us we could have as many as we wanted, which they shouldn't have done, because two or three of us got carried away. We were kidding amongst ourselves and telling stories, and there were probably some swear words that were heard farther up the plane by the regular passengers. But other than that, I didn't see anything that was out of the way.

*Paul Lindblad:* The few Scotches Lulu had wouldn't be enough to get him high. Heck, no. He was all right.

*Lew Krausse:* I'd already eaten, so I felt I could handle the drinks. I was doing nothing more than sitting around and talking and relaxing. Aker was a little high probably, but that was all. At that time he was having a lot of problems off the field, so he might have had a reason to have a couple of extra drinks. Even then, nothing happened, because Jack gets peaceful when he gets high.

There was a report that manager Dark, tipped about the tippling by the traveling secretary, who had been informed by broadcaster Monte Moore, took a brief peek at the rear of the plane, asked a stewardess if there were any problems, and was told, "Oh, no. They're a great bunch of guys." So Alvin returned to his seat. Dark said that he was the first off the plane at Kansas City after the approximately four and a half hour flight. Aker may have been among the last to disengage himself from Flight 85.

*Paul Lindblad:* Sure, Aker was hurtin'. But he walked off the plane.

*Dick Green:* I didn't see Lulu drunk on the plane or bothering people.

*Lew Krausse:* We landed at Kansas City without any incident.

*Jack Aker:* I was a little drunk, but I got off the plane. And I didn't have to be physically helped off.

Fifteen days later there were calls from the insurance office in Chicago to two fellows in Washington's Shoreham Hotel—Lew Krausse and Alvin Dark. The calls were about Flight 85, by then known to the Kansas City Athletics as Flight What?

Alvin says that someone on the plane told Charlie that Lulu had used "deplorable language" overheard by a woman with a small child aboard the flight, and that the woman had written Charlie. Yet neither Krausse nor several other players questioned could recall seeing this heartwarming mother and child on Flight 85. But, as noted earlier, the athletes admitted to a few expletives. Most of the ballplayers thought that Finley was using whatever it was he heard about the events of the August 3 flight to deal with Lulu's Bellerive shoot-'em-up. Aker says, "Lew was being punished for something else." Lindblad suggests that "Krausse's name was brought up in the report to Mr. Finley, and Mr. Finley had told Lew a few weeks before that he was gonna get him good if he ever heard Krausse's name come up in anything connected with trouble."

Aker says he was rather surprised the shit didn't hit *his* fan. But Jack was the player representative, and Marvin Miller might have looked askance at an owner messing with one of his reps. Lulu had something coming. Lulu was vulnerable.

*Lew Krausse:* My phone rings at eight in the morning there in Washington. Finley. I should have known right away from his tone that something was wrong. He said, "I'm fining you five hundred dollars for carrying on and drinking on that flight." And seriously, I had to wait and think what flight it was. You know, if you do something wrong, you remember. And Finley and I are screaming and hollering at one another and I'm denying everything. And I slammed down the phone on him. I went into the bathroom to get a drink of water and tried to wake up and came back into the bedroom, where the phone is ringing again. Finley. He says, "As of today, you're suspended indefinitely without pay. You're to go directly to Kansas City." And this time, *he* hung up on me.

Alvin says Finley called to tell him about Krausse's fine and suspension. Dark says Finley wanted him to tell Lulu. Dark says he told the Owner: "I know nothing about this [the flight problems]. If I suspend him without knowing why, he can sue me and you and everybody." Alvin was worried about the reaction from the rest of the players. "I can't go along with you," the manager told the Owner.

Krausse phoned Alvin and says the manager suggested he return to Kansas City, as ordered by Finley. "So there I was sitting out in the cold in Kansas City while all this was going on back in Washington," says Krausse.

"All this" turned out to be quite a lot.

> *Jack Aker:* Finley had prepared this statement to be posted in the clubhouse. It was a memo announcing Lulu's fine and suspension and a rule that there'd be no more drinking on future team flights. Fine, that's Finley's prerogative. However, about fifteen minutes after I heard about the memo, I found out that he planned to issue that statement to the wire services. So I called him and asked him to hold his memo out of the media, that we accepted his notice. And he informed me that he'd already given it to AP and UPI.

> *Finley's statement* (in part): The attitude, actions and words of some of you have been deplorable. As members of Organized Baseball, you have certain responsibilities and obligations to yourself, your family, your club, and most important of all—the fans.

Oh, yes. Charlie signed it "sincerely."

> *Jack Aker:* I told Finley the players would probably be upset about him giving out the statement to the press. Which they were.

The statement insinuated, in effect, that all twenty-five of his ballplayers had a drunken brawl on a plane. So we started our player meetings and decided to draft our own statement.

Aker says that "about seven or eight of us essentially worded it. Harrelson worked closely with me on it." But Aker, the solemn part-Indian, wrote the final draft.

> *A's players' statement* (in part): We feel that an unjust amount of pressure has been brought to bear on several members of the club who had no part whatsoever in the so-called incident on the recent plane trip from Boston to Kansas City. The overwhelming opinion of the players is that the entire matter was blown out of proportion. Mr. Finley's using of certain unauthorized personnel in his organization as go-betweens has led to similar misunderstandings in the past and has tended to undermine the morale of the club. We feel that if Mr. Finley gave his fine coaching staff and excellent manager the authority they deserve, these problems would not exist.

Broadcaster Moore was the target of the "unauthorized personnel" euphemism. A few players said he blew the whistle on the players' drinking on Flight 85. Moore has always denied the allegation. As of 1975, he was still a play-by-play man on Athletic broadcasts. And at the Shoreham in that week of August, 1967, he was on Charlie Finley's air.

> *Jack Aker:* At a meeting in Mr. Finley's room in the Shoreham, I think I mentioned that some of us thought Monte Moore had instigated the thing and spread some false rumors. Now Moore was in the room at the time with all the coaches and Finley and Dark. I can remember very vividly what Finley said after I said that about Moore. He jumped up and said, "If you or any of these son of a bitchin' other ballplayers ever say anything to this man right here"—and he pointed to Monte Moore—"I'll have your ass."

*Lew Krausse:* I don't know if Monte said anything to Charlie about the flight. But I do know that after all of this happened, everybody refused to go on Monte's pregame radio show. And Finley sent a note down to the clubhouse saying that anybody who messed with Monte would get fined a thousand dollars.

Moore turned down a request to be interviewed for this book. He, like Charlie, said his refusal was "nothing personal."

Alvin Dark was as much caught in the middle of the Flight 85 brouhaha as Lulu Krausse. Obviously, Dark had to go because he wouldn't back Charlie 183 percent. Yet, there was a report at the time that Alvin intended to quit at the end of the 1967 season anyway, a rumor that can be viewed as academic, for the way the club was struggling that season Charlie—following precedent— would probably have bounced Dark in late September. Instead, the dismissal came in the Shoreham on August 19. And again on August 20. In the space of about eight and a half hours, Charles O. Finley fired his manager, rehired him with a two-year contract extension (with a raise in salary), then fired him again. At times one has to feel that the Owner is actually Chekhov's casting director.

Charlie at least handled the Dark dismissal in person, as he does most dramatic encounters. Finley will not duck the hard moments. After his telephonic suspension of Lulu, Charlie flew to Washington to confront Alvin. Another day, another manager.

*Alvin Dark:* He said, "Alvin, I'm going to have to let you go. I want my manager to back me on this, and you're not doing it." I was fired, and still we just sat there talking.

What they didn't talk about was the fact that Dark knew the players were preparing that "unjust amount of pressure" statement. Alvin had told a couple of his lads to let him look at the statement before they released it because "it might get you in trouble." But the statement was already on its way to the media as Dark and Finley chatted—and Alvin was the one who ended up getting in trouble because of it.

As Dark spoke with Finley after the early evening firing, the ex-manager reflected on the nature of Charlie's athletes, their abilities and prospects, their future as potential contenders. Alvin figured the A's could win the American League pennant by 1971 with such young pitchers as Jim Hunter, John Odom, Chuck Dobson, and Paul Lindblad, such sound infielders as Dick Green and Bert Campaneris, and such budding bodies as Reggie Jackson and Sal Bando. Dark's guess was accurate, as Dick Williams will be glad to remind him.

Charlie was so touched and enthused by Alvin's Pollyanna gushings that he decided to change managers in mid-firing.

> *Alvin Dark:* He said, "How'd you like to manage two more years?" I told him that he just fired me. He said, "How about two more years?" I said, "Fine."

Enter the press, with a request for a Finley response to the recently released players' statement. (Pause for a Richter scale reading of Finley's surprised simmering.) Finley wondered if Dark knew anything about this mysterious statement. Alvin said he told the Owner that he "knew they were planning a statement, but I hadn't read it." And Charles O. Finley spoke unto his subjects and said, "Get me Aker."

Jack wasn't gettable for several hours. He'd gone to Baltimore and didn't reach the Shoreham until about 2:00 A.M. Finley questioned his pitcher about the players' statement, asked if Dark knew about the statement in advance. And Alvin couldn't deny he was aware the statement was being prepared.

> *Alvin Dark:* So he fired me again.

Aker called another players' meeting. "We kept having meetings and meetings and meetings," says Chuck Dobson. Several players remember more about what followed this succession of team meetings than what occurred at the meetings themselves, which continued even after the club had returned home to Kansas City.

> *Dick Green:* Fifteen minutes after a meeting was over, Mr. Finley knew about it. And there was nobody but just the twenty-five players in the meetings. I guess somebody got on the phone after every meeting and told Mr. Finley what happened.
>
> *Chuck Dobson:* We thought he had the place bugged.
>
> *Jack Aker:* We had some meetings in an old equipment room set back under the stands in the Kansas City ball park. One day we took a vote on something or other, then we went right out on the field and played the game. Soon as the game was over, I had a message to call Mr. Finley. He asked me about the meeting, and I told him as much as I thought he should know and that we'd taken a vote on a certain matter. He proceeded to tell me how I had voted and also he named some of the fellows who had voted the same way I had. From then on at our meetings, I informed the players that if they had any personal opinions and didn't want Mr. Finley to hear them that they should maybe reserve them in the meetings. Finley had his favorites on that club, just like he does now. And that's always been one of the problems with his teams. He has a few players who are just like sons to him. He treats them very well financially. Now there's nothing wrong with that, but it tends to alienate certain other players on the team. And before you know it, you have a split.

There was little if any split, however, at a players' meeting to consider issuing a statement in reaction to Dark's firing. Alvin had popped by the clubhouse in Washington for a final conversation with his lads. He spoke emotionally ("they were like sons to me"), and they reacted with feeling. Their statement expressed a sense of "deep personal" loss. And there was a discussion about striking. Dick Green says the strike conversation "was just talk." Aker can't recall that "a strike was ever mentioned." There was no strike, although there was one player who never again showed up for work with the Kansas City (or Oakland) Athletics.

> *Lew Krausse:* Finley has done a lot of nice things that people don't know about. Like with Ken Harrelson. Finley bailed him out more times than you can even talk about. Finley helped him on a complicated house deal and loaned him all kinds of money. Then Harrelson was traded, and Charlie got him back to recover his loan—deduct it from his paycheck. And Ken hadn't been back with our club too long before all of this airplane flight business happened.
> *Finley* (in 1968): Harrelson kept coming to me to borrow money. Two thousand. Twenty-five hundred. Seven thousand in all. I was glad to lend it to him. And then he did a thing like that to me.

The "thing" was a statement to a Washington writer who asked Ken what he thought of Dark's dismissal. Harrelson was quoted as saying "Finley is a menace to baseball." Finley phoned Ken, asked him to verify that quote. Harrelson denied calling Charlie "a menace." Harrelson told Finley that what he actually said was that Charlie's actions were "bad for baseball."

The Owner asked his outfielder to write a retraction. Before Harrelson's creative juices flowed fully, Finley was back on the phone to tell Ken he'd been released.

Harrelson was a free agent. He had been fired. Mike Andrews can look it up.

Four clubs were in a remarkably tight race for the American League pennant in that ten-team, single-division season of 1967. (The A's at that moment were in tenth place.) As soon as the news of Harrelson's nonstatus was announced, the Twins, Tigers, White

Sox, and Red Sox were calling him. The Red Sox were desperate for an outfielder because of a serious injury to Tony Conigliaro and gave Harrelson a reported seventy-five thousand dollars to sign. From the ranks of the unemployed, Ken Harrelson was instantly a reborn bonus baby. Finley could have sold Ken to any of the four interested teams and kept the cash for his club. Instead, he chose to enrich the object of his disaffection. Charlie said he would rather not profit from such a transaction. "It would have been blood money," he said.

With Harrelson, the Red Sox knocked off the Twins on the final weekend of the season to win the American League pennant. Of course Boston also had a fellow named Yastrzemski for the heavy hitting. And a second baseman named Andrews. And a manager named Dick Williams. The Red Sox' remarkable championship season was described as "The Impossible Dream." Ken Harrelson had a similar 1967.

The A's players fought harder off the field than on in the final weeks of that season, their last in Kansas City. They had in mind the simple little task of throwing Charlie Finley out of baseball. They hoped that Players' Association boss Marvin Miller would help. He arranged a hearing with Commissioner William Eckert, and Finley began seeking allies among his players.

> *Jack Aker:* Finley threatened me with something: to disclose my personal life on the road to my wife. I informed him that at that time my wife and I were going through a bad part of our marriage. In fact, at that particular time I had asked for a divorce already. I told him I wasn't worried about what he told my wife, because I'd already informed her of my activities. And this kind of upset him a little bit, I think. He had no leverage then. He tried to use the whole arsenal.

A's pitcher Jim Hunter recalls that "a bunch of guys we'd never seen before seemed to be following us players around everywhere we went" in the weeks following the Krausse-Dark-Harrelson fuss. Hunter says he never had any proof the followers were private detectives—"but they sure acted like it."

Marvin Miller began receiving word from some of the Athletics about being "intimidated and coerced" by Finley in hopes the hearing before Eckert would be cancelled. So Miller invoked a baseball first, filing a complaint of unfair labor practices against the Owner with the National Labor Relations Board.

Commissioner Eckert moved faster now to give the players a hearing, and Charlie was forced to seek a compromise. He would agree not to pressure his athletes over grievance rights. He would agree not to be vindictive against any of the fellows opposed to him in the aftermath of Flight 85. And the players accepted his deal. Most of the voting in the earlier player meetings was lopsidedly anti-Finley. But in this final vote, the tally, after much rancor, was 14–9. Baseball was off the hook with the NLRB. And about a month later, on October 18, 1967, the A's were out of Kansas City.

Aker says his salary was cut by ten percent for the 1968 season. "Finley offered no explanation for the cut," he says. "I asked to be traded, and he refused." One year later, Aker was sent to the Seattle Pilots in an expansion draft. And he eventually did get that divorce he was talking about.

Harrelson and Dark were reunited with the Cleveland Indians. Dark involuntarily left that club to become an amateur golfer. Harrelson departed Cleveland in hopes of becoming a professional golfer.

Krausse says Finley never did fine him. "I lost four days' pay, that was all," says Lulu. Krausse survived to pitch the A's home opener in Oakland in 1968 (losing to Baltimore). After the 1969 season, Charlie traded him to Seattle/Milwaukee. Lulu says he and the Owner "are on great terms right now. I mean, really super." At the start of the 1974 season, Krausse was ticketed to pitch for the Atlanta Braves' farm club in Richmond, Virginia. Lulu preferred throwing for Oakland's farm down in Tucson and says Charlie was kind enough to oblige. "Mr. Finley is the kind of guy, you know, if he wakes up in the morning with a hard-on, boy just don't get near him that day," says Lew Krausse. "But if he wakes up with a smile on his face, he'll do anything in the world for you. There's no pattern to him. No consistency."

After Krausse went to the Pilot/Brewers, Paul Lindblad was sent to the Senator/Rangers, thus breaking up one of your better little games of five-point Missouri Mule Pitch.

(Postscript: In February, 1975, Finley signed a pitcher who had been released by Atlanta. One Lew Krausse. "He's glad to be back with his old team," Charlie said.)

# VI

# THEY ALSO SERVE
# WHO PAY AND SIT

Tom Corwin, a young man whose father worked in the mills with Charlie in Gary, insists that one of Finley's strong points is his ability to empathize with fans, to understand how the working man makes plans to attend a sporting event, when the working man can afford the tickets. "Charlie was there once, so he knows," says Corwin.

But somewhere along the line, one gets the impression that Charlie's caring about the needs and desires of the fan was overwhelmed by Charlie's caring about Charlie.

> *Roe Bartle* (mayor of Kansas City in 1961): Charlie Finley has put more spirit into the city than anyone [in the past decade]. He holds the heart of the city in the palm of his hand.
>
> *Bonnie Howard* (an Oakland A's fan in 1974): I wish that he could move out here or sell the club to somebody out here and then the team would get better support. It seems not to affect him at all, the fact that people don't come out and support the A's. Mr. Finley is

116

out to make money, that's what it looks like. Everyone isn't like Finley; everyone doesn't have money like he has. He can just throw it away, and we can't. He should be more free-minded toward the fans.

Between Mayor Bartle and Ms. Howard—in those thirteen seasons—the Finley empathy toward the paying customer diminished. Not completely, but enough. The hunch is that he thought he gave them all he could and that when they failed to respond to this giving, Charlie lost interest in responding to them. He must have felt that he did so much—and received, as the years went by, so little in return. The surface sullenness has always obscured the inner need for adulation and attention and affection. A million people buying tickets in one season could have bought this man's heart. Only once (1973) did he get his million.

Right away, in 1961, he started doing things for the working man in the Kansas City ball park, things he thought the paying customer would want because these were things that Finley wanted. He installed new citrus yellow field boxes, had the reserved seats and bleachers painted desert turquoise. The dugouts were lowered, lengthened, and lighted so the working man could better see his heroes in meditation. Quartz lights were installed every fifty feet outside the stadium so the working man could feel safer. The wall outside the park was sandblasted and painted yellow. The ball park beams were yellowish orange. Pink fluorescent lights marked the ends of the foul poles. There was a new scoreboard device carrying special messages called "Fan-A-Grams." Picnic grounds were built behind left field and shaded by ten sugar maple trees. Special tunnels were built to make it easier for fans to walk to and from their seats. Radio broadcasts of the games were piped into ball park rest rooms. Sheep nibbled on an embankment just beyond right field. A mechanical rabbit handed baseballs to the umpire. An air vent dusted off home plate. There would eventually be fireworks and the mule and a man ringing an old railroad bell and pretty ball girls down the foul lines and a Dixieland band and a Hot Pants Day and a Bald-Headed Day and a Mustache Day and Family Nights that would draw thousands at two-for-the-price-of-one rates. And always the organ music.

Finley was selling baseball in the smallest city in the major leagues—and trying to sell a very bad baseball team. Frank Lane said the ball park would be filled by victories, not mechanical rabbits.

When there was talk of moving the franchise, the heart of the city began slipping from the palm of Finley's hand.

> *Richard Mendahl* (an Oakland A's fan, in 1974): We used to live in Kansas City when Finley had the team there. And I felt so badly toward him there that I thought I'd never go to another game that Finley had anything to do with. A couple of things happened to my kids and me at the ball park that made me feel the club didn't want me or my support at all. But when the A's came out here to Oakland, I kind of relented a little. And now I don't feel so badly toward Finley anymore. I think he's done a lot for baseball.

Charlie never politicked enough in Oakland or Kansas City. The absentee nature of his ownership prevented that. Research indicates he spent more time kibitzing with the folks in Kansas City than he did later in Oakland. Perhaps because Kansas City was closer to Chicago/LaPorte. Perhaps because by the time he got to Oakland grass roots sentiment seemed less important than winning. In terms of population, Oakland was smaller than Kansas City. Charlie could have covered his second city quickly and thoroughly had he ever bothered to go beyond the Chamber of Commerce and friendly restaurateur approach. If he had roamed the stands of the Oakland Coliseum, he would have discovered a different breed of sports fan in the West.

Deron Johnson, who played for Finley in K.C. and, much later, in Oakland, called the Missouri-Kansas fans "real good country people who really were enthusiastic about the game. At the beginning, we couldn't do anything wrong as far as they were concerned." Oakland does not have real good country people in the same proportion as Kansas City. Oakland lacked the solid base of middle class that feeds on a day at the old ball park, and its sizeable black population had already built up an emotional interest in the San Francisco Giants starting a decade before Charlie's arrival. The people who drove across the Bay Bridge to watch Mays and McCovey would have little interest in zipping a shorter distance down the Nimitz Freeway to see the likes of unknowns such as Rick Monday and Mike Hershberger. Loyalties would not come until Vida and Reggie truly arrived. Early, extra selling was needed and not provided with sufficient impact, with the impact that the persistent presence of Finley might have had.

Somehow, an Oakland A's Booster Club got started, and survived. By 1974, the club had about 375 members. "We have nine luncheons and four night game meetings a year, and our members like it real good," said club treasurer Earl Arehart. "But we could do a lot better here if we had local ownership, where somebody would take an interest in the community." Or at least, suggested Arehart, an interest in the Booster Club.

> *Jack Summerfield* (Booster Club board member): All the things we try to do for his team bring no cooperation from Finley whatsoever. After the A's won their first Series, we gave him an expensive set of cuff links and a tie bar. All gold, custom-made. And we didn't even get a thank-you note. The team never gives us any free items to give out at meetings, as other professional sports clubs do in the Bay area.

We have to do everything on our own, without any cooperation from the team. But we have a good Booster Club, despite Charlie Finley.

Yet Summerfield and Arehart do not truly represent the attitude of all Booster Club members toward Finley. At one meeting in 1974, I spoke with several of the members, asking their attitude toward the Owner. A little grass rootsing.

And their concerns were the types of immediate, personal problems that Charlie might have assaulted head-on—if this had been Kansas City in 1961 or 1962.

Mrs. Joe Cannon wondered why the Owner didn't have special ticket price discounts for senior citizens or ladies. "We're retired and we like to go to the games, but it would be more to our liking if we did get a price break on certain days."

Dorothy Barbat wanted Charlie to "encourage the children to come a lot. After all, they're going to be growing up and be fans pretty soon." Charlie was staging occasional Little League, Scout, and knothole days, but observers always had the feeling that all those empty seats might have been put to better use with more frequency.

Had Charlie talked to his Booster Club the evening I did—when they assembled to watch a film of the 1973 World Series—he would have learned that most of them liked him because he gave them winners, that many of them thought the press was too hard on him ("Knife him on every turn of the road they possibly can," said Lillian Bauer), that several felt he treated Mike Andrews unfairly, that he brought color and exciting players into the game, that he seemed to be the only owner in the majors "who participates so much," in the words of Alice Naps.

Or he might have heard Joe Sandoval tell me, "I think his desire to get as much publicity as he does hurts the attendance at the ball games. I'm in business [in Richmond, California] and a lot of people that I talk to complain that Finley interferes too much. The controversy he creates alienates people against going to the games. I think they take it out on the team. They want to hurt Mr. Finley in the pocketbook, so they don't go to the ball park."

Or from Mrs. Joe Sandoval, who has never met the Owner: "I think he's a schnook. I think he's at the point that he's so self-centered that everything he has and owns belongs to him, and nobody else can have it."

Yet when the film was shown and Charlie's form filled the little screen in the banquet room, the applause for the Owner was as enthusiastic as the cheers for some of the players. I would assume that Elmer Swanton applauded Charlie, for earlier Elmer had said to me, "He has done a great job in bringing exciting baseball to the Bay area. The man is a businessman, and whether he is a crude businessman makes no difference to me. He has brought us good baseball. That's my full opinion."

He had given them winners. The mechanical rabbit was gone. The ball girls had been eliminated. He was still getting players, but then, too, he was still keeping the money he had. No one was beating down the doors of the Oakland Coliseum to get in, just as bodies had been sparse in the stands at Kansas City.

In the early Oakland days, as in Kansas City, Charlie suggested that "you can't ballyhoo a funeral." For reasons inimical to the Owner, consecutive championships couldn't be ballyhooed either.

They were a long time coming, those titles. Thus, into reverse, an Oakland–Kansas City–Oakland round trip. Clap hands, there goes Charlie.

Three years after he became owner of the Kansas City Athletics, Charles O. Finley was asking approval of the American League owners to move his team to Louisville, Kentucky. He kidded, "We have these caps that have K.C. on the front, and we don't want to throw them away, so I think we'll call ourselves the Kentucky Colonels. And before every game, after 'The Star-Spangled Banner,' everyone will sing, 'Oh, the sun shines bright . . . ' " He kidded around, but he was deadly serious; getting the hell out of Kansas City was the most serious thing in the world to Charlie. He felt abused, unloved, taken. Particularly taken. And you do not take the Owner and General Manager, no, sir.

> *Joe McGuff* (sports editor of the Kansas City *Star*, in a letter to American League club owners in 1967): In any proposal to move a franchise, the most important single consideration is whether the owner has acted in good faith. Has he honestly tried to establish himself in the community where he is operating and has he tried in every way to make his operation successful? Has he been honest with the public and responsible officials of local government? Has he conducted himself in a responsible manner?

McGuff went on to outline, chronologically, the "major events since Charles O. Finley purchased the Athletics. A pattern of behavior is clearly evident."

Some people say that Charlie "had a lot of problems with the press in Kansas City." Just as Richard M. Nixon had a lot of problems with Bernstein and Woodward. If McGuff and veteran Kansas City baseball writer Ernie Mehl chose to scrutinize the Owner and General Manager, they were well within their professional rights. Another newspaperman close to the situation told me, "There was no policy on the *Star* to *get* Charlie." McGuff and Mehl were working to keep a viable major league baseball franchise in Kansas City, for whatever reasons: Good for the city's economy, good for the sports fan, good for the sportswriter, good for national identification of their community. They did not want

Finley to move the club. Move himself and sell the club, sure, but keep the ball club in Kansas City.

McGuff has written a well-documented case on Charlie's attempts to leave Kansas City. Joe's letter to the American League owners deals more with fact than malice. His early chronology alone is sufficient to denote that "clearly evident pattern of behavior." What is missing from McGuff's outline is an instance of Charlie meeting with executives of a beer company who had been pushing the A's in Kansas City before he bought the team. They offered to continue their broadcast sponsorship and help him with season ticket sales and promotional matters. A man who was at the meeting said Finley told the beer people that he did not want their help and that he did not like their beer, either—at which point he summoned a waiter and ordered another brand of brew. Well, maybe he was just teasing, huh?

*McGuff's letter to the owners:* To sum up briefly: Finley purchased controlling interest in the A's in December, 1960. He made elaborate promises to leave the franchise here. By the following August he was attempting to move to Dallas–Fort Worth. On May 18, 1962, he made another attempt to move to Dallas. On September 19, 1962, he asked for a new stadium here. On September 30, 1962, he said the city was justified in being angry about his attempts to move but requested that he be given an opportunity to make a fresh start. On July 9, 1963, he made his first attempt to move to Oakland. Negotiations for a new lease on Kansas City's Municipal Stadium started in December, 1963. Finley promised he would operate here regardless of the outcome of the negotiations. On January 7, 1964, Finley signed a conditional lease in Louisville and announced plans to move the A's there. On January 16, the American League ordered Finley to sign a lease in Kansas City. Finley then asked for a new meeting for the purpose of requesting permission to move to Oakland. On February 29, Finley signed a lease here under threat of losing his club. He later instituted a suit against the city to have the lease voided in favor of a previous lease that he claimed was the only valid lease. In the meantime Finley's name was linked with possible franchise moves to Atlanta and Milwaukee. In the autumn of 1966 stories appeared about the possibility of the A's being moved to Oakland. . . . Finley did not comment on any of these stories. On May 7, 1967, stories appeared in the New York *Daily News* and the *New York Times* about the possibility of the A's being moved to Oakland. Finley, contacted by the Associated Press in Chicago, declined to comment. His unwillingness to comment . . . has created the definite impression here that he will attempt to move.

*Calvin Griffith:* Charlie definitely made a mistake not living where his ball club was located. When my team moved from Washington, I brought my whole family to Minnesota. Every one of us live there year-round. We moved because we had to become part of the community. I felt if we were part of the community, people would realize that we weren't out there to milk them. We joined civic clubs, we donated to every local charity humanly possible. There's no question about it—if Charlie had moved to Kansas City or Oakland, he'd have a more successful operation. And that was one of the things he said he'd do. But he told me that he had to stay with his insurance business in Chicago because that's what made everything else go.

When Charlie purchased the balance of the Athletics' stock from local interests in February, 1961, he promised to eliminate a clause in the club's lease with Kansas City Municipal Stadium. It was an escape clause that provided the lease could be cancelled if attendance dipped under 850,000. He said at the time, "I'm going to strike a match and set fire to the contract. This will prove I am not in the slightest concerned about the 850,000 minimum. I am not concerned, as a matter of fact, with attendance at all."

There was a public burning of what appeared to be the lease. In mid-August Charlie was peeking around the Dallas area, engendering rumors that he wanted to move the A's. He said he knew nothing about the rumors, in fact called the stories "disgusting." The Dallas *News* reported that Charlie said he was not obligated to stay in Kansas City, that he was confident in the future of the Athletics, if not in Kansas City then somewhere else. And he confirmed his lease still contained the escape clause—"but that doesn't mean I will move the club." He was quoted as saying, after touring the Dallas territory, "A team here would be a tremendous asset to major league baseball." About the escape clause, he added, "I would have to pay the remaining two years rental on the stadium if I decided to move the club. The contract or the attendance would not have any influence on me if I decided to move the club."

In Charlie's seven seasons in Kansas City, the attendance never did approach 850,000. The closest it came was 773,929 in 1966. In fact, Finley's A's did not surpass the 850,000 mark until 1971 in Oakland, the year of Vida Blue.

A week after his trip to Dallas in 1961, Charlie said he would sign a provision deleting the escape clause from the lease. Perhaps the league was getting a bit miffed. On August 26, he signed the provision—and didn't think about Dallas again for fully eight months.

The Associated Press reported in May, 1962, that Charlie was talking to American League club owners about "the possibility of moving the Athletics to Dallas." Charlie would not comment. That September he asked the Kansas City city council to approve a new fifty-thousand-seat baseball stadium to be built from general obligation bonds. He said, "I am convinced that without a new stadium, Kansas City cannot much longer have major league baseball."

It may have been about that time that Charlie first started peering westward. Bill Cunningham, general manager of the Oakland Coliseum, recalls that "in 1962 or 1963 Finley indicated some interest in coming to the Bay area. He had had exploratory meetings with Bob Nahas [a wealthy Oakland builder who was ramrodding efforts to form a public corporation that was to develop the Oakland Coliseum project]. He was exploring the possibility of using Candlestick Park [home of the San Francisco Giants] or Youell Field [pre-Coliseum home of the Oakland Raider football team]." But bonds for the Coliseum were not committed until 1964; the ball park would not be opened until the fall of 1966.

On September 30, 1962, the day after Hank Bauer became the second ex-manager of Finley's Athletics, Charlie asked Kansas City for a fresh start. His attendance had dropped nearly fifty thousand from the first season to a 1962 mark of 635,675.

*Charlie's appeal:* When I first came to Kansas City, everyone was on my side. They were on my team. Then I started working on this Texas thing and they got down on me. I don't blame them. Kansas City had a major league club and here was a threat that the team might be lost. I would have been mad and upset myself if I had lived here. But on my side, I believe everyone will agree we have started to build a winning club. [The 1962 A's had won eleven more games than the 1961 team.] Our trades have been good ones and we have been careful not to tear down. We have tried to build. So I am asking that bygones be bygones, that the past be forgotten and that we start over again. I am convinced I can build a winner here. Contrary to what some might think, I like Kansas City and I applaud the loyalty of its faithful baseball fans. . . . One reason I am urging the erection of a new stadium is that I believe it will do a great deal to arouse new interest. The fans here have been justified in their criticism because, understandably, they do not want to lose the

Athletics. And I can't blame them. And now I want them back on my team. We'll all join forces and see if we cannot make 1963 the biggest season in the history of this city.

In the middle of the biggest season in the history of Kansas City, there were firm reports that Charlie was fiddling out West. Horace Stoneham, owner of the San Francisco Giants, told the Associated Press that Finley "was in to see me. He asked me if his club could play in Candlestick Park as a starter" until Oakland built the Coliseum. "But I told him it would be better to establish himself directly in Oakland."

Finley apparently had told American League officials about his interest in Oakland. Both he and American League president Joe Cronin denied that report, but then there surfaced a story written by Charlie's friend David Condon of the Chicago *Tribune*, a story in which Charlie was quoted as saying, "I think I could have gotten permission [to move to Oakland]. But I didn't make a formal request. Besides, I know there are two or three owners who believed I might louse up the Oakland franchise." In the same Condon story, Charlie said, "We need a larger park [in K.C.] so we can capitalize on the good draws. Right now when the Yankees come to town we are limited to capacity attendances from thirty-two thousand to thirty-four thousand. If we had a stadium that seated fifty thousand we could fill it for games with the Yankees. That would mean a difference of more than a hundred thousand in season attendance."

The crunch was beginning. His lease at Kansas City Municipal Stadium had expired. He said that he had lost just over one million dollars in his three years in Kansas City. He wanted a more favorable lease. He was adamant that the city fathers were not as cooperative as he felt they should be.

He said the city had not yet reimbursed him on money he had

spent to improve the stadium. "It was a pigpen when I arrived," he told a magazine writer, "and now it's the sexiest park in baseball."

A story in the *Saturday Evening Post* in 1964 said that Charlie had spent five hundred thousand dollars to refurbish the stadium. In 1968, *Life* quoted Charlie as saying the Kansas City city council "pleaded poverty" when he asked them "to fix up" the stadium. "But they told me they would give me credit if I did something. So I spent $580,000 of my own money on it. They gave me nothing."

Joe McGuff would later report to American League owners that Finley's refurbishing expenditure was three hundred thousand dollars. The city would ultimately set aside a portion of Finley's rental payments as restitution for his refurbishing costs.

But what bugged Charlie more than that lingering debt was the treatment Kansas City gave the professional football Chiefs, newly arrived from Dallas and owned by a fellow with a bit more money than Charlie, one Lamar Hunt. The city council provided funds so the Chiefs could have a practice field, training quarters, and office space. The *Life* writer reported the Chiefs were given $650,000 by the Kansas City city council and quoted Charlie: "My god, our offices were so cold my employees had to wear stadium boots and sit on heating pads in the winter and I was paying $120,000 for the privilege. How much rent did the Chiefs pay for the stadium? ONE . . . DOLLAR . . . A . . . YEAR."

McGuff reports that Charlie's rent in the first three Kansas City years ranged from $59,030 to $71,818. The football team's rent was in fact a buck a year plus a percentage of the concessions. *Time* reported the Chiefs' rental totalled fifteen thousand dollars in the 1963 season.

Whatever Charlie was paying, there was no question the football team was being treated very, very kindly by the city council. In the sixties and seventies in America, communities were doing financial backflips to attract professional sports franchises, and pro football teams were accorded the same respect as mom, apple pie, and the flag.

Finley was entitled to his outrage. Kansas City may have hoped that Charlie would get so damned mad he would sell his club to local interests. But the town did not totally reckon with his perseverance and energy.

The matter of the renewal of his stadium lease ping-ponged throughout the final nine months of 1963. One contract was approved by an outgoing city council and then voided by new councilmen.

Toward the end of the year—the contract expired on December 31, 1963—there were arguments over the length of a renewal, the matter of a new escape clause, the actual rental price. There seemed no area for agreement and on December 24, Charlie said, "Rather than yield on any point, I will rent a cow pasture and put up temporary stands for the team to use next year. The A's will play in Kansas City and that's definite, but they won't use the stadium unless they are given what I consider a fair lease."

There was one report that Charlie sent right-hand man Pat Friday to inspect a sizeable cow pasture in a place called Peculiar, Missouri.

Negotiations broke down completely on January 4, 1964. Charlie would later tell *Life*, "I got so mad I walked out of the meeting [with the council] and got on a plane and went to Louisville and signed up to play ball there for two years. That was my big mistake. Some of the [American League] owners had been on my side. But now the city council went to the American League and said, 'Look at this damned fool!' So the league told me to stay in Kansas City for four more years or get out of baseball. They sentenced me to four years at hard labor. The mayor of Kansas City told the owners, 'If you will keep Mr. Finley in our city we will go out and sell tickets for him.' What a con man *he* was. They did nothing. They wanted the team but not Finley. They figured: 'We'll starve him out!' So I sweated blood for four years. I lost sleep. I lost hair. I lost money. You name it. I lost it."

Of course he could have sold the team after the 1963 season and not lost sleep, hair, or money. But as he said at one point in the Kansas City turmoil: "Baseball is more than a hobby for me. It's a total commitment." He was desperate to hang on but to take his balls, bats, and gold and green uniforms (unveiled in the 1963 season) elsewhere.

He told *Saturday Evening Post* that American League president Cronin knew he was investigating possible moves to Dallas and Oakland. "I was encouraged by the league to look around," he said. "Cronin let me take the abuse. He never had the red blood in his *veins* to stand up and say, 'We knew Finley had problems in Kansas City; we knew he was looking in Dallas and Oakland; we contributed financially to this.' " Charlie said the league reimbursed him for most of his travel expenses.

Cronin's response: "Baseball has a dual obligation—to both the owners and the fans. On Finley's request, we made surveys. But those we made in Dallas, Oakland, *and* Kansas City convinced us we weren't justified in letting Finley move. Before we abandon a city we have to consider its history—the quality of the team and its public relations and the effect they might have on attendance."

Cronin and Charlie would tangle for years. The Owner berated the league president, abusively, in front of a newspaperman when Cronin called off a playoff game on a rainy day in Oakland in 1973. Cronin's last act before retiring in 1973 involved Finley's attempt to prevent Dick Williams from leaving the A's to manage the Yankees. But interestingly, at the 1967 baseball winter meetings in Mexico City—just after the American League permitted Charlie to move to Oakland—it was Finley who spearheaded a resolution approving a raise for good old flaccid Joe Cronin.

Back in January, 1964, however, Cronin had his hands full with Charlie. On January 6, Charlie was checking stadium sites in Louisville, meeting with the governor of Kentucky and the mayor of Louisville. The next day Finley signed a contract with the state of Kentucky to play in Louisville's Fairgrounds Stadium, subject to the approval of American League owners. (A minor league team had failed in Louisville.)

Charlie said he believed the club owners "will approve the move when they hear my case." The American League owners would meet on January 16. Advance indications were that Charlie wouldn't be permitted to budge an inch out of Kansas City. Chicago White Sox owner Arthur Allyn said, "Finley is a fool."

Three days before the league meeting Finley hinted he would sue his fellow owners if they didn't let the sun shine bright on his new Kentucky home.

> *Finley* (on January 13, 1964): I will take on each American League owner individually or I will take them on collectively. I have taken it on the chin from the American League long enough and I will say this: If the league pulls the rug out from under me, the league is going out with me. . . .

Meanwhile, fans, Missouri Senator Stuart Symington suggested that Congress just might take a fresh look at baseball's tidy exemption from antitrust laws if the American League permitted Finley to move from Kansas City.

On January 16, the American League owners met in New York and voted nine to one to keep Charlie in Missouri. The minority vote was cast by Charles O. Finley.

He had lost, but he would not surrender unconditionally.

*Finley* (on February 1, 1964): My plans will be to go to court to find out if the American League has the power they think they have to restrain me from moving my club to Louisville or any other place.

He had hired a fair country lawyer named Louis Nizer. He also had vocal support from feisty old Brooklyn congressman Manny Celler, who said Charlie "has a perfect antitrust suit against organized baseball."

"This is still a free country," Charlie said, "and I don't believe that anybody can force me to operate my business in a city where I've lost a million dollars in three years."

On January 27 he asked for another meeting of league owners to hear his request to move the A's to Louisville. He was pushing things to the limit, but the owners were more fearful of Stu Symington, and they ordered Charlie either to sign a new four-year contract to play in the Kansas City stadium or be expelled from owning the franchise. He backed down at the end and on February 29 signed a new four-year lease. He would tell a *Saturday Evening Post* writer that the owners "picked me clean . . . tarred and feathered me. When Cronin sent me the telegram telling me to sign, I smelled the pine box. It's one of the greatest injustices in baseball history. I'm saddled with the only noncancellable contract in the big leagues."

More than one year later he would tell a man from *Sports Illustrated*: "I don't feel anger or hatred [toward the other owners]. When they can't see the handwriting on the wall I feel sorry for them. When they're all against me I am disappointed but never discouraged. Anything that is worth having is worth fighting for. When they vote against me it encourages me to fight more, because I know they need help. . . . If you know anybody who is interested in getting into baseball as an owner, and he wants to get along with the other owners, then here is my advice for him: Do not go into any league meeting looking alert and awake; slump down like you've been out all night and keep your eyes half closed, and when it is time to vote you ask to pass. Then you wait and see how the others vote, and you vote the same way. Suggest no innovations. That way you will be very popular with your fellow owners."

As much as he must have otherwise wished, Charlie was not very popular with anybody in 1964. He most certainly had recognition, but no affection. No matter what he might do while reclining in that "pine box" in Kansas City four more years, he was suspect.

> *A former A's executive:* Charlie brought the Beatles to Kansas City once and promised to give the profits to a children's hospital. And he was charged with staging the event to bail himself out. He broke even but he still gave twenty-five thousand to the hospital.

If the town was down on him personally, its Establishment had no interest in destroying his baseball team. In his letter to American League owners in 1967, sports editor McGuff made these points on the community's behalf: "Since being forced to remain in Kansas City in 1964, Finley has done nothing to promote the season ticket sale. He has never had one salesman on the street. The A's do not have a ticket outlet outside of Greater Kansas City. Promoters who formerly promoted bus and train trips to the A's games for groups report they get no cooperation from the A's. In 1964 and 1965 it was assumed here we [the Kansas City *Star*] would help the club conduct its season ticket sale. The club did nothing, other than send out a form letter to previous season ticket holders. In 1966 a group known as the Greater Kansas City Sports Commission was formed. . . . More than one hundred of the leading businessmen in Kansas City devoted several full days to selling A's tickets. Finley cooperated to the extent of running several ads [and] we sold well over five thousand season tickets. A similar drive was conducted this year. Mr. Finley's actions are most significant. The A's did not assist in the drive in any way other than to send out their usual form letter. Finley ran no ads. . . . Under these extremely difficult circumstances, thirty-eight hundred season tickets were sold. Again there was no expression of appreciation on Finley's part. The major civic clubs in Kansas City held a luncheon for the A's at the outset of the [1967] season. Mr. Finley, who was in town the previous night, not only did not stay over but did not even have the courtesy to send a message to be read at the luncheon. . . ."

Then McGuff detailed what he described as Charlie's nonattempt to sell radio-TV rights for the 1967 season. The A's, wrote Joe, "put the rights up for bids among the stations here and when no bids were offered the club made no further effort to sell the rights. . . ."

McGuff was attempting to suggest a deliberate pattern of actions by Charlie—a pattern Finley hoped would convince the other owners to let him move at the end of the 1967 season. He could plead poor attendance. He could plead insufficient broadcast revenue. He could say: I served my four-year sentence, now let me try it someplace else.

In those four seasons (1964–67), Charlie was building toward that conclusion. In the last week of 1964 he criticized the city for failure to support his club and two days later instituted a suit to have his stadium lease voided so that an escape clause could be added. The suit was eventually dismissed in court.

In July, 1964, he denied a surfacing report that he was going to sell the A's to a Milwaukee group. In September he offered to sell the A's if the American League approved the purchase of the New York Yankees by the Columbia Broadcasting System; he asked for a Justice Department investigation of possible antitrust violations in the proposed CBS purchase. Charlie may have been motivated by his antipathy for the Yankees (i.e., their overwhelming clout in the affairs of the entire league), but he also was talking on rather solid legal grounds. As Bill Veeck points out in *The Hustler's Handbook*, CBS, as owner of the Yankees and broadcaster of sporting events, could be "sitting on both sides of the table at the same time. It is both the buyer and the seller" of radio-TV rights.

In protesting the intended sale (which was completed and not later voided by any governmental action), Charlie at last gained the support of another American League owner. Arthur Allyn of the Chicago White Sox was the only other franchise holder in the league to vote against the CBS deal. In succeeding years, he and Finley would become companionable. (It was reported that the two once discussed the possibility of "trading" teams: Allyn would sell the Sox to a group of Oaklanders, Charlie would move his players to Chicago, the new owners of the Sox would take their athletes to Oakland. The story may be a joke. But remember, Charlie always did want to own the Chicago White Sox.)

*Sports Illustrated* reported that Finley put an eight million dollar price tag on the A's during the CBS uproar—"A price that kept him in baseball, after all." Two Kansas City groups apparently were interested in talking to him about buying the A's, but not at that figure.

There was another flurry of reports that he would sell to a Milwaukee group in late 1964. At about the same time he issued a statement saying he was going to meet with the board of directors of his company (Shirley and the kids) to discuss the possibility of moving the A's to another city. The minutes of that meeting are not available.

So it went those last four years. Tantalized by the prospect of a large new ball park in Kansas City, yet dispirited by the lack of attendance. The old Durante song was applicable—having the feeling that you wanted to stay but still having the feeling that you wanted to go. One must assume that Charlie expected baseball to make money for him in Kansas City. When it didn't, he thought that he could take his team somewhere else—almost *anywhere* else—and make money.

> *Bill Cunningham:* He came out to take a look at construction in mid-1966 and then came back to see the first Raider game in the Coliseum in 1966. Then he financed a report that measured Seattle, Oakland, and Kansas City. While we thought we had the inside track, it was never a certainty. He kept going back and forth between Seattle and us. But they didn't have a stadium ready in Seattle. We knew Charlie pretty well and we weren't counting on him definitely coming here until we had a long-term contract. Although our board of directors had heard some of the criticism [about Charlie] emanating from Kansas City, they felt that he might change some of his ways. He was just fine with the board in meetings. That's part of Charlie Finley—he's a master salesman. At first blush when you meet him, you say what's everybody so teed off at Finley for? He seems like a nice guy who says he's gonna do all these colorful and exciting things and make the fans wanted and appreciated. He told the board president and me that he was considering moving his family and his insurance business out here. We had a definite impression he said that. The similarities between his early speeches in Kansas City and what he said to us are amazing. At the Oakland welcoming luncheon for him, he said the A's would forever have OAKLAND across their shirts because he was proud to be here. That lasted one year.

On October 18, 1967, the American League owners met in Chicago to consider the transiency of Charles O. Finley. He had given notice that he would no longer require the facilities of

Kansas City Municipal Stadium; the lease had finally expired. He would need votes of seven of the other nine owners to come to Oakland. On the first ballot, he was short, but not by much. Three owners (Cleveland, Washington, New York) abstained. And only one (Baltimore) voted against him.

> *Frank Cashen:* We didn't really believe that moving the team to Oakland was the answer to Charlie's problems. Very frankly, we felt the A's had not done the proper market studies to look at the various places that were available. And we thought it would certainly hurt the San Francisco Giants to put another team into the Bay area.
>
> *Cedric Tallis* (in 1967 an executive with the California Angels): Everybody in the American League was sick and tired of the uncertainty and thought it would be better to let Charlie move.
>
> *Calvin Griffith:* I voted for Charlie to move to Oakland. I've gone on record as saying I'd vote for any club that feels they have to move because I needed help to move from Washington to Minnesota [in 1961]. If an owner feels he has to move, he knows more about it than me.

On the second ballot on October 18, the Yankees changed their abstention to an aye, and Charlie was sprung. At the same meeting, the owners ruled that they would expand the league no later than 1971. And that seemed to be that. For an hour or so.

Around the corner from the league meeting waited a delegation from Kansas City that included Senator Stuart Symington and Kansas City mayor Ilus Davis. They did not care about Finley's departure. But they did not want to wait until 1971 to regain a franchise in Kansas City. Symington, who would describe the Finley-winning Oakland as "the luckiest city since Hiroshima," said he might just move to strip baseball of its antitrust exemption if the American League didn't hustle a club into Kansas City. Mayor Davis threatened to enjoin the A's from moving.

Cronin had to be a wee bit shook. In one of the more decisive moments of his reign as league president, Cronin quickly reopened the earlier adjourned meeting of the owners and put together a vote to add a club in Kansas City for the 1969 season. The league would also have to add a twelfth team in 1969 (the ill-fated Seattle Pilots) to ensure orderly if unplanned expansion. And naturally the National League could not stand still. It also would go to a dozen teams in 1969 (hello, Montreal and San Diego). There no longer would be the old-fashioned pennant races. Instead, each league would have two divisions and thus playoffs leading up to the World Series. Thanks, sort of, to Charlie.

> *Frank Cashen:* One thing I'll never understand is the events of that day. Voting in the morning to allow Finley to leave Kansas City. Then voting in the afternoon to expand into Kansas City because we considered it one of the hotbeds of baseball. As an American Leaguer, I have to say I think that was a disgraceful proposition to have occurred in one day. Expansion was forced, and I'm not sure at all that it was good for baseball—as far as comparing the caliber of the game before that expansion and now.
>
> *Cedric Tallis:* The American League never would have permitted Finley to move if they hadn't conceived of having an orderly expansion and another club in Kansas City. Expansion was a good thing at that time. We got the growing pains over quickly, and the hoppers are full. We [the Kansas City Royals] became contenders quickly. All in all, I think it was best that the marriage between the A's and Kansas City was dissolved.

The day after the league owners did their double duty in Chicago, Senator Symington, under the protection of legislative privilege, told his fellow senators that the absence of baseball in Kansas City for one season "is more than recompensed by the pleasure resulting from our getting rid of Mr. Finley." The senator from Missouri called Charlie "one of the most disreputable characters ever to enter the American sports scene."

Back in Oakland, as Coliseum boss Cunningham recalls the mood, "We were delighted to get baseball and felt we would learn to live with the A's and with Charlie."

Oakland had its team. Symington would have his team. Cronin would get Symington off his back. The American League owners would have Charlie off their backs. As for the Owner and General Manager after being paroled from Kansas City: "I feel like I have unloaded two hundred pounds of sand I've been carrying on my back for six years. I feel like I can take off and fly any minute—just keep me pointed West if I do. You know, you're supposed to pinch yourself and see if it's a dream, but I'm going to wait several days. If I'm dreaming, I don't want to wake up."


Stu Symington was right rather than president: Kansas City did deserve a major league baseball team. Kansas City could support a major league baseball team.

In January, 1968, Ewing Kauffman, a Kansas City resident, became owner of the town's new franchise. Kauffman was a self-made gentleman who had grown up on a farm and at the age of eleven spent a full year in bed because of illness. After working for a pharmaceutical firm for several years, he founded the K.C.-based Marion Laboratories and built it into one of the most successful pharmaceutical firms in the country.

Among the original members of the new Kansas City team's board of directors was Charlie's old sportswriting friend from the *Star*, Ernie Mehl. And the first manager hired by Kauffman was a fellow named Joe Gordon. No, Frank Lane was not the first general manager of the Kansas City Royals. That job went to one Cedric Tallis.

The largest home crowd of the Royals' opening season (1969) was on April 20. The count was 31,872, for a double header. With the Oakland Athletics.

In August, 1969, Kauffman made a firm commitment to lease the baseball stadium segment of the Harry Truman Sports Complex for twenty-five years. The new ball park, called Royals Stadium, opened April 10, 1973, and seats 40,762. The press box is air-conditioned.

When the A's come to visit the Royals and Charlie accompanies them, he is introduced to the crowd, and is booed.

The gentlemen who ran the Oakland Coliseum were determined from the start of their relationship with Charlie to prevent an in-and-out atmosphere. As Coliseum general manager Bill Cunningham puts it: "Our approach was to tie him down in the lease to provisions that would protect the Coliseum and our community against the repetition of [another Kansas City] happening."

Finley's rent was to be $125,000 or five percent of the gate up to an attendance of 1,450,000—a figure never approached in Charlie's first seven years in Oakland. His largest one-season attendance in that time was 1,000,736 in 1973, and a good chunk of those bodies attended the half-priced family nights. Thus his rental did not exceed the $125,000. (The last year at Kansas City he paid stadium rent of $51,085, according to one reliable balance sheet.)

Charlie would receive twenty-seven cents of every dollar parking charge and twenty-five percent of the concession revenue. He also would be required to pay the costs of maintenance and cleanup at the ball park and share in the general overhead there. "Stadium operating expense" ranged from just under $300,000 in 1970 to nearly $450,000 in 1972. In his final K.C. year, that expenditure—again, according to a reliable balance sheet I have seen—was only $225,166.

These financial elements of his Oakland contract are not as fascinating as another segment of the proposal—an injunctive relief provision. This was the Coliseum's protection against a Kansas City-like exodus. In this provision, as Cunningham describes it, "Finley agrees to have the A's play exclusively in our stadium and no other place, except as a visiting team, for a period of twenty years. He is further specifically bound by the contract not to enter into discussions with anybody or any city about the transfer of the A's to another location during the life of the contract. The contract runs for a firm twenty-year period with four additional five-year options. So it could be a forty-year commitment."

Could be.

One might assume that Charlie would have protested this provision. Cunningham says no. "He wanted the long-term commitment," says Bill. "And his attorney felt that was a fair and proper thing for a publicly owned stadium to ask for. As I recall, the only contract items that remained up in the air were just the nitty-gritty matters. You know, like whether you pay $250 or $150 for the lights. Not specifically that, but things like that. Charlie is a tough negotiator and he hangs in there until the end all the time. We had some difficulty in getting him to put his name on the document. The A's had moved into their Coliseum offices before we signed the contract. They were already selling tickets [for the 1968 season]. Finally, we had, in effect, to put a gun to his head and say that if he wanted to open up in April in our ball park he'd better put his name to that piece of paper. If not, we would have rented him the stadium on a day-to-day basis. The difference would have been about double the rent. And on that basis, the tenant doesn't get a percentage of the parking and concession revenue. I agree that it's proper for him to fight for everything he thinks is right when he's negotiating, but you've got to reach a deadline point unless you want to trigger another action on our part. And he didn't sign that contract until just a couple weeks before the season opened."

There have been rumors—generally touched off by the San Francisco newspapers—that Finley could buy up his contract from the Oakland Coliseum and get out of town. "No way," says Cunningham. "Our board of directors would not consider a buy-up under any circumstances because they don't feel they have the right to negotiate away the public's right to see baseball in the stadium they're paying for with their tax dollars. Under our terms, the first time there's even a public discussion about moving, we could go to court."

> *Question:* How soon after the A's came to Oakland did you get a report that Charlie was looking at another town?
>
> *Bill Cunningham:* Oh, within two or three years. Probably Toronto in 1970. There have been cases of him talking to other cities that have come to our attention. Toronto, New Orleans, Washington, Dallas. We've heard about some of these first-hand from people who supposedly talked to him in other towns. We know stadium managers and politicians in other cities, too. In some cases, we heard through hearsay. But we really couldn't punish him for doing this. We really wouldn't want to.
>
> *Question:* But doesn't this represent a contract violation?
>
> *Bill Cunningham:* Uh, yes. But there are other minor contract violations, too. If there were a really serious effort to move the franchise, then of course we would be seeking an injunction the very day that happened. But when you get involved in hearsay and things you think are very remote, there's a limit to how much you can take people on. You have to think about the consequences you're looking for. Are you looking for a declaration of a default of the contract? Of

Oakland dignitaries came to the airport to greet the man who moved his ball club from Kansas City in 1968. When Missouri Senator Stuart Symington heard about the franchise shift, he called Oakland "the luckiest city since Hiroshima."

*World Series hospitality room guests at Oakland Coliseum in 1973 included all-time-great player Stan Musial (standing left) and all-time-great mule Charlie O. (unencumbered at right). While Finley's guests sipped and supped, Finley's animal strolled amongst them in hostly fashion. Its presence was questionable, but its behavior was exemplary.*

en Charlie O. (the
n) is away from Oak-
d, Charlie O. (the mule)
ys with trainer Stan
ca. Stan says the mule
ns to like anyone who
ls him. Stan says base-
's best-known animal
s children and FM
ic.

Owner and GM
ls most of his work-
ime, which is all the
on the phone. Since
961 days as owner of
Kansas City A's,
ie has switched to a
hone, a new cap and
e comfortable speak-
osture.

*Shirley Finley joined hubby in welcoming guests and Hoosier friends to World Series festivities in both 1972 and 1973. But in 1974, Shirley stayed on the farm.*

*Mrs. Onassis was just plain First Lady when she welcomed 1961
Christmas Seal National Campaign chairman Charlie to the White
House. Ten years later the Owner and his entire ball club would be
back to see new occupant Nixon.*

On January 16, 1973, the Oakland Chamber of Commerce opened its heart to Charlie with a gala testimonial dinner saluting his world title. Gifts included this bust of the Owner, sculpted by Nolan Hibbard, a security guard at the Oakland Museum. Charlie seemed to be touched, perhaps perceiving a small step toward Mt. Rushmore.

A cheery cluster around the 1973 American League pennant hardware. Manager Dick Williams (left) would quit within ten days; League President Joe Cronin would retire within two months; pitcher Jim Hunter (right) would soon be talking to Charlie about a deferred-income contract.

*On his rare appearances in Oakland, Charlie employs the services of an off-duty police sergeant, Carl Ivey (right), to allay untoward folk.*

course not. We're looking to keep the A's here. Finley has never made an attempt to break that provision of the contract. Never. He has never indicated any desire he wanted to break that. He has always indicated he wants to stay in Oakland. He has indicated—after he lost his big radio-TV contract [after the 1972 season]—that he'd need some help here. He thought the Bay area could support only one team and he was hoping it would be him. But he didn't ask for lower rent.

For the purposes of noninjunctive relief, it might be valuable at this juncture to glance at the other Bay area baseball team's attendance since Charlie's arrival. Since moving from the Polo Grounds in New York to San Francisco's bandbox Seals Stadium (1958–59) and thence Candlestick Park, the Giants' annual attendance ranged from 1,795,356 (1960) to 1,242,480 (1967). In their first head-to-head year in the Bay area, the Giants drew 837,220 and Oakland 837,466. (One has to wonder about the coincidence of Charlie outdrawing Horace Stoneham by 246 in that 1968 season. It must have been the challenge, I guess. The A's, not the Giants, finished that season at home, a factor that had to have helped in the counting.) In only one season after the arrival of the A's did the Giants' attendance exceed a million (their division-winning year in 1971). By 1972, Giant owner Stoneham was starting to peddle high-priced athletes (Mays, McCovey, Marichal) in order to survive. One cannot totally blame Charlie for Stoneham's slim pickings. The Giants brought a sense of prehistoric creativity to their promotional exercises.

In July, 1974, when Charlie was attacking a Bay area sports columnist for suggesting he was moving to Seattle, the Owner and General Manager also expressed sorrow for Stoneham and said the press had hurt Horace, too. "I have the greatest respect for Stoneham," said Charlie. "He is a very fine person and knows baseball inside and out." Horace Stoneham, through 1974, had never made a player deal with Charles O. Finley.

National League president Chub Feeney, once general manager of the Giants, told a writer that when Finley moved to Oakland "baseball still drew a million and a half in the Bay area, but the two teams drew it between them. There was no more traffic on the Bay Bridge."

Feeney's estimate might be a little low, but not by much. If both teams are playing well at the same time—as occurred in 1971—they could draw some two million fans combined. Something the Los Angeles Dodgers do all by themselves.

Were either Finley or Stoneham to move their clubs from the Bay area (hypothetically speaking), the survivor might wish to split his schedule between the Oakland Coliseum and Candlestick Park, some forty dates on each side of the Bay. More logical, at least in terms of fan interest, would be a reshuffling of the leagues so that both the A's and Giants would end up in the same division of the same league and play each other eighteen times.

The Coliseum's Cunningham will not speculate on those possibilities. He feels he doesn't have to speculate, that the injunctive relief provision will keep the A's in Oakland through 1987. "The American League is not involved in the A's contract with us," he says. "However, the league unofficially told us both before and after Finley got approval to move here that they looked upon this as Charlie's last opportunity to make a successful franchise, that the American League was committing itself to the Bay area. The implication was that in permitting him to make the move, it was their intention to have a franchise here. They hoped Finley and the A's would be successful, but they weren't closing the door to other possibilities if things just didn't work out."

Which could mean whatever you might want it to mean. Which

could mean a repetition of Kansas City—Finley moving and the American League immediately putting another franchise in town. It would all depend on the Coliseum's appetite for an all-out court fight on the injunctive relief provision. Or, for that matter, baseball's appetite.

> *Bill Cunningham:* Believe it or not, and I'm obviously measuring my words here, Charlie Finley has not been an extremely difficult person for us to deal with. We've had our disagreements and some real verbal outbursts, but we respect him for what he did by bringing the team here and giving us world championships. It hasn't been a difficult relationship. We just wish he was more personally involved or had someone with the authority to be involved.

One of Cunningham's major disagreements with Charlie involved Finley's debts to the Coliseum. "In the early years," says Bill, "Charlie didn't agree with some of the bills and he was meaning to protest them, and on his next trip out he would meet with us. These things just dragged on and on and on. And the bills really got out of sight. Primarily, these were staffing bills, money we had been laying out to pay ushers and ticket takers for his games. We said, 'Hey, we got a cash flow problem, too.' We said that it wasn't a matter of dispute, that we had standard labor pay rates and staffing patterns. But the thing just kept dragging, and we finally reached the point where we went to arbitration on a number of these questions. His highest delinquency at one point was almost two hundred thousand dollars. It stayed at that peak for about two months. It was at the over one hundred thousand dollar level for more than six months once."

Thus to arbitration. "We came up with a supplemental agreement," says Cunningham, "so we don't have delinquencies now." The little supplemental agreement that convinced Charlie to pay the Coliseum on time says that if he isn't current in bill payment he doesn't get his concession and parking revenue for that particular month.

> *Question:* Is it Charlie's business theory that if he's holding the cash, he can collect interest on it rather than give the money to you?
> *Bill Cunningham:* That's right. And with the numbers I'm sure that he must deal with in his various businesses, if he owes us a hundred thousand and some other people that way, he's drawing some pretty nice money.

Finley has said he lost more than four and a half million dollars in his seven Kansas City seasons. From the looks of an authoritative balance sheet, he has more than recouped in Oakland. The ledger reflects a loss in the final Kansas City year of nearly four hundred thousand dollars and "net income before F.I.C." in Oakland the next year (1968) of $604,279. Each Oakland season through 1973, the "net income" exceeded one million dollars—except 1970, when it dipped to $616,920. The A's total net income through the first six Oakland years was just under seven million dollars.

Charlie's income from broadcasting was the key source of his breakthrough into the baseball black. Broadcasting revenue in Kansas City in 1967 brought the A's seventy-five thousand dollars. But for the first five years in Oakland, the radio-TV revenue never fell below $1,290,000. With the help of one-time network sports boss Tom Gallery, Charlie was able to land an amazingly lucrative five-year broadcast contract with the ARCO oil folks. His arrangement with them also included advertising on the "million dollar scoreboard" he had built in the Coliseum.

> *Bill Cunningham:* The original contract he had with the Coliseum required him to put in the scoreboard. And it did cost him about a

million. The scoreboard becomes the property of the Coliseum after the expiration of his contract. But I don't think you could have convinced him to spend the million dollars if it wasn't to his advantage. I think he has certain tax advantages in whatever way he has amortized it. Plus that scoreboard advertising money from ARCO—one hundred thousand dollars a year for five years.

After the ARCO contract expired, Charlie's broadcast revenue dropped in 1973 by some $450,000. And ARCO gave him ten thousand instead of one hundred thousand for scoreboard advertising. In the 1974 season, the A's were selling "commercials" on the giant computerized message board to all comers—for $125 per minute or $5,000 per season (eighty-one minutes).

Oakland had not filled Charlie's ball park. But it did make him money. It was not Kansas City. Neither, to Charlie's regret, was it White Sox Park in Chicago.

**VII**

# MASSA CHARLIE

The press enjoys labeling. Hell, we all do. It is just easier to affix a description to another human being—accurate or no—and burden him with that label in perpetuity.

Some keen writer once thrust "plantation owner" on Charles O. Finley. The phrase may have come out of Finley's acrimonious contract dealings in 1972 with Vida Blue, who suggested at the time that his boss was treating him "just like a damn colored boy." No matter. The image of Charlie as Big Daddy was there before, and remains, because Finley wants it that way. I am certain he would thrive as the owner of a real plantation. This is not to suggest the man is a raving bigot. Many of his white athletes feel he treats *them* like "damn colored boys." Charlie has no more, no less, antipathy toward blacks than any other white man who grew up in Birmingham in the twenties. He tells racial and ethnic jokes in public, but so do car salesmen from Keokuk. He will not hire a black manager for his baseball team, but neither did any other major league owner until 1974.

Sure, he once complained to an official of the Oakland Coliseum about a black security guard standing duty in "a white section" of the stadium. But that was in Charlie's first year in Oakland. He was genuinely surprised—just as he was by the fact blacks had been able to buy tickets behind the A's dugout. He couldn't understand what they were doing there. Chalk it up to environment, to a southern Wasp heritage. Try, as Vida Blue does, to understand "why some people like to wear one color shoes and others another. Everybody's got reasons for what they do, and you can't judge 'em without thinking about those reasons first."

Blue doesn't peg Finley as a bigot. And neither do most of the other blacks who have played for the Owner. In fact, one white Athletic told me that Charlie "bends over backwards for some blacks on this club to prove he's *not* antiblack."

Yet the plantation owner peg sticks—misconstrued by the public perhaps but accurate in a nonracial sense. Charlie does enjoy the role of "favor dispenser," ceremoniously portraying the sturdy, handsome man in the white suit and black string tie standing on his veranda blowing kisses and favors into the wind and watching them fall on deserving subjects kneeling in the soft grass below.

The giving of gifts, the granting of favors denotes superiority. Dispensing makes one "a nice guy." It is very important to Charles O. Finley to feel superior, and appreciated, and needed. And I don't think necessarily in that order. Inside the giver is a taker pleading to be let out, not understanding why everybody always seems to be taking the gifts for granted, taking advantage of the giver. Seems to be. Being Big Daddy ain't always fun, baby.

*Mary Barry* (former A's ball girl): I think the world of Mr. Finley. I think people overlook the good he does and just talk about the mistakes they think he makes. I got to know Mr. Finley pretty good during the 1972 playoffs and World Series, when he took us ball girls to Detroit and Cincinnati with the club. He told us to call him Dad if we wanted to. It was unbelievable the way he took care of us. He said if we ever needed anything, come to him. He was just like a second father to us.

If permitted, he would be father to the world, as long as he could not only grant the wishes of the children but make up the wishes, too. The necessity of doing it his way is part of the benevolence. And if you happen to dig his way, marvelous.

From the beginning in baseball, Charlie went overboard to do nice things for his players. At spring training in Kansas City in 1961 he told his athletes to come to him with their problems. He took all of them to dinner in an expensive club in Palm Beach, Florida. He gave each an expensive clock-radio. He annually flew wives and girl friends to a team picnic in LaPorte. His first general manager, Frank Lane, said that the Owner's benevolence was preposterous. "Let the ballplayers show Finley how much they appreciate him, not the other way around," he said. Lane of course was fired. In the Kansas City days, Charles O. Finley was a loser on the field but having one helluva time spreading joy.

*Ted Bowsfield:* I went into a liquor store business in Redondo Beach, California, just about the time I came to Charlie's club and I asked him if he'd give me a salary advance. I needed about thirty-five hundred for the liquor store. And he surprised me and said he would. You know, I was not that good a ballplayer that he had to do it. He gave me a chance to do things financially that I otherwise would not have been able to do.

*Lew Krausse:* He used to give us twenty-five bucks if we won a double-header. And Christmas presents. He did all kinds of nice things in Kansas City. I know of three situations where Charlie got guys out of problems they were having with women. In one particular case that I was the closest to, he paid off the girl this player had a problem with. The baby was born and the girl wanted a thousand dollars a year for eighteen years. Finley went in and settled with the girl for ten thousand. He's done things like this that people don't know about.

*Sal Bando* (A's team captain): A lot of the things he's done for players he doesn't want publicized. Maybe he doesn't want that side of him seen. Maybe he doesn't want people to feel he's a soft touch. Or maybe these things are so personal, and just done for people he likes, that he doesn't think they should be publicized.

*Tom Corwin:* The supervisors' club at the U.S. Steel Mill in Gary had a monthly meeting. My dad was in charge of the program once, and he asked Charlie to be the speaker. There were only about eighty people in the club. Well, Charlie did speak and, according to reports, it was one of the best meetings ever because it was a combination of a speech and a bull session. And a lot of the members Charlie had known either from high school or from his days working at the mill. My dad said it really was enjoyable. Charlie enjoyed this kind of contact. I think he knew that without his insurance business idea, he could have still been working in the mill. And he knew how much *he* would have enjoyed that kind of program—hearing a person of this stature. He was doing my dad and the club a favor, sure. But it was a great gesture. And that's the sort of thing you don't hear about. Something he did that had no publicity angle or monetary glory connected to it.

*Alvin Dark:* The thing about Charlie Finley is that he is basically a very generous man. He'll do anything for you. Just don't demand it.

The only one who makes demands on Charles O. Finley is Charles O. Finley. He was particularly unsparing of himself in chasing hot prospects. A most vintage year for that artful pursuit was 1964, when Charlie wooed such budding luminaries as Willie Crawford, Johnny Lee "Blue Moon" Odom, and Jim "Catfish" Hunter, the first two blacks and the latter a good old Carolina country boy.

Willie Crawford was one of the nation's sultriest baseball prospects in 1964. Representatives of every major league club visited the southwest Los Angeles home of the young man who had batted .600 for his high school team. The Cleveland Indians, quite properly assuming that the Crawford family would like to eat better than it had been, took Willie, his two brothers, and a cousin, budding basketball star Curtis Rowe, to a fashionable Beverly Hills restaurant. The Baltimore Orioles heaped prime ribs of beef upon the Crawfords. And the Dodgers loaded the Crawford table with that delightful soul food favorite, pastrami sandwiches.

Charlie, despite his food fetishism, turned to other tactics. The senior prom was coming up, so Finley bought Willie a tuxedo. Plus a gown for Willie's prom date. Plus the rental of a Thunderbird for Willie to drive on dance night. The Dodgers obviously sensed trouble, for they countered with a bit more than Charlie—a hundred thousand dollar bonus. Presumably tucked inside pastrami sandwiches. And Finley lost Willie Crawford. But not "Blue Moon" Odom.

Charlie likes to tell the story of cooking a meal for Odom and his mother while trying to recruit the young pitcher in Macon, Georgia. Odom has become one of Finley's favorites, a leading "son," down the years. "Blue Moon" never achieved the classic results for which Charlie yearned, but the Owner nonetheless has gone out of his way to show affection for the volatile, confused young black from Macon.

> *John Odom:* My father died when I was five, and there was just me and my mother living in this place in a housing project. Not really the ghetto, but close. My mother was a maid in other homes. Made about twenty-five, thirty dollars a week, I guess. I was almost nineteen years old when the baseball scouts came around. The San

Francisco Giants had offered me about forty thousand. The A's offer was real low. So their scout, Jack Sanford, got on the phone with Finley, and Finley came down to see me personally. I knew I might be talking to him eventually, but it was a surprise to see him turn up in my neighborhood. When he got there to my house, he waited for his turn to talk to me, just like the other scouts. And before I knew it, there was a truck outside with all kinds of fruits and vegetables and stuff. He just got all the neighbors to come up to the truck. I don't know how they got there, but they were there. And he passed out Kansas City A's jackets to them, too, after I had signed. I got seventy-five thousand. I was happy that an owner had come to see me, because I could bargain more with him than I could with a scout. I think if I'd asked for a hundred thousand, I could have got it 'cause I was in the driver's seat. I know about the story of him cooking a meal in my house. I wouldn't say exactly that he cooked, but I remember that he was in the kitchen with my mother and I think he kind of turned over some chicken or something that she was frying. He helped out a little bit in the kitchen. My mother really cared about him. She talks about him now. He helped me and helped her by signing me so that I could stop her from working. I think he helped her out extra, too, because she told me he had given her money occasionally. I had a home built in Macon with my bonus money the next year, and now in the off-season my family and I live there with my mother. I don't think I could have got a better deal from any other ball club. The way he's treated me, I really don't want to go with another ball club. It wouldn't be the same as the A's.

Pitcher Lew Krausse was Finley's first big bonus baby in 1961. The Owner offered to invest a big chunk of the hundred grand plus bonus, says Lew. There was a hot stock, as Krausse recalls it. And Charlie guaranteed there would be no loss. But Krausse said no, and now regrets that he did—although later the pitcher did accept another no-loss investment offer, but for fewer bucks, from

Charlie. That sort of proposition became a standard Finley favor—to favored players. Second baseman Dick Green may end up with the largest house in the state of South Dakota partly because of his stock profits under Charlie's no-loss-guaranteed deal. Green gave Charlie nearly thirty thousand dollars to invest. Dick Green's house in Rapid City will cost about one hundred thousand.

*Joe Rudi:* After the 1972 Series, I gave him about fifteen thousand to invest for me. But the stock market fell off the table right after that, so I got the fifteen back. Charlie's done a lot of good things for me. He'd advance me money. And when I was coming up and down from the minors, he used to take care of the family moving expenses.

*Sal Bando:* I've given him about twenty-five to invest. I'm not sure what it's worth now. There had been a pretty good profit. But, you know, there's no loss guaranteed when he does this. Some players don't accept his offer to invest because they don't want to owe him any favors when they negotiate at contract time. But he's sharp, and I felt that because of his knowledge of business and his connections, it was a logical investment to go into with him.

*Chuck Dobson:* I was thinking about giving him some money to invest in the stock market one time, but I decided not to. I'm stubborn that way and probably foolish, because he's made a lot of people a lot of money. But I didn't want to bother him with that. I asked him one day if it was a pain in the ass for him to do, and he said yes. I figured also that if I gave him my money I couldn't talk about him openly.

*Vida Blue:* The players shouldn't have to put themselves in a position to accept special favors from Mr. Finley. None of us are that poor that we have to reach back and call Uncle Charlie for something like a salary advance. I once gave him a small sum for the stock market. I did it because I was trying to end the civil war we had in 1972. Like, have peace. So I figured why not. He wanted to do it, and I think it was a good gesture. But as far as borrowing money from him, you can go to the bank and get that. You may have to pay interest, but you *can* go to the bank.

Which brings us to Jim "Catfish" Hunter, a bonus baby pitcher who became one of the more ranking "sons" of the plantation owner. Not to mention one of the best pitchers in baseball. "Catfish" was just a Carolina farm boy who took his money, pitched his game, kept his mouth shut, competed fiercely but never controversially. Not until Charlie fired Mike Andrews during the 1973 World Series.

"I don't like things that are bad for the game," said Jim Hunter in front of the dugout in Shea Stadium on an evening the Andrews fuss was at its most vocal level. "And what Finley did to Mike Andrews is bad for the game."

You learn values in Hertford, North Carolina.

Hunter's life and tastes are remarkably simple: The game, farming, hunting, fishing, corny jokes. He is a difficult interview for many because he has little to say to strangers. He is old school. He also, in my opinion, represented by 1974 the best "money pitcher" in baseball, the arm you would call on in a game that you had to win. Finley paid him one hundred thousand dollars in 1974. Finley was getting off cheap.

*Jim Hunter:* It was Thanksgiving Day in 1963. We had just won our state championship in football. I was an all-state end and linebacker. My brother and I were out hunting and he accidentally shot me. Went through my boot and my right foot and shot my little toe off. Most of the pellets just lodged in my foot. I hadn't had any firm baseball offers yet because I still had my senior year to pitch. Even with that accident, I won twelve games, so a lot of scouts came to see me. They weren't worried about how I was pitching but if my foot was all right. I lost the little toe. Can't work the one next to it now, and haven't got real good working of the other two. I signed with Finley purely for money—seventy-five thousand. I think the Mets would have come past that but they couldn't get in touch with the head man at that time. And when Mr. Finley offered that seventy-five, it was more money than I'd ever seen in my life, more than I'd ever heard of. So I signed right away. Right after I signed he offered me a free operation on my foot. He was protecting himself, 'cause if the doctor said I couldn't play he'd get his contract money back. All or nothing.

At the Mayo Clinic doctors said "Catfish" could play. Charlie brought the young pitcher to the farm in LaPorte and wined him and dined him. Rather, shaked him and steaked him. "Lots of milkshakes, and everything we ate was steak, and more steak. I'm off a farm, but I'd never seen a beautiful farm like that with such a big house. Almost looked like a hotel to me."

From then on Hunter would be seeing bigger hotels in bigger cities. He never had to pitch a day in the minor leagues. Hunter moved into the starting rotation in the Athletics' final few years in Kansas City. He would be one of Charlie's important pitchers along with Odom, Dobson, Krausse, Jim Nash.

By 1973 four of the five hurlers were finished as effective starters. Only Hunter survived. In 1973 he won at least twenty games for the third consecutive season. But the greatest game in his career came in early 1968, when in the Oakland twilight he threw 107 pitches against the Minnesota Twins, not one of whom reached base. It was the first perfect game in a regular American League season in forty-six years. Finley wanted to give "Catfish" a five thousand dollar bonus. But baseball regulations prohibit performance bonuses, so Charlie added the money to Hunter's contract. (The bonus provision always did seem fuzzy to Charlie, as we shall see later. Four years later.)

Hunter was brilliant in both the playoffs and World Series in

1973. He had no problem getting that hundred grand contract for '74, and the Andrews business seemed to be forgotten by him when he arrived at Mesa for spring training. Then traveling secretary Jim Bank passed out the World Series rings, and "Catfish" got totally pissed.

The rings for the 1972 Series victory featured a full carat diamond set in a green stone. Estimates of the ring's value range from fifteen hundred to twenty-five hundred dollars, depending on which player went to which jeweler. "Catfish" and the other A's recalled that when Finley handed out the diamond-set rings at spring training in 1973 he promised the players that if they won the Series again, their next rings would make these look like dime store novelties. Well, the '73 rings also had a green stone. Just a green stone. No diamond.

Relief pitcher Darold Knowles said the new rings "have to be the worst in World Series history." Reggie Jackson said, "They're trash." He said the new rings, which one player said he had appraised at about four hundred dollars, were "a backlash to our protest over the Mike Andrews thing." And "Catfish" said . . . Well, to begin with, he said he'd seen better rings back in high school. He said it was a joke. He said Finley was a cheap so-and-so, except he didn't say so-and-so.

After Charlie read Hunter's comments, he phoned the Mesa clubhouse and spoke with his star pitcher. Then Finley called a newsman to inform the world of the following: that he had given Hunter the five thousand after the perfect game in May, 1968; that on January 5, 1970, he loaned "Catfish" $150,000 interest free for the purchase of a farm and that Hunter had repaid this loan in one year; that after the 1971 season, Hunter received an eighty-five hundred dollar bonus; that in 1972, Hunter gave the Owner twenty thousand dollars plus the eighty-five hundred bonus for investment in the stock market at a no-loss guarantee—an investment, Finley said, that returned Hunter an after-taxes profit of nearly fifteen thousand dollars; and, finally, that before the start of the 1974 spring training Finley advanced Hunter ten thousand on his salary.

> *Finley:* So if somebody's going to call me a cheap so-and-so, he better get the adjectives right. I may be a dumb so-and-so, but I'm not a cheap one.

The writer to whom Finley spoke spread Charlie's accounting of Hunter's financial activities to the rest of us, and I quickly cornered "Catfish" seeking verification. He said that everything Charlie said was correct—except the information about the farm loan. But Hunter did not want to talk about it. Then. A few months later, back in Oakland, he did. Finley had said it was a no-interest loan. Hunter said otherwise. That is not particularly significant, however, in light of other incidents connected with that loan.

> *Jim Hunter:* I wanted to buy a farm close to Hertford. My brother was working this land I was interested in. Corn, soybeans, peanuts. Same as on my dad's farm. It was five hundred acres. So I got the loan of $150,000 from Mr. Finley. Hell, a lot of owners do this. When he first lent me the money, we had a verbal agreement— never anything written down. He sent the money straight to my bank, and it went in the bank under my name. He didn't have any attachments to it. The only agreement was that I was to pay him back twenty thousand a year and six percent interest. Then after three or four months, he started calling me. And the days that he would call me would be the days that I was gonna pitch. He would call and say, "Jim, you know you owe me $150,000, and I need the money." And I'd say, "Mr. Finley, how do you think I'm gonna get it playing ball? Lemme go home in between starts and I'll make

arrangements to get the money." Mr. Finley would say, "No. You gotta stay and pitch. You can't worry about that." And so the next time I was gonna start, he was right there on the phone again. "Jim, you know who this is?" "Yes, sir, Mr. Finley." "You know you owe me $150,000?" "Yes, sir. Lemme go home and I'll make arrangements." "No, you can't go home." He did this about five or six times—every time on a day I was pitching. I tried to tell him that he deliberately called me on my pitching days, but he said no, he didn't know when I was gonna pitch. But he knows more about the ball club than anybody else, even the players on the team. Finally, I just got out of my room on those days I thought he might be calling. I just got smart enough to get out, to not even answer the telephone. He acted like $150,000 meant a lot to a millionaire. As much money as people say that he's got, that shouldn't have bothered him that much. As soon as the 1970 season was over, I went straight home right away and tried to get a loan. I couldn't get a loan right away, so I said the hell with it, I'll sell the farm. I sold four hundred of the five hundred acres and paid him back—interest and everything. I remember during that year I used to call my father and tell him I needed that hundred fifty. Hell, my father never had that kind of money in his whole life put together. We were just cheap farmers. That's all we were. We didn't have any money. Finley would keep telling me to get my father to sell the farm. I'd like to worry my father to death about that farm. If I still had all of those acres today, hell, it'd be worth three to four hundred thousand dollars. But I did come out a hundred acres ahead. I think Mr. Finley goes out of his way to do nice things for ballplayers. He's been good to a lot of us. That farm loan is the only thing I've held against him. I was bitter against him. My father was—still is.

Hunter says Finley eventually refunded his interest.

Mrs. Mary Botto of Stockton, California, in a 1974 letter to the sports editor of the San Francisco *Chronicle*, wrote, "I chuckle over the attitude of the Oakland A's and their World Series rings.

For mature men to act this way is hard to figure . . . it's real easy to label other people 'cheap.' These malcontents should pool their salaries, buy a big league franchise, and then have all the rings their little hearts desire. . . ."

Dennis Touros of Fresno, California, wrote the same newspaper: "The nation waits hours in line to buy gas, pays high prices for food, and watches a government scandal unravel, and the Oakland A's gripe about their World Series rings not having a diamond in them.  Come on now, let's keep things in perspective."

The next manager of the Finley Athletics is expected to be named shortly. Leading candidates are Mary Botto and Dennis Touros.

Charlie was wrong. He's not a dumb so-and-so, either.


Stocks, loans, salary advances, goodies. Charlie dispensed where and how and when he wished. Nobody could tell him how to be nice. Nobody until Bowie Kuhn, that is.

The Owner was so devastatingly elated after the A's took the first two games of the 1972 World Series in Cincinnati that he immediately began dispensing. Gene Tenace became five thousand dollars richer after hitting two home runs in Game One. Joe Rudi was similarly endowed for making a remarkable catch and homering in Game Two. Reserve first baseman Mike Hegan picked up five big ones for his work earlier in the year, although he did make an outstanding fielding play in the ninth inning of Series Game Two.

As soon as Commissioner Kuhn heard about these gifts, he decided to check them out, to make certain the monies weren't performance bonuses. World Series rule 46A reads: "Neither of the contesting clubs shall give or pay a bonus or prize to any or all of its players before or after completion of the Series. . . ."

Finley said the financial cheer for Tenace, Rudi, and Hegan

were nothing more than salary increases, "raises for performances this year . . . not bonuses." He said that Rudi was one of the best hitters in the American League in 1972 and deserved a raise. He said that Tenace had become the club's regular catcher in the final six weeks of the season and deserved a raise. He said that Hegan batted well over .300 during the season and deserved a raise.

On November 1, the Commissioner fined Finley twenty-five hundred dollars "because increased compensation promised to [Tenace and Rudi] was related to their performances during the recently concluded World Series." But the Commissioner's decision "was not intended to affect the commitments made by Finley to the players." Charlie had to pay for paying. He continued to insist the payments were retroactive pay raises, not bonuses.

Charlie delights in giving retroactive pay raises. A's equipment manager Frank Ciensczyk joined the club in its first season in Oakland but did not receive a salary increase in neary five years. Then one day in September, 1973, Frank said he was given a raise of $150 a month—retroactive for two years. "I got nothing but good things to say about the man," says Frank Ciensczyk.

Broadcaster Harry Caray, who lasted one year (1970) in Oakland, remembers that Charlie "offered to put three years' salary in the bank for me and let me draw it out any way I wanted to. And he offered me an interest-free loan to buy a home and live in Oakland if I wanted to." The Owner also asked Caray to rephrase his traditional air bellow of "Holy Cow!" to "Holy Mule!" Caray never took the salary offer, loan offer, or mule proposal.

Reggie Jackson feels the Owner "thinks people can be bought with things." Not necessarily. Finley is too wary to count on anyone staying bought. Besides, it's the thrill of the giving, not the buying.

For no reason whatsoever, Finley once sent booze to the

Oakland press box in the umpteenth inning of the second game of a Sunday double-header. True, he never repeated that gesture. But I don't recall the second game of a Sunday double-header ever stretching that long again.

Little things mean a lot. Even to Charlie.

Insurance executive Bud Gillespie, a friend of Finley for many years, has a son who was injured while a Marine. Paul Gillespie is a quadriplegic. "Charlie's always asked me about him," says Gillespie. "He once got Paul a baseball cap and team jacket, and another time an autographed ball. Now, he had no reason to do any of that. I was just a business acquaintance. He even gave me a pass to the ball park for my son. Why, Charlie could have used that for people who might have done him more good."

Gillespie remembers a day in Chicago that Finley spent about a hundred dollars flying a tureen of the Finley family's secret broth to a sick doctor. "Typical of Charlie," says Gillespie.

Finley's high school friend and steel mill coworker Howard Corwin died in 1966 at the age of forty-eight. Charlie used to entertain the Corwins at the ball park, or take them out to dinner, or just drop over to their house and chat about the old days.

> *Tom Corwin:* A lot of times, when there's a death in a family, everybody says, "If you need anything, call me." Which you, of course, never do. But Mr. Finley didn't wait for my mother to call. He would phone her at two- or three-day intervals and ask how everything was going and if he could get us anything. He'd have us out to the farm sometimes. And if he didn't call, Shirley Finley would. They were very comforting.

Lester Hineline was the bailiff in the Indiana circuit court in which Shirley Finley filed for divorce against the Owner in the spring of 1974. When Charlie popped in for a preliminary hearing on the case, he promised to send the bailiff an A's cap and World Series souvenir bats. Within a few weeks, Lester Hineline had his cap and bats, and Charlie said that if the A's won another World Series he'd send Lester another bat. All that in White Sox country.


Ah, the White Sox of the immediate prewar: Appling, Lyons, Kreevich, Bullfrog Dietrich, Kuhel, Kolloway, Kennedy. For a young man in the mills the Boys of Summer. My goodness, Luke Appling could foul off pitches with great charm. My word, Teddy Lyons was some smart pitcher because he had been to college. My god, Bob Kennedy could handle those hot smashes to third base. Bob Elson would tell you all about it on the radio. Pitching, defense, no punch. But, oh, the characters. Not the Dodgers. Just the South Side of Chicago, the closest major league park to my neighborhood, and to Gary, Indiana.

Appling was Charlie's last manager in Kansas City, succeeding Alvin Dark the final few weeks of the 1967 season. As one player who was a rookie then recalls things, Appling spent moments of those managerial weeks eating in the dugout. During one critical point in one meaningless game, Appling wasn't even in the dugout. "He'd gone upstairs for another sandwich," says this player. Luke—Luscious Luke—did not follow the Owner to Oakland. His successor was quiet, fastidious, patient Bob Kennedy, a Marine pilot in two wars and the perfect manager for Charlie's baseball kids, if not for Charlie.

The A's were no-names to Bay area baseball fans in 1968. Finley had been promoting his hundred grand bonus baby, Rick Monday, only twenty-two and lifeguard-handsome. Rick had hit fourteen home runs in 1967 and was touted as the A's big power man for 1968 (when he would hit eight). Kennedy's pitching staff averaged just twenty-four years of age; the other players rounded out to twenty-six. Only two players, pitcher Diego Segui, and catcher Jim Pagliaroni, were as old as thirty. The young pieces were being assembled and honed. Reggie Jackson stumbled and struck out through 151 games. When Kennedy wasn't trying to give him confidence, a coach named Joe DiMaggio would. Sal Bando played every game at third base and displayed an instant awareness of the game's nuances. He was only twenty-four and in his first full season, but soon would be captain. Charlie liked a gaunt fellow named John Donaldson at second base, but Dick Green would start to prove more reliable and productive and get the job.

Bert Campaneris was already a fixture at shortstop: a withdrawn, very cagey Cuban with Charlie's ear and fleet, mincing steps. Kennedy wanted to play Campaneris in left field, and did for three games. One could get more attention at shortstop than left field, and Charlie had his manager return Campaneris to the limelight of the infield. The Owner would one day comment, "I didn't need any manager who was wet behind the ears telling me about Campaneris."

A California country boy, one Joe Rudi, was tested in left field. He was twenty-one and shy and awkward. He and Monday, the center fielder, worked out signals on calling for fly balls hit to left center. They decided that if Monday was to make the catch, Rick would shout, "I got it," but that if Joe thought he could grab the fly he would yell, "I'll take it." And of course one day on a fly hit to left center, Rudi called out to Monday, "Uh, you got, uh, I got, uh, I'll take . . ." Double. Rudi would someday become the best defensive left fielder in the American League.

Veteran pitching coach Bill Posedel had some equally ingenuous arms with which to deal. But the roots were there. Jim Hunter was there, and John Odom (16–10 in 1968), and Chuck Dobson. Paul Lindblad was in the bullpen, as were Jack Aker and very, very briefly twenty-one-year-old Rollie Fingers. They tried to label him "the Cucamonga Kid," which happily never caught on. In 1968 Fingers threw one inning and gave up four hits, a walk, and four runs. His time would come.

Hunter's great moments came sooner, however, when he pitched his perfect game. Within a week, though, Hunter was bombed by the Twins in the first inning in a start in Minnesota.

Kennedy's devastation came the day the season ended. The A's had lost the final game by a run, costing them a tie for fifth place. But they did finish 1968 with a record of 82–80, the first time any of Charlie's clubs played better than five hundred baseball in a season and the best record by any Athletics' team since 1948. But Kennedy, who had signed a two-year contract, was canned. The team had won four more games than he had predicted. No matter. He was not satisfactory to the Owner. Hank Bauer was coming back. The man Charlie had summoned from the outfield to manage in Kansas City in 1961 had gone on to lead Baltimore to a world's championship in 1966 and then been fired by the Orioles in the summer of 1968. He was out of baseball when Charlie hired him. Perhaps, with his gruff demeanor and penchant for rules, he could put the pieces together faster than Kennedy. Perhaps he could do better. Which he did in 1969, the year of Reggie Jackson's emergence as a home run hitter, the season in which the A's led the West in the American League's new divisional setup until a disastrous early July series in Minnesota. Two new faces would appear late that season. Catcher Gene Tenace would arrive for sixteen games and bat .158. Pitcher Vida Blue would give up thirteen home runs in forty-two innings. They would come around. Eventually.

> *Hank Bauer banquet joke:* One day, I got a call in the dugout. It was Charlie. He said, "Mr. Bauer, I noticed that when you took the lineup card out to the umpire before the game you had a grass stain

on the seat of your pants. I don't think it befits a big league manager to be seen with a grass stain on the seat of his uniform pants." I said, "Charlie, that ain't no grass stain. That's mistletoe."

With thirteen games left to play in the 1969 season, the Owner flew West and fired Hank Bauer, who had an 80–69 record. His successor was ruddy Sacramento Irishman John Francis McNamara, a manager on the Finley baseball farms for several years and an A's coach under Kennedy and Bauer. McNamara had tutored many of the young Athletics in the minors. If the players had been able to select a manager after Kennedy's firing, their choice would have been McNamara. He was only thirty-seven years old and lusted for a big league manager's job. In the final fortnight of 1969, McNamara was 8–5 as a manager. The A's finished second in the West at 88–74. Bauer and "Johnny Mac," as some called him, were six games better than Kennedy. Or, if you prefer, the Charlie Finley of 1969 was six games better than the Charlie Finley of 1968. Still building—on the field. The Oakland home attendance dropped nearly sixty thousand in the second season to 778,232. Across the Bay the Giants ended with 873,603, and second in their league's West.

Reggie Jackson and Vida Blue have only two things in common. Each is black. Each endured hellish emotional turmoil following remarkable seasons with the Oakland Athletics. The source of the turmoil in both cases was Charles O. Finley, who had his point of view. On paper, Finley won in each instance. Off paper, it is another story; repetitive, but very Charlie Finley. You had to be there to absorb what the Owner wrought. You could read about Reggie in 1970 and figure it was just another baseball salary fuss. You could read about Vida in 1972 and figure it was just another baseball salary fuss. But you had to be there, all along, to understand that there was more involved than just money. Tender psyches staggering; an iron, adamant will refusing to buckle. Winning and losing became irrelevant. Both times it was more a matter of survival, and eventually all three of the men did. Each in his own way, in his own time. Charlie got his championships, Reggie got his MVP award and his big bread, Vida got . . . Well, you have to know Vida Blue, sense the delicacy there. Everybody needs more than milk.

One summer evening in 1970 in the clubhouse of the Oakland Athletics, Reggie Jackson was within ten feet and a split second of beating the living shit out of me with a baseball bat. There had been an argument over an official scorer's decision. Another player and another writer were the center of the petty beef, but Reggie and I foolishly intruded and in a few moments were in a screaming encounter session of our own. The other writer and other player stopped their beef to listen to ours. Things really got hairy. Reggie told me I talked too much. I told Reggie he talked too much. He raised a bat over his head. I shut up. Everybody in the clubhouse watched, waiting for their first look at slaughter. It was like that old kids' game where you're ordered to freeze. Not an eye blinked, not a word was said. After five seconds of the game, Reggie lowered the bat and I got the hell out of there. Around the batting cage the next day, several of Jackson's teammates tiptoed up to me and said, "Don't worry about it. You know how fucked up he is this season." I knew, I knew.

In 1969 Reggie Jackson, son of a black tailor, flirted through midsummer with the home run records of Babe Ruth and Roger Maris. He ended that season with forty-seven homers and the promise of superstardom. Since his high school days in Wyncote, Pennsylvania, everything about sports had come preposterously easy to Reggie. Life itself was a different matter, and would continue to be. But he flourished on the game, on statistics, on the desire to excel as no player ever had. And here in only his second full major league season he had hit all those home runs. Surely there would be compensation accompanying the adulation. Surely. He was thinking in terms of a forty-seven thousand dollar salary for 1970. A grand a homer. That made sense to Reggie. Playing the negotiating game also made sense.

> *Reggie Jackson:* I had made twenty thousand in 1969. I asked for seventy-five for 1970. I lowered it to sixty, then to fifty-five, then to fifty-two. Finley offered forty, and he wouldn't budge at all. Not at all. I was only twenty-two, twenty-three years old then, and I was intimidated by him. But I don't think I made any mistakes in those negotiations. None. Not any. If I was treated fairly, everything would have worked out fine. I felt he just should have sat down and said to me, "Hey, Reggie, look. I'm the owner of the ball club. I can't afford to pay the money you're asking for. But look. You're a tremendous investment for me, and I gotta get dividends from you. And I'm too smart a businessman to have this kind of money invested in something and not get any dividends from it. You're out of line, but let's get together. Let's sit down." That's what he *should* have said to me. I mean, he's almost thirty years my senior. He's been in business longer than I am old. He should *know* what's right and what's wrong and be able to convey it to me. And I think that it was largely—grossly largely—his fault that we didn't get together. It got so emotional and dragged on for so long, I guess I was almost at the point of saying screw it. But I never would have said screw it, really.

Ten days before the opening of the 1970 season, Reggie signed for forty-five thousand dollars and a rent-free apartment in Oakland. Jackson chose luxury digs, Finley balked, Reggie threatened to quit, Finley grudgingly agreed. Jackson was just about getting the forty-seven he wanted. Finley was giving only forty-five on paper.

When Reggie failed to hit early in the season—and until 1974 he never was much of a spring sensation—Finley had him platooned, benched, replatooned, rebenched. Manager John McNamara kept saying the decisions bearing on Jackson all were his. McNamara, a baseball-savvy, patient veteran of Finley's farm system, was saving face. John wanted to continue as a big league manager. Let somebody else make waves. Somebody else did. Finley suggested that if Jackson didn't start earning his keep with the bat pretty damn fast "there's only one thing left. He might have to go down to Triple-A. . . . I'm not knocking him, mind you. He's busted his ass. Lately, however, he's just not an aggressive hitter."

In Baltimore, the Oriole front office read about Finley's dissatisfaction with his young slugger. Frank Cashen, a top executive with the Baltimore club, recalls an attempt to make a deal for Reggie. "Charlie was offered a pretty sensational package," says Cashen. "We were going to give him a left-handed pitcher, a second baseman, and an outfielder. All front liners. But Charlie turned it down. He said that Jackson was a friend of his and that he couldn't trade him because he couldn't trade his friends."

By mid-June McNamara asked Reggie to go willingly to Oakland's farm club in Des Moines, Iowa. Jackson simply could not believe it. He said he wouldn't "travel roads I've been on." He told a writer, "If Finley would have signed me right away, I would have been ready. If he would have cared about this club, he should have signed me on time."

*Reggie Jackson:* There was almost a point during that 1970 season when he talked about farming me that I was thinking of forgetting about the game. I was sick of it. I was tired of it. I was *sick*. It was a pain in the ass. It was sickening to have to listen to someone tell me something that I knew was not true—me going to the minor leagues. I had as much business in the minor leagues then as Joe Palooka does in the ring with George Foreman. One night in Oakland we talked for four, five hours in Mr. Finley's apartment about my going down to Des Moines. He tried to do everything to convince me to go down. I was still married to Jenni then, and she said, "I'm sticking with you. I know you're right. I know I'm right. Forget the minor leagues." Finley was playing small games with me, just like he had all that spring. He'd offer to give me six crates of oranges, stuff that had no relationship to playing baseball. He even called Jenni about me while the club was on the road.

Juanita Campos met Reggie Jackson at Arizona State University at the end of their freshman year. He rarely dated blacks. In the spring of 1965 they began seeing each other regularly and were married in 1968. She hated what she calls the superficiality of the baseball life and says she couldn't cope with the changes in Reggie. She felt totally insignificant in a marriage that finally ended, after a series of glum separations, early in 1973. But during the turmoil of 1970, Juanita, by then calling herself Jenni, was considered rather significant to the baseball fortunes of Charles O. Finley.

> *Jenni Jackson:* Finley called me while the A's were on a road trip and wanted to know if I had any information to offer about Reggie. His approach was, like, wondering what he could do to help. He wondered if I knew why Reggie was in such a slump, why he was so down. I remember he asked me if Reggie and I were getting along, because we had separated for a while right after the 1970 season got started. Finley said he was glad we were together again because the separation seemed to have had an effect on Reggie. Finley kept asking me if there was anything that Reggie was still really upset

about—anything that Finley could work with. And the thing I didn't appreciate about it was that Finley's approach seemed to be *kind* on the surface, but what he really seemed to be looking for was something he could use *against* Reggie later. He was asking me some things that he really should have been asking Reggie. I mean, Finley owned the man, and if he couldn't go directly to his employee and try to figure things out, then it was a sly thing to ask me. I told Finley that Reggie vitally needed his approval. He kept saying that his concern was Reggie's well-being and that he thought Reggie was just a *good* person. He used all of these compliments.

During the All Star break in the 1970 season, the rarely played but still major league Jackson telephoned the Owner and pleaded for a slate-wiping. He promised to behave himself, to hustle, to do or die for Finley U. And he was restored to the starting lineup. For two weeks. His slump had not abated, and he was now reduced to spot duty on defense or as a pinch runner. One evening he disgustedly left the dugout before the game ended, and a day later there was an edict prohibiting such early departures. "If I were a ballplayer," said Charles O. Finley, "I'd certainly try to see all nine innings of a game. If there is anyone who needs to learn what the game is about . . . it's Jackson."

On September 5, 1970, Reggie hit his first major league grand slam home run and told Finley to go fuck himself. Both events occurred before a crowd of 9,824 in the Oakland Coliseum. As Reggie saw his drive headed for the seats, he trotted slowly toward first base, looked up at the Owner sitting in his mezzanine box, raised his fist high in the air and shook it in Finley's direction, then lip-synched the epithet. An instant course in lip reading. Finley smiled and extended his arms upward—a figure of pleasure and appreciation.

For forty-eight hours.

In the meantime, Jackson had been plunked back into the starting lineup and delivered six hits, two of them homers, in ten trips in three games. The A's were within six games of the division-leading Minnesota Twins and on their way to Bloomington for a showdown series. But first, after a Labor Day doubleheader in—where else—Chicago, Charlie had planned a showdown of his own.

Manager McNamara, the coaches, team captain Sal Bando, and Reggie were ordered to report to McNamara's room in the Ambassador West. Finley joined them. He was seeking a formal apology from Reggie for the "fuck you" gesture.

> *Reggie Jackson:* What I did after that grand slam homer just came to me. You can't plan something like that. The gesture I made was not meant in harm. It was only, "Look. See what I can do?" Charlie wanted me to sign a statement of apology at that meeting. I never felt so alone and helpless in my life in that hotel room. It was just like going to a police station and being put under a lamp and being whipped. It was either sign a statement or be fined and suspended. I think it was to be a five thousand dollar fine and suspension without pay for the rest of the season. During that meeting, Charlie said I'd embarrassed and humiliated my teammates, my manager, my family, my wife, the fans, the American League president, the commissioner of baseball, and the game of baseball. He got all of those people involved. He said I owed them all a public apology. I didn't owe 'em shit. Because what I did *he deserved.* I was getting fucked.

Coach Vern Hoscheit remembers that the only speakers at the session were Finley, Jackson, McNamara, and Bando. "None of us coaches said anything," he recalls. "I don't get myself involved in controversy," says Hoscheit, once president of the Three I League.

> *Sal Bando:* I don't know why they called me in there. I guess just because I was captain. Finley said that if Reggie didn't sign an

apology that Joe Cronin [then American League president] would suspend him. I didn't believe that stuff about Cronin, but I don't think that was important. What I believed was that Reggie should apologize. He was wrong for doing the gesture. But also I couldn't blame Reggie for being upset because of the way they handled him that year. Still, you have to treat your boss with respect in public. It just got to the point, though, that it was one pride against the other. Reggie's pride for not wanting to apologize and Finley's for not wanting to be ridiculed. Reggie was very upset. There were tears. I wasn't there to take sides. I wasn't anti-Finley or anti-Reggie. I just wanted to be fair.

*Reggie Jackson:* I finally signed because everybody in the room was against me. Everybody.

*The statement:* Last Saturday, I made gestures and comments I wish I never made. I would like to apologize to the fans, my teammates, John McNamara, and Mr. Finley.

In the especially crucial series that followed in Bloomington, Minnesota, Jackson struck out five times and went hitless as the A's dropped three straight and out of the division race for 1970. The next evening a rookie pitcher named Vida Blue defeated Kansas City on a one-hitter. Before the month ended, Blue pitched a no-hitter against Minnesota. He probably would be something, this young left-hander from Mansfield, Louisiana. Yep. In 1971 he probably would be something. That was the year that Richard Milhous Nixon gave a soul handshake to Vida Rochelle Meshach Abednego Blue, Jr.

Vida remembers the day of Reggie's expletive-included grand slam home run in September, 1970. The pitcher was too green, too unsure then to do anything more than sit back quietly and observe. Sitting back and observing remains his wont, but on that day Vida was so perturbed at what seemed to be the lack of security in baseball—for himself—that he didn't attempt to analyze the Jackson explosion.

*Vida Blue:* Now that I think back, I'm sure Reggie was feeling the same way then as I did two years later. There had to be something inside of him that gave him that hatred at that moment for Charlie Finley. Reggie's the type of person that anything he believes in, he believes very strongly. I'm the same way. And that gesture of his then was his way of saying, "I should be playing regularly." Yep, I know now how Reggie felt then. It was the same thing for me.

Anybody who caught for Vida at DeSoto High School in Mansfield had to sit out for three or four days afterwards. As a kid pitcher, Vida Blue had two major problems: he was wild, and he destroyed catchers with welt-creating fastballs. Reggie Jackson had been all-everything in Pennsylvania, and in Louisiana Vida was throwing touchdown passes of fifty-five yards and longer, plenty of swift strikes and more than his share of balls. He was the eldest of six children of an iron foundry worker and a certain prospect for a college football scholarship. When Vida was seventeen, his father died, and Sallie Blue told her son he was now the Man. She still called him Junior, although perceiving sudden maturity.

The A's selected him in the second round of the 1967 free-agent draft, and the need for money (the bonus was about twenty-five thousand) was more imposing than Vida's love for football. Forget college and quarterbacking. Feed the family. While pitching for the A's farm club at Birmingham, Vida Blue dined steadily on Crystal burgers, also a favorite snack of one Charles O. Finley.

Blue had a cup of coffee in Oakland in 1969 and was called up twice more late in the 1970 season, with sufficient schedule remaining to throw that one-hitter and no-hitter. One year later Vida Blue stepped out of store windows and counters all over America. His smile was fetching, his pitching devastating. By the All Star break he had won seventeen games. He obscured everyone else in baseball that season, allowing Reggie Jackson a sabbatical from the furies. Vida was twenty-two years old and eight thousand feet tall. Larger even than Charles O. Finley. In 1971 Vida won twenty-four games and the Cy Young (best pitcher) and Most Valuable Player Awards in the American League. Plus, from the Owner, a Cadillac (blue), a gasoline credit card, and two thousand dollars for a wardrobe. His actual salary for the 1971 season was something around fifteen thousand dollars. Of course the pay would have to be increased mightily in 1972.

Here was a fellow who had drawn nearly one out of every twelve fans who attended an American League game in 1971, who added about a million and a half dollars to the treasury of the Charles O. Finley Company. There were three teams in the American League that season that did not attract as many customers to their eighty-one home games as Vida Blue did to his thirty-nine pitching starts. Surely Vida was in for a lot of bucks. He would need advice. Back in high school, Coach Clyde Washington was his quasi-business advisor. Vida got his sizeable bonus, but Washington wanted no part of it.

Now, though, Vida would need a bit more professional expertise than Clyde Washington could provide. Blue asked A's teammate Tommy Davis for advice. Davis put Vida in touch with a Los Angeles contract lawyer named Robert Gerst, who had been an advisor to professional basketball superstar Jerry West.

> *Vida Blue:* I had Gerst because I needed advice. The type of season I had in 1971 was so unusual that I couldn't come up with an asking figure by myself—even a moderate figure that I thought would be fair to me and fair to Finley. Six figures seemed to be a nice round number, though. But I was ready to settle for less. Not much less, but less.

Blue's settlement point was seventy-five thousand, and there was no way in the world the Owner was going to go that high. Vida was not aware at the start of negotiations in 1972 that Finley was paying another A's twenty-game-winning pitcher, Jim Hunter, fifty thousand dollars. Hunter wanted a bit more but settled for the fifty when, he says, Finley promised him that Vida wouldn't make more than fifty either.

Irresistible force, meet immovable object.

> *Vida Blue:* Mr. Finley puts everything he's got into everything he does. But he still wants it to be beneficial to Charlie Finley. Which is what the world is all about, you know. Maybe you shouldn't be concerned with the other guy, but you still got to draw the line as far as humanity is concerned. I do respect Finley as a businessman, but he does have his little hangups about misusing people and treating people the way he wants to treat them without any type of dignity whatsoever, without any consideration for their feelings.

Finley's feelings were hurt because Vida brought Gerst into the contract talks. Finley had never dealt with a baseball player's representative in this manner. But Vida said that behind closed doors, Charlie was civil to the attorney, that the two men began to respect each other in the series of talks that started in January, 1972.

Gerst's opening bid was $115,000. That, he said, was the average salary paid to the game's ten top pitchers. Finley countered with forty-five, rose to fifty, stopped. He told Blue and Gerst that they had as much chance of getting $115,000 as he did of jumping out of his insurance office window, which was on the twenty-seventh floor. Gerst and Vida didn't budge, and Charlie didn't jump. There was nothing more to discuss.

> *Vida Blue:* I'll tell you what really turned me off more than anything in that whole business. Finley is sitting at his desk with all

of his insurance policies and his lists of doctors and his bills and everything and he reaches into that pile of papers and picks up this stat sheet with the final 1971 season averages. And he looks right at my face and says to me [Vida speaks very slowly, attempting to imitate Finley, to recapture the moment]: "Well, I *know* you won twenty-four games. I *know* you led the league in earned run average. I *know* you had three hundred strikeouts. I *know* you made the All Star team. I *know* you were the youngest to win the Cy Young award and the MVP. I *know* all that. And if I was you, I would ask for the same thing. And you *deserve* it. But I ain't gonna give it to you." All that bullshit, right there. I almost cried when he told me all that. *"I ain't gonna give it to you."* I was through right there. That's why baseball is just a job to me today, because of that statement. Look at Nolan Ryan. He goes and strikes out four hundred people or something and gets a hundred thousand dollars. But you can't blame it on a black-white world. It's not that. It's just that Charlie Finley is Charlie Finley, and he's going to continue to be Charlie Finley.

*Reggie Jackson:* I don't think either Charlie or Vida was right. Vida was asking for too much. It would have upset the morale of the ball club for Vida to get paid twice what guys like me and "Catfish" Hunter were making. We'd already been there a few years. You can't do that. Vida should have got fifty to sixty thousand as a salary, and Charlie should have given him a twenty-five thousand bonus on the side. Charlie should have said to Vida, "Son, you're a wonderful guy and I love you. But you're out of line. I gotta have you to win. You're the greatest thing going since M and M's. But I can't pay you a hundred thousand. I can't pay you ninety. I can't. You're out of line." If Charlie had talked to him like that and given him a good salary and a good bonus, then he would have kept Vida mentally sound and helped Vida's pride. But I couldn't persuade Vida or Charlie. I guess you could say that Charlie was just repeating what he did to me, and it was unbelievable that he was doing it again. But if the same thing happened with another player next year, he'd probably do the same thing.

Jackson, in reflection, feels that Finley always "made me look bad in the press" during their contract fuss. "I always looked like I was out of line—a young kid who didn't know what he was talking about. That's the biggest thing I didn't like. Finley had the press on his side, and he used it."

And he used it again with Vida. Quite effectively, too.

Finley's main contention during the nearly four months of stalled negotiations was that Vida didn't deserve all that money on the basis of one season's performance. Let him prove himself over several seasons, said Charlie, and maybe then he would be worthy of six figures. How can a man on any job expect such an instant reward? That never happened in the steel mills, said Charlie. And baseball wasn't all that much different. There are rules, he said, and there are rules.

> *Vida Blue:* Mr. Finley is always afraid of those high salaries. But I try to see two sides to everything, and the other side of the case was that he was doing this from a business standpoint. And I've told people that as far as every little angle and aspect of business goes, he's among the best. He does it cruelly, but he plays it by the book. He'll do the most cruel *legal* things that you can do to a person. And what can you do? In 1972 I thought he was wrong in not showing gratitude by paying me a salary on which we could have compromised. I would have been happy, and he would have been happy. But we both had to come out with statements trying to save face.

Charlie appeared to be saving more.

One evening during that struggle I played the devil's advocate in my favorite Oakland neighborhood bar, a cafe of planned rinky-dink shabbiness called The Alley, run by a tough ex-waitress from Texas, Jody Kerr. She draws the kind of crowd that digs Finley's logic, which is to say business people. They understand his arguments. They thought Vida was making a fool of himself. They didn't care how many tickets I said he sold in 1971. They didn't care how much money he made for Finley. How could I be so stupid as to agree with Blue?

"What if he's just a flash in the pan?" said Jody. "Let him stay around a while. Then he'll get his money."

Charlie was scoring heavily in Oakland. But his adamancy was having a different effect on the leaders of the game. As spring training came and went without Vida Blue, it became obvious that a middleman was needed. Nobody truly believed that Vida intended to retire to take a fifty-five thousand dollar a year job as vice president of public relations for a manufacturer of bathroom fixtures. But on the other hand, there was no reason to believe the young man would buckle under the Owner's will.

Summitry was necessary. By god, Commissioner Bowie Kuhn was necessary. The season had already begun. Fans who would have paid to watch Vida Blue pitch did not want to pay to see anybody else pitch.

And so, Chicago's Drake Hotel, late in April. Kuhn, Finley, Gerst, Blue. For twenty-two hours. Finally, compromise. Finley wouldn't have to go over his fifty grand basic salary ceiling, but he would have to come up with some extras. Say a five grand bonus as a head-pat for 1971. Say eight grand in sort of retroactive college scholarship money. A nice little sixty-three thousand dollar package. Not the seventy-five for which Vida would have settled on January 8. Not the fifty that Charlie would have handed over that day. Just a tidy, Bowie Kuhn–induced compromise. A bending of principles, fellas, and let's play baseball.

> *Vida Blue:* That whole long meeting was done in a childish, unbusinesslike, unmannerly manner. The commissioner was trying to be very diplomatic about the whole thing. He was trying to get it solved. But I think, and maybe Mr. Kuhn didn't realize it, he had

unintentionally taken sides. The first few hours especially he seemed to be speaking more in my favor. I could sense the tone of his voice. Like, let's get this out of the way because it's bad for baseball, let's get it solved. But as the time moved along, he started to speak in Charlie's behalf—and that's when I left and went back to my own hotel room. I went in and out twice. I just needed some fresh air. Finally toward the end, I figured the sixty-three was all I was ever going to get from Charlie Finley. When we got it settled, Charlie wanted to say in an announcement that I signed for fifty, which would have saved face for him. But Gerst and I didn't want that announcement made. So things got stalled again.

Kuhn *ordered* Finley to keep the offer open for three more days and asked Vida to accept. The commissioner's "order" to Charlie was made "in the best interests of baseball," and the Owner bitterly resented the commissioner's participation. "It's ridiculous," said Charlie, "for the commissioner to get involved." Three months later Kuhn fined Finley five hundred bucks "for public remarks made by Mr. Finley prior to his signing of Vida Blue. The remarks . . . were found by the commissioner not to be in the best interests of baseball." Before 1972 was over, Bowie would tap Charlie's till again for giving extra compensation to other A's players. But back on April 30, the only thing concerning Kuhn was to get Vida the hell signed.

That day President Nixon, who had met Vida at the White House the previous summer, told a reporter, "He's got so much talent, maybe Finley ought to pay." I've always meant to show that quote to Jody Kerr and the folks at The Alley.

Finley said he always had been an admirer of Mr. Nixon, and on May Day the revolution ended. Finley said he hoped Vida would win twenty. Trying to get his arm and head back together, Blue won only six. When he made his first pitching start of 1972 about four weeks later, Blue drew some thirty-three thousand paying fans to the Oakland Coliseum. A sportswriter figured that Charlie got a return on his investment in one pop.

At no time during the 1972 season was there any front office talk of sending Vida Blue down to the minors. Some things do change.

Blue did not flip in 1972 as Jackson had in 1970. Vida was not whole, but he was reasonable. Immediately after signing and joining the club in Boston he nearly jumped a team flight but changed his mind at the last moment because, he recalls, "One of the players was late boarding and I had some time to think. I still wasn't totally sure I had done the right thing by signing that contract." He attempted some sort of early reconciliation with the Owner but never quite managed. He knew that most of the players believed he was asking for too much; two of them, in fact, had been dispatched to Oakland from spring training to convey Charlie's arguments. And Vida's closest friend on the club, Tommy Davis, the veteran who had suggested that Blue give lawyer Gerst a buzz, was cut by the A's in training camp. Davis had batted .324 for Oakland in 1971 and was hitting over .500 in Arizona. In 1973 Tommy would be the most productive designated hitter in the American League—but as a Baltimore Oriole, not an Athletic.

Without the benefit of spring training, Blue was not at all sharp. There was a sense of indifference to his performance by the fellows in the clubhouse and a tinge of fan animosity built by Charlie's case in the papers. Blue faced lonely times. In a year he switched from being baseball's biggest surprise to the game's leading disappointment. He was moody, but rarely abrasive; silent, but infrequently hostile.

The difference between his behavior and that of Jackson two seasons earlier was chiefly the difference in the men, plus the fact that Finley didn't attempt the same intimidating tactics with Vida.

Reggie was separated from his mother very early in life. Reggie cries out for affection, attention, people. Reggie came from a relatively more affluent and sophisticated background than Vida. And Reggie went to college. But Blue emerged from Louisiana with a greater ability to cope. He lacks Jackson's articulateness; he cannot dazzle the press with his metaphorical footwork. And his seeming aloofness is translated by the casual inquisitor into an "indifferent Vida Blue."

Finley took something from the innards of each for one year. Yet he could not excise their desire to succeed. "You cannot doubt their physical abilities," says a teammate. "They both want to be the best at what they do. Reggie does it more demonstratively. That's how he satisfies his own need for greatness. But as far as Vida is concerned, it's a misconception that you have to show affection for the game *outwardly*. When Vida goes out there to pitch, he tries as hard as anybody. And he might come off the mound saying that it's no big deal. But he wants to excel, believe me. I don't think either of them feels that he has to show Finley something. They just have to show themselves. They don't know how to do anything but excel. That's all they want. And both of them are able to get along publicly with Charlie now by not saying anything. That's their way."

> *Vida Blue:* There is confidence and there is cocky confidence. I have confidence. Charlie Finley has cocky confidence. But he's capable of respecting people. He *can* do it—without force or anything. He's shown respect to me once or twice. Like here in 1974 asking me if it was okay to announce my contract signing to the press. The only thing I think he owes me is respect. I just want him to respect me, whether we ever get into another contract hassle or not. And I think that's the only thing we owe each other. Just respect.
>
> *Reggie Jackson:* What I owe Charlie Finley is a good performance.

I owe him the best of my ability, all my knowledge, all my leadership. And what he owes me is honesty and respect. I think he should make me someone he can confide in on our ball club because I can do a lot for him. I think he owes me that. I can help the club and I can help him. He wants to be number one in everything. That's his craving. And there's nothing wrong with that either. I feel that way, too. He's let me know some things I should do to help my public image—that I should be more appreciative to the fans, think before I talk, do things that'll constantly make me look good. And sometimes I follow his advice. He'll never give you advice that'll harm you.

Vida signed without incident in 1973 and again became a twenty-game winner. In 1974 Blue was satisfied with the Owner's offer, but not Reggie. He thought the league's Most Valuable Player Award winner should make well over the hundred grand Finley was offering. Because of the new arbitration procedure, there would be no more one-on-one traumas. Reggie asked the arbitrator for $135,000, but eventually felt he was underselling himself. "I could have gotten $160,000 easy," he says. "It's completely beyond my comprehension why I had to go into arbitration with Finley. Because he did not have a snowball's chance in hell of winning."

Charlie's major argument to the arbitrator was that "someone" had to win the MVP award. Yes, and that someone cost him thirty-five thousand more than he wished to pay.

I used to wonder if Finley had a special deal with the people at Greyhound, if he bought a bundle of those "See America" economy tickets, those ninety-day, ninety-dollar, you can ride anyplace things. Players kept popping in and out of Oakland with such frequency—and such repetition—that one assumed Charlie hired a special bus to pick up and drop off athletes. Pinch-running toy Allan Lewis spent more time traveling than playing.

One day in the late summer of 1973, Reggie Jackson took a look around the clubhouse at three new arrivals and suggested that he didn't really mind playing for Oakland "because sooner or later everybody in baseball walks through these doors." Through, and out, and through, and out. Manager Hank Bauer walked into the clubhouse one Sunday morning in 1969 and ordered three strangers to get their asses out of there. The three strangers were baseball players, brought up from the minors the previous evening by Charles O. Finley, who had failed to pass along this information to his manager. At least in the military service they give you written orders.

In the space of three years, Charlie had all three Alou brothers playing for his club, but never more than one at a time. The moves were sequential, too. First came the eldest Alou, Felipe; then the middle brother, Matty; then the baby, Jesus. Who says the Owner and General Manager is an illogical man? Surely not John Donaldson, who came to Oakland from Kansas City, left Oakland for the expansionist Seattle Pilots, then to Milwaukee, back to Oakland, to the minors, and, in 1974, back to Oakland. John needed only forty-nine more days to be eligible for a four-year pension, and Charlie was giving him that chance. "If necessary, I'll board myself up in my locker for forty-nine days," said John.

Finley keeps bringing them back. And back.

*Ted Kubiak:* From the day he first traded me, I kept hearing rumors he was trying to get me back. Wherever I was playing, every time I saw one of the A's they would say to me, "Hey, you're coming back." And I finally did. Maybe he brings back a lot of guys 'cause he's worried that he's made a mistake getting rid of them.

*Paul Lindblad:* Charlie knows he can probably get you back whenever he wants to. So he's not afraid to make a deal for you if he thinks it'll help the club.

*Frank Fernandez:* I don't have the slightest idea why Charlie keeps bringing me back and hanging on to me. I've asked him several times. He told me once that I was his catching insurance. Another time he told me that nobody else wanted me. And once he said, "You're one of my favorite poeple. That's why I like to have you around."

They call him "Broadway Frank." Because, of course, he's from Staten Island. Born, raised, learned to pull the ball on Staten Island. A little college (Villanova), a little fishing, a few girls, a contract with the New York Yankees. "Broadway Frank" goes to Broadway, and on opening day of 1968, Fernandez' first full season in pinstripes, he hits a home run for a 1–0 Yankee win over the Angels and his greatest sports thrill. Or maybe his only sports thrill. In 1970, Frank Fernandez leaves old Broadway for new Oakland, for Charlie Finley, for four years of, well . . .

Finley trades him to the Washington Senators in 1971; before the year is out, Frank is back with the Oakland organization in Des Moines. Briefly. He finishes that Oakland-Washington-Iowa year with the Chicago Cubs, and plays three games for them at the start of 1972, a year in which he later visits Wichita and Syracuse. He makes a vague appearance with Toledo to open 1973, then, hello Charlie. Frank is off to Tucson, an A's farm club, for a restful summer. Fernandez *must* have had a "See America" pass. He and Allan Lewis surely crossed paths at a rest stop.

*Frank Fernandez:* I was really supposed to start 1973 in Tucson. But instead they sent me to Toledo, a Tiger farm. I couldn't take it. I went home after a week. But Tucson called me back, so I went. And I sat on the bench in Tucson most of the year. Now tell me: what the fuck is the good of having a catcher nearly thirty years old with about four years of major league experience sit on the bench with a minor league club? But that's Finley. I tell you, it's frightening. Finley's just toying with your life. To be honest, I'm resentful. And he keeps saying that he's breaking his ass to make a deal for me.

For reasons not quite clear to Frank Fernandez, or many others, he was invited to train with the A's at their Mesa, Arizona, camp in the spring of 1974. "Broadway" assumed they wanted him around to catch batting practice, or work with the rookie pitchers, or bring a little class to the clubhouse. Handsome, wistful-eyed Spaniards glow under Arizona skies; a reverse Midnight Cowboy.

> *Frank Fernandez:* Every time Finley has sent me someplace else, it's been a loan, I think, not a trade. When he sent me to Chicago, I asked the general manager of the Cubs, John Holland, if I was there on a loan or on a deal. And he said it wasn't a loan. But I found out later that it was a loan, because I saw a sheet of statistics from the A's office that showed a list of loanouts. And I was on that list: a player on loan. And I also heard that a couple of clubs wanted to get me from the Cubs, but of course they couldn't make a deal because I was just on loan from the A's. The specter of Finley is always hanging over your head. How many guys has he done this to? He sits back like he's laughing at you. I keep saying to him, "You don't want me in Oakland and you don't want me to play while I'm in Tucson. Why not just get rid of me?" I'll take my chances in the minors someplace else. Finley is not the kind of guy you want to get hooked up with—if you had your choice.

A few days later, Frank asks if anybody has said anything nice about Finley to me yet. I tell him that some say Charlie has been helpful in monetary matters. "Money, huh?" says Frank, who has been using his minor league salary—"under the fifteen grand major league minimum"—to pay college tuition in the off-season. "Money, huh? That's what makes him nice, huh? That's real swell."

Shortly before the end of spring training in 1974, "Broadway Frank" was put in a position to remember himself to Herald Square; the A's presented him with an outright release. And within a few days catcher Larry Haney was added to the Oakland roster.

Charles Thomas Dobson, three months older than Frank Fernandez and a teammate of "Broadway" at Tucson in 1973, also came to Mesa to train with the A's in March, 1974. The right-handed pitcher had seventy-two major league victories, not one, however, since 1971, when his arm went bad. Finley sent him to the Mayo Clinic for surgery and then to the farm system for restoration. About the only pleasant moments for Dobson in Birmingham in 1972 resulted from inspecting cocktail lounges with another struggling pitcher, fellow named Denny McLain. "I've had experiences other people only dream about," said Denny when Finley was going to lop him off the Oakland roster. "But I'm going to stay in baseball until they rip this uniform off me." And Chuck Dobson felt just about the same. A good spring in Mesa, and he could be back with the big club, with Charlie, with some of the people he'd known since his Kansas City A's days of 1966. Dobson was comfortable playing bridge in the Mesa clubhouse with three other pitchers. He would have liked to play bridge with Knowles and Fingers and Holtzman every day in 1974. But he could not be certain what plans Finley had for him.

*Chuck Dobson:* He's been kind to me, you might say. But not because we're great, great friends. He's just trying to get his money's worth out of me, I think. He's treated me funny in the last couple of years. After the 1972 season, he called to tell me that he wasn't going to give me a World Series ring. Not that I thought I earned one. Before he could say too much, I told him, "I'm glad you didn't order me a ring, because I don't want one." And he went into a big apology. He likes to bring people back. My theory is that Charlie feels: I've got it and you don't and I'm hiring you and don't give me trouble because someday you're gonna need me again—but you're gonna do it my way next time. But he's a kind-hearted man when it comes down to bringing people back. Look at Alvin Dark this year. Why did Charlie hire him? As a kindness to Alvin to get him back in baseball when Alvin was down and out and looking for a job? Or because he can have his thumb on Alvin? Charlie gets everybody back. People know that once you've been in Charlie Finley's employ, it's not hard to come back.

Chuck Dobson's father worked an auto assembly line in Kansas City, and his mother handled financial matters, including the twenty-five thousand dollar bonus from Charles O. Finley in 1964. By the 1971 season, Chuck was making twenty-eight thousand dollars a year from the A's. And even after the surgery for his aching right elbow, Chuck was offered an eight thousand dollar raise by the Owner. "I knocked over six chairs and two tables trying to find a fountain pen," he says. "I guess Charlie thought I could come right back in 1972 and throw. He made a mistake." For a minor league pitcher, Dobson was uncharacteristically affluent.

> *Chuck Dobson:* Finley's sticking with me because I don't cause problems, don't make waves. I usually do what he tells me to do. Anyway, now I can't make waves. He's holding the strings. People don't make waves unless they're secure. With Charlie, I've felt more lucky than grateful.

In Mesa, the Dobson family lived far more prudently than those Athletics guaranteed of a big league job in 1974. His bridge buddies were across town in expensive golf course rental units. Chuck and Kay Dobson were in a noisy apartment complex, with swings for the kids and community barbecue grills. He would come home from a day of practice and attempt to relax with a drink. Kay watched him nervously as he spoke. Dobson is high strung. He did not want his uniform ripped off him that spring.

We shared his Scotch, barbecued his hamburgers, knocked off the wine that Kay quickly picked up at a corner market. The Dobsons should not have been removed from the campus of Kansas University; they remain beautiful and should be frozen in collegian time.

> *Chuck Dobson:* The most enjoyable time I ever had with Charlie was when he and I went out to dinner by ourselves in New York in 1972 during the players' strike negotiations. I was the A's player representative that year, and Charlie at least took the time to look into the negotiations and see what our strike was all about—unlike the other owners. He said to me, "I can lose money in cancelled games over this little bit of difference [in pension benefit and other player demands that year]." Over dinner he suggested that the two of us should break the strike. He said, "If we can get them to agree to end the strike now, we can open the season on time." We had a real nice dinner, but I think he was trying to sell me on the fact that *I* should stick *my* neck out to end the strike, which I ended up doing. But it was a very comfortable dinner. We were just like two little kids. No pretense in our conversation. I had more personal contact with him that night than I've ever had, maybe because there was nobody around to recognize him.

Toward the end of spring training, Chuck Dobson was released by the Oakland Athletics. He was free to make a deal for himself and signed a 1974 contract with a team in Mexico City.

# HOCKEY
# AND BASKETBALL

The Seals in their first three seasons of National Hockey League play seemed to have as many stockholders as Polaroid. At times, starting in 1967, there appeared to be an owner-of-the-week club. There were notes, notes on notes, entangling alliances that would have stumped Henry Kissinger. Attendance was not what one would call breathtaking. True, the club did reach the playoffs in two of its first three years, but a dynasty was obviously not forming in Oakland. That is why, when financial difficulties ensnared whoever owned the team on the first full moon day of 1970, the NHL looked benignly toward an obvious savior of the franchise: The Man Who. And who better than Charles O. Finley? One man, one vote, one pesky, nagging problem cleaned up for the clubby gentry of the league's board of governors. Those fine fellows were unaware at the time, but they were about to destroy the Seals in order to save them.

Finley and Munson Campbell were your basic odd couple. Here was the guy from the mills and insurance mailing lists tiptoeing

through hockeydom with a Yalie. One of Campbell's classmates at
New Haven in the early 1940s happened to be Bruce Norris, who
happened to be the son of a man who, in effect, happened to
control the fortunes of three of the six teams in the National
Hockey League at one time—Detroit, Chicago, New York. Bruce
Norris has described Munson Campbell as being "like one of the
family. He knew everything that was going on [in hockey]." And
then he got to know Charlie Finley. The entree was white shoes.
Campbell's Manhattan advertising agency was handling the advertising and marketing for a Japanese-made imitation leather called
Clarino ("which sounds like an Italian detergent," says Campbell).
The "Albino Kangaroo" shoes Finley gave his lads in Kansas City
were losing their whiteness in the Oakland ball park, and Charlie
wanted a look at Clarino. So early in 1969, Campbell and a shoe
manufacturer's sales boss went to Chicago. They spent a few hours
hashing over a few minutes of shoe business in Charlie's office, and
Campbell departed the meeting with the feeling that he didn't
want to do any business with Finley. The shoe salesman did,
however, so there were more sessions on Michigan Avenue.

At one of these meetings, the subject turned from baseball
footwear to an entirely different sport.

> *Munson Campbell:* I was getting impatient at this session. I had to
> meet Bill Wirtz [boss of the Chicago Black Hawks] and Bruce to go
> to a hockey game, and the matter of hockey came up. I asked Finley
> if he knew anything about it, and he said he thought he liked it but
> really didn't know if he did. He said he'd been to one hockey game
> in his life. Mr. Finley knew *nothing* about hockey. Mr. Finley didn't
> know how to tape a hockey stick.
>
> *Prescott Sullivan* (sports columnist with the San Francisco *Exam-
> iner* and a fancier of Finley): Finley shouldn't have been expected to
> know all there is to know about hockey. Expert knowledge of a

particular sport, while desirable, isn't a rigid requirement for ownership.

*Bill Torrey* (general manager of the New York Islanders of the NHL and executive vice president of the Seals, 1968–70): When we were in the playoffs in '69, Finley called my box office manager and asked for tickets, so the box office man asked me what to do. I told him to leave four tickets for Finley at the will-call window to pick up and pay for. I said, "He can afford it." The day after the game, Charlie called me, thanked me for the good seats and asked if I was the reason why he had to pay for the tickets. I told him I was. He said, "Good, that's the way I like to do business." I had heard that he had seen hockey and that he thought it was a commercially viable enterprise.

*Munson Campbell:* In the fall of 1969, I knew from association with the Norris family that the Oakland franchise was in trouble. So in the course of one of my conversations with Finley, I said, "There's an opportunity in the sports situation in Oakland, and you seem to me to be the one to take best advantage of it."

Campbell was suggesting that a man who already owned one sports franchise in a city could buy a second one there and combine the administrative functions for both clubs. Campbell said he asked if Charlie was interested in this endeavor, and to Munson's temporary delight—and eventual grief—Finley said, yes, indeed, but only in terms of the Seals being a financial investment.

The moment had arrived, the tentacles were being unfurled. As Kurt Vonnegut would appraise it: "So it goes . . ."

*Munson Campbell:* I sat down and drew up a master plan for a twelve-month-a-year administrative operation. Finley could hire the top people in the country for front office work and pay them better than anybody else could, because, in effect, they'd be doing two jobs. He could have group and season ticket incentive plans and special sales promotions combining the two teams. Baseball players could sell hockey tickets and vice versa. He could have become a total sports czar in the Bay area by following this plan. He really could have. I felt that he had an excellent chance to get the franchise, that I could do the things for him he couldn't do, because he knew nobody in hockey. Not one single human being in hockey at all. And most of hockey's leadership were my friends. Hockey was my avocation.

*Bill Torrey:* Without Munson Campbell, Finley couldn't have swung the votes to get the franchise. I think Munson's relationship to Bruce Norris was the key to the whole thing.

The big thrust toward obtaining the franchise began late in 1969. Campbell says that both Bill Wirtz and Bruce Norris told him to get an agreement in writing with Finley before he went to work on Charlie's behalf.

*Munson Campbell:* In conversations with Finley, I was led to believe that if I could get him this franchise at a very low price—and remember that expansion franchises in Buffalo and Vancouver at that time were going for six million dollars—that I would expect in return from him an interest in the franchise. I would also not be above and beyond coming out and running the thing for him. We had numerous discussions about that. He leads you to believe that he's agreeable, and I assumed he was. Obviously these assumptions of mine were erroneous. Maybe that's my fault.

Even without any advance formalized agreement, says Campbell, he began lobbying for Finley among the members of the board of governors of the NHL. Charlie, says Campbell, didn't give him "a dime of advance expense money for all my traveling." Munson was a bit pushed by these stirrings of insecurity but not sufficiently concerned to stop working for Charlie. Both of the men were full of enthusiasm; the Seals obviously could be had for a bargain price—"like at a firehouse sale," says Bill Torrey. And the odd couple of hockey began making their social calls. It was a pure case of sports-business politics: the smooth, glib Campbell paving the way for the smooth, shrewd Finley. Charlie had been through this kind of thing with other "betters" years earlier; he had sold himself to the medical world, now he would peddle Finley to the icemen.

> *Munson Campbell:* The people in hockey knew nothing about Finley except that he was an eccentric, controversial sports figure. Maybe hockey was too mid-Victorian; maybe the game did need him. There are a lot of capable men who are eccentric. I think the members of the board of governors assumed—and I think Finley led them to believe—that I would be in the forefront of the franchise, so they need not worry about him. And he was a different person when I took him to meet Wirtz, Norris, and several other team owners. I think Finley's always different when he's insecure, when he doesn't know how the field is marked off or what he's supposed to say. Then he's just peaches and cream—totally charming. All he would keep saying in these meetings with these men was: "Yes, indeed. Yes, I'm vitally interested in hockey. Yes, I'm going to move out to Oakland if I get the Seals." He gave them all the right answers. He would quote some of the platitudes from my master plan. Mr. Charles O. Finley can be a remarkably smooth salesman when he wants to be. Don't forget that insurance is never bought, it's always sold. He was mellow, he was peaceful, he was very deliberate; he knew all the right answers. He was following my advice one hundred percent: where he should be, when he should be there, what he should say, how the person he was meeting fit into the master plan.

It was by now February, 1970. Bill Torrey was sitting in the

Seals' offices in Oakland with less than comfortable posture. The tangled financial status of the club's multiple ownership left the future of the team's top executives clearly in sticky limbo. And one day that month, Charlie—one would guess unbeknownst to Campbell—phoned Bill.

> *Bill Torrey:* Charlie tried to pick my brain on the phone. He obviously wanted to get more information about the club so that when he went before the board of governors he would appear to be more knowledgeable and intelligent than somebody else. That shows you how smart he is: he thinks ahead. But at the time, he knew nothing about hockey and he admitted that to me. That didn't make any difference, though. Even after he got the franchise, he admitted he didn't know anything about the game—but he still wanted to do things his own way. The fact he didn't know anything about anything never stopped him from doing things his own way.

At that point, early in 1970, everything seemed to be going Charlie's way. Finley, says Campbell, had established excellent rapport with the hockey Establishment, never ceasing his servings of peaches and cream. Still, as the likelihood of Finley's success increased, you had to figure that somebody out there didn't like him, that somebody would step on the unrolling red carpet. Oh, yes, indeed.

> *Munson Campbell:* The only organized resistance was from the Salomon family in St. Louis [owners of the Blues of the NHL]. They're very close to the Symington family [one of whom happened to be that United States Senator from Missouri who blasted Charlie after the A's whisked out of Kansas City]. When it appeared to the Salomons that Finley was going to make it with the franchise, they sought organized resistance.
> *Jerry Seltzer* (son of the man who invented Roller Derby, later

impresario of that game until its 1973 demise, and best man at my
second wedding): Early in 1970, Sid Salomon III, an old friend,
called and told me the NHL was about to make what he thought was
a very bad mistake, that is, awarding the Oakland francise to Finley.
He thought there should be competition, and suggested I try and get
a group together.

Try he did. Roller Derby was going well at the time, and
twitting Finley was nothing new to the Oakland-based Seltzer.
Hours after an A's Farmer's Day game at the Oakland Coliseum,
Seltzer would stage a Farmer's Daughters' Night game at the
adjacent Oakland Arena. Finley once had a Hot Pants Day game,
and that evening the Roller Derby promised free admission to
anyone wearing "no pants." But Seltzer, for whom I moonlighted
and later full-timed as propagandist, was not being merely waggish
at this stage. Roller Derby did not fulfill all of Jerry's cultural
yearnings. He truly wanted to run a "regular" sports franchise.

> *Jerry Seltzer:* Initially, I met with a great deal of resistance in
> trying to get a group together to bid for the franchise. Many of the
> people I talked with in the Bay area couldn't see hockey having any
> possible success in Oakland—no matter *who* was running it. But I
> felt that if there was a representative team and good promotion,
> hockey could be a huge success, because even as it was being run
> then it was outdrawing the Warriors [of the National Basketball
> Association]. As time went on, getting the Seals became quite a
> challenge to me.

Despite the monetary morass on the top, the Seals weren't doing
too badly on the ice in the early spring of 1970. They would finish
in fourth place in their division under Coach Fred Glover and
reach at least the first round of the Stanley Cup playoffs. In that
final pre-Finley season, the team won twenty-two games, a

less-than-dazzling height never to be reached in the four succeeding seasons of Charlie's ownership. Well, that's baseball.

And while the Seals were skating their way toward a first round playoff sweep by the Pittsburgh Penguins, Seltzer was huddling with Wayne Valley, one of the big money men of the Oakland Raider franchise of the National Football League. Jerry's group was starting to form. Several of Valley's friends, particularly Bay area car dealer John Buono, were caught up in Seltzer's enthusiasm. Rounding out what was coming to be known as the Seltzer syndicate were such football associates of Valley as Lamar Hunt, Bud Adams, and Ralph Wilson, owners, respectively, of the pro football teams in Kansas City, Houston, and Buffalo. Each of the three had a couple of bucks. They would be investors, as would Seltzer to a lesser—much lesser—extent, but Jerry and Buono would be running the franchise.

The battle lines were drawn: Finley and his lonely millions against Valley, Hunt, Adams, Wilson, et al, and their gregarious millions. For this sort of combat there is no Malthusian theory.

Seltzer chose to deal with Trans National Communications, the on-paper owner of the Seals. The odd couple, meanwhile, was romancing previous owner Barry van Gerbig, who still had a stake in the club and was tied in with several other stake-holders. Lack of an advanced degree in World Bank Management prevents elaboration at this point.

*Bill Torrey:* It seemed ludicrous to the board of governors that Trans National Communications was trying to promote a successor [Seltzer] after not being able to run their own shop. Jerry's affiliation with TNC killed any chance he had of getting the franchise, and I'm sure the governors weren't greatly thrilled by Seltzer's association with Roller Derby. I think that Seltzer is one of the best promoters in the country, although I thought the makeup of his group was cumbersome. One of the reasons the league liked Finley was because he was one man, and the NHL has always preferred to deal with one man. And that was a big factor in Charlie getting the franchise. The key governors felt that they could control one man—Finley.

*Jerry Seltzer:* While we were getting our group and money together, I kept hearing that Finley and Munson Campbell were going to each of the owners with the story that Charlie was their kind of guy, that he was a strong individual, that he was white Anglo-Saxon, that he could identify with the game, that he loved the game more than anything. We rather naïvely believed that we would be going in with the best group and that that fact would come across to the NHL. We knew that because of the reasonable rent situation at the Oakland Arena, hockey could be successful with less attendance than in the rest of the league. And I knew that Valley and Buono and their Oakland friends were people who could push season ticket sales personally. I got intensely involved trying to get that franchise.

*Munson Campbell:* The offers from Finley and the Seltzer group were even, about $4.3 million, so it was up to the board of governors to pick which owner they thought would best support hockey in the Bay area. Finley kept seeing this as a fine business investment, a bargain. He thought he might expand his fine television contract for the A's into hockey. The combination of the two-franchise plan was absolutely perfect. All he had to do was follow the master plan.

In late June of 1970, the board of governors met in a hotel near New York's Kennedy Airport to unsnarl the Seal situation. Their finance committee had studied the credentials of Finley and the Seltzer syndicate. Finally now, there would be a vote. The odd couple was confident, but so was Seltzer.

*Jerry Seltzer:* I knew that some of the governors were calling me a hippodroming promoter, but I thought that our group was so strong that we had a chance to win. Even the directors of the Oakland Coliseum Commission had recommended the NHL give us the franchise. But there were only four votes for us.

After the vote, I went up and congratulated Finley. That was only the second time I'd ever seen him in my life—the first time was just before the meeting that day. When I congratulated him, I said that, like everyone else in the Bay area, I was interested in the Seals being a success. I told him that if he wanted to utilize my services in any way, he should certainly feel free to do so. He said he certainly would, and that was the last time I ever spoke to the man.

*Bill Torrey:* Right after the vote, Charlie went up to his room and spent the next two and a half hours telling the Bay area media how happy he was about getting the franchise. Then when he finally hung up the phone, he turned to me and said, "Now how the fuck do I get out of Oakland?" To me his intentions were very clear: he wanted to move the franchise.

## And not be sports czar of the whole darn Bay area?

*Munson Campbell:* As soon as he got the franchise, his whole tone changed. Before then, I'd been conducting meetings. Now he was. He started going around me to people. The authority shifted to him. You can tell when the complexion is changing by the tone of his voice: it becomes arrogantly authoritative instead of just "I'm selling insurance."

*Bill Torrey:* Charlie asked me if I'd stay after he got the team. I said that as long as my present contract was honored, I would remain. My contract said I was responsible for all player dealings and couldn't be interfered with. But within a month, I knew I couldn't live with him. As soon as I started negotiating the player contracts, I knew I had problems. He continually interfered. I eventually signed them all but it was with extreme difficulty. I could have gone out and signed them anyway without going through him, but I was trying to educate Charlie about hockey. And we felt we had the best material in the history of the franchise. At first he told everybody he was going to spend money and leave no stone unturned. And he did spend a lot of money. He printed up a big, elaborate, four-color brochure for season tickets. Spent a ton of money on it, and we got a huge mailing list. But then he wouldn't let it be mailed out until late August. He just kept making changes on it for the sake of making changes, and the brochure went out too late to have any value.

His idea of using white skates for hockey was obviously awful. He asked me what I thought of white skates, and I said, "Charlie, you like white baseball shoes. They look nice in baseball because they're on a green infield. But now you're going to take white skates and put them on white ice. It's going to wash out." He liked white skates, anyway. He also wanted to bring in colored sticks and an orange puck and make the ice surface green. Maybe I'm a puritan, but to me there's a limit to what you can do.

Charlie's limit was "Polar Bear White" skates, green and gold uniforms, player names on the backs of the uniforms and a new name for the club. In its first two NHL seasons, the franchise was called the California Seals. In year three the name was changed to Oakland Seals. Then came Charlie and the California Golden Seals, which was one way to get the fuck out of Oakland.

*Munson Campbell:* It didn't take him long to rub the hockey Establishment wrong. I don't recall the specifics, but one by one I would begin to get word back from other owners that he had made one of them furious. His approach began to seep through the entire hockey hierarchy.

*Bill Torrey:* He violated the noninterference clause in my contract so often that it got to the point where I had to have my lawyer talking to his lawyer. And my lawyer told me that I could either keep letting Charlie interfere with me or go to court and get the matter resolved. I told Charlie that, and he had another contract drawn up. But I wouldn't sign it and told him I'd go to court. So he said, "Well, there'll be a lot of publicity on this one. I won't mind that." He just has a craving for publicity. He loves it. Then he said, "Do you have your lawyer on a monthly retainer? Jesus, they're expensive." He said he had lawyers working for him full-time, so he might as well "throw another case in the hopper." He was, in a sense, trying to tell me that I couldn't afford to take him to court. I discussed it with NHL president Clarence Campbell [no relation to Munson], and he felt that I was young enough and had enough experience so that at some future date I would have a chance to come back into hockey. That I should leave it in his hands. I left the Seals in December of 1970, and about a year later I got my job with the Islanders.

The Seals were last in their division in the 1970–71 season. Coach Glover stayed, but general manager Frank Selke departed early on, then Torrey, too. Munson Campbell was gone before the 1971–72 season was over, as was Glover. New coach Vic Stasiuk elevated Oakland—excuse me, California Golden—into sixth place in Charlie's second season but did not return for the 1972–73 campaign. Glover did—first as executive vice president and then, thirteen games into that season, as coach, too, succeeding Garry Young, who had become the Seals' general manager in 1971–72 before starting the 1972–73 season as coach. Finley was furious over Young's handling of player contracts in the wake of competition from a new league. Under Young-Glover in 1972–73, the Seals won only sixteen games and finished last (eighth) in their newly expanded division. Attendance, which had been at club record-setting proportions in 1971–72, dove in 1972–73, and late in the season Finley halved the ticket prices.

Anyone for peaches and sour cream?

*Munson Campbell:* The league became painfully aware that Mr. Finley had no intention of trying to build hockey at all and, in essence, was letting the franchise deteriorate, because he wanted to move it. He wants to move all of his franchises. The NHL had never moved a franchise in its life and was not about to. In no way was the board of governors going to let the Seals leave the Bay area.

Charlie had Indianapolis all lined up. Ah, the Indianapolis Golden Somethings. But no. The NHL, undaunted by Finley's threats of an antitrust suit if they kept him in Oakland, wouldn't budge. The league was looking for a buyer. And there is every reason to believe that one of the people suggesting the governors find an antidote to Finley was a man named Munson Campbell. His old friend Bruce Norris had by now become chairman of the board of governors. If a buyer for the Seals couldn't be found, the league would take it over. For the National Hockey League, two seasons of Finley had been akin to Mao's march over the mountains: a bit fatiguing.

> *Jerry Seltzer:* Starting in 1972, I had about half a dozen contacts asking if I still had any interest in putting a group together to buy the Seals. These contacts came either directly or indirectly from the NHL. At various times I've run into some of the people who voted against me, and they told me they thought they made a bad mistake. It must have been frustrating for them.

Charlie talked of titanic hockey money losses, later said that poor health would probably necessitate his selling the Seals. It was no secret by mid-1973 that the NHL was prepared to buy him out and run the club itself, if necessary. The only question was the purchase price, and that question became a nagging one for months until, finally, in February, 1974, Charlie got almost $6.5 million from the board of governors.

> *Bill Torrey:* I think he stuck the NHL, if you want my honest opinion. The Islanders didn't vote for that transaction, but the

league thought it was worth all that money to get rid of him. I know what it costs to operate a franchise in the Bay area. I know what Charlie put in, and I know what his costs were. There's no way his losses were as great as he claimed. It came to the point that to save the Bay area franchise, the league just had to step in once and for all. I'm just sorry they didn't do it a couple of years sooner.

*Prescott Sullivan:* To use his own colorful phraseology, Charles O. Finley stepped out of the Bay area hockey scene one day last week smelling like a rose. Try as we might, we couldn't get him to say how much he'd made on the deal. But the smile, even on the pallid face of a sick man, suggested a cool million. . . . Anyway, Finley is well rid of the NHL. And vice versa. It's a tossup as to which of the two parties to the transaction is the happier.

The 1973–74 Seals finished with the worst record in the team's big league history: last in the division with only thirteen wins in seventy-eight games. The club played thirty-nine times on the road and lost thirty-seven. Home attendance averaged about 4,900 per game.

To run the club under its caretaker league ownership until a new franchise could be found, the board of governors named as Seals' president one Munson Campbell, who appointed as his player personnel boss one Garry Young. Their first day on the job they announced the acceptance of the resignation of Coach Fred Glover.

The program table of contents for a March, 1974, game between the Seals and Islanders listed a profile of Charles O. Finley. When one turned to that page, one found instead a profile of Munson Campbell, in which he was described as "a proven winner. A dynamic individual capable of turning around an entire hockey organization."

*Finley* (to a newspaperman a few days after selling the Seals): I feel great relief since getting the Seals off my back. I only purchased the team in the first place because I wanted to bring the Seals to San Francisco. Unfortunately, that never worked out. [An expected arena in San Francisco was not built in that time.] I poured a lot of money into the hockey team, but the NHL was awfully good to me. They not only gave me a good price, but they also met all my expenses for this year [1974]. Let's put it this way: I didn't lose anything on the Seals.

*The Memphis Tams 1972–73 press guide:* The self-made million-aire purchased the Pros last summer, rescuing the franchise from certain death just minutes before the ABA owners were to vote in favor of [the team's] dissolvement. [Finley] took over a financially drained basketball club.

Before the Tams of the American Basketball Association were in fact the Tams, they were the Memphis Pros, who in a previous incarnation were the New Orleans Buccaneers. The ABA was like that, with its red, white, and blue basketball, three-point field goal, outrageous bonuses and franchises that lifted a leaf from—of all places—the Roller Derby by representing not one or two cities but entire states. In the early 1970s, this league's most representative success was establishing an out-of-sight salary scale in professional basketball and instilling the older National Basketball Association with a sweaty case of antitrust jitters.

The ABA seemed an awfully freaky locale for the Owner and General Manager. But he got in cheaply and had visions, one must assume, of quick profit. For at the time the Memphis Pros fell unto Charles O. Finley, an ABA merger with the NBA figured to be just around the corner—with exemplary TV and gate revenue to follow. And certainly if an ABA club suddenly became an NBA club, the franchise itself would greatly increase in value. The Owner had to believe—with some measure of realism—that there was nothing to lose by buying the Memphis Pros.

Artistically, the club was less than successful with records of 41–43 and 26–58 in its first two Memphis seasons, 1970–71 and 1971–72. The town could not complain too much because the town kind of owned the Pros, at five bucks a share in a public stock sale. The fact that the fans were able to keep the team in town by buying it was referred to as "The Miracle of Memphis."

Memphians would have been better off sending the whole team to Lourdes.

The people who ran the ABA were meeting in New York in the summer of 1972 trying to figure out what to do with this floundering miracle. Folding the Pros seemed to be the most judicious course. Just as the secretary was about to call the roll—or some such dramatic moment—one of the Pro owners phoned Finley, and for twenty-five thousand dollars in cash and a pledge to absorb existing Pro debts, Charlie had himself a red, white, and blue basketball of his own. A real mogul now in three different professional sports.

One of his initial promotions was a "Name the Team" contest, with a first prize of twenty-five hundred dollars. William Barrett of West Point, Mississippi, suggested TAMS—an acronym for Tennessee, Arkansas, and Mississippi—and thus defeated 21,999 other entrants. Good start, Charlie.

One of his early personnel moves was to employ as club president seventy-one year old Adolph (The Baron) Rupp, recently retired as head coach of the University of Kentucky and at that point the "winningest" college basketball coach in all of Christendom, not to mention the history of the Southeast Conference. Another good start, Charlie.

Rupp would be to the Tams what Joe DiMaggio had been to the A's when Finley first came to Oakland: a stunning public relations gesture.

Finley and DiMaggio were never quite sure what Joe would do

as an "executive vice president" of the A's. Tired of waiting for definitive duties, a void made even more ephemeral by the lack of a desk, the Yankee Clipper became a coach and departed after two seasons. But early on, he did draw publicity for the A's, merely by being in the ball park with them. And truly, it was not that bad a deal for DiMaggio, who felt sadly snubbed in terms of front office job offers by the Yankees. Joe was fifty-three years old when Finley hired him. Dignified, yes. Gracious, yes. In need of pride-salving attention, yes. He quietly put in his two years, then quietly left.

Rupp stayed just one year at Memphis, although all was harmonious for The Baron at the beginning. In the Tam press guide that first season, Finley was quoted as calling his hiring of Rupp "the happiest moment of my life."

*Adolph Rupp:* Charlie Finley is a magnetic man. A great man. Trying to top him is like trying to get the sun past a rooster.

*A former Tam employee:* They seemed to have a lot of respect for each other. Rupp always called Charlie "Mr. Finley" and Charlie always called him "Coach Rupp." After a team meeting one time, Rupp said to Charlie, "Now, Mr. Finley, if our coach [Bob Bass] should ever get sick for a day or two, who's the coach?" And Charlie says, "You are, Coach Rupp." Then Rupp says, "Now, Mr. Finley, if Bass gets fired or quits, who's the coach?" Charlie says, "You are, Coach Rupp." And Rupp says, "Fine, fine," and walks away. Charlie looks over at one of us and winks with a big grin. He was having fun with Rupp. No way he ever would have made Rupp coach, and I don't think Rupp would have taken the job, anyway. The real problem was that Rupp's duties were never outlined. [Hello, Joe.] I think Charlie wanted Coach Rupp as a figurehead—a name, a speechmaker to drum up support. I think both Charlie and Coach Rupp believed that the Tams would draw thousands of people just because of Rupp's name. A lot of us thought so, but we were all wrong. It didn't take long for Charlie to realize that nothing would work there.

The Tams in their first Finley year had an average attendance of thirty-two hundred as they lost two more games than they had in 1971–72, finishing at 24–60 but setting a sort of ABA record for most players used in one season: twenty-five. As one former front office employee says, "Even the players admitted we had a horrible team."

By the end of the season, it was apparent to Charlie's staff in the Mid-South Coliseum in Memphis that the Owner had lost interest. Rupp apparently was no longer the happiest moment in Charlie's life, for The Baron rarely heard from the boss anymore.

Although the Tams press guide noted that Charlie "insists he didn't buy the Tams to make money," there was every indication the Owner had no interest in losing too much in Memphis. A sale was likely, and Charlie did have an offer of one and a half million dollars from a group in Providence, Rhode Island. But the league refused to sanction the franchise-shifting deal, and Finley was unwillingly stuck in Memphis for the 1973–74 season. Until only a few weeks before the opening of the exhibition season that fall, Charlie appeared on the brink of folding his basketball club. But when hotshot commissioner Mike Storen threatened to take the club away from Finley, the Owner hired a coach and a front office staff. The Tams were all set for a dismal year: in 1973–74 they turned in their poorest record (21–63) and, despite an eleventh hour surge in season ticket sales (five hundred in one week, according to an ABA press release), were unable to equal their sparse attendance average of the previous year. Charlie had signed two popular Memphis State players, Larry Finch and Ronnie Robinson, but to no avail. Even Santa Claus ignored the Tams; their thirteen-game losing streak did not end until December 26, 1973.

There was frequent conversation about an ABA-NBA merger during Finley's final year in professional basketball. The anticipation of a merger agreement must have dazzled Charlie. A Congressional bill seemed in the works. North Carolina's Senator Sam Ervin was going to champion the merger. But then he got busy with something called Watergate, and the NBA owners became increasingly convinced that the ABA would perish—and thus backed off. The NBA began granting expansion franchises for six million dollars.

> *A former NBA club executive:* If there had been a merger, the existing ABA franchises would have had to take on additional value. I don't know if it would have been six million dollars, but it probably would have been a substantial figure. Who knows?

Charlie sure would like to have known.

In the spring of 1974, Finley kept edging closer to selling the Tams to a Memphis-based record company, Stax, which brought you Isaac Hayes and just about more soul than any other label. Charlie reportedly was asking for a million dollars. A Stax vice president said the firm had reached agreement on a purchase price. But by mid-June, the deal appeared to have collapsed.

Finley told a Memphis writer that he couldn't communicate with the Stax people. "Hell," he said, "they won't even return my telephone calls."

Butch van Breda Kolff, Finley's coach in Memphis in year two, said, "I just wish to hell someone would tell me what's going on. But no one knows."

Charlie came to Memphis to pick up the club's financial records and tell the press that he had no further interest in professional basketball. Finley predicted that before the month was out the league would buy the Tams and fold them.

Memphis *Commercial-Appeal* sports columnist Roy Edwards said ABA Commissioner Storen had vetoed Finley's sale to Stax because of too much uncertainty and instability in the record business. "It's really far out for anyone to be termed too unstable for the ABA," wrote Edwards.

By June 20, the Tams belonged to the league. The price paid to Finley was not disclosed. Various reliable reports said Charlie got at least three quarters of a million for a club that cost him some twenty-five thousand dollars (plus existing debts) two summers earlier. One former Tam employee estimates that Charlie spent between seven hundred thousand and a million dollars on the Tams.

"We are extremely sorry to see Mr. Finley leave the ABA," said Commissioner Storen. Charlie said he sold because of doctor's orders. He said he was very happy with the sale price.

Within the month, Mike Storen had quit as commissioner of the ABA to take over the Memphis team, which would now be called the Sounds. There was no indication how much, if anything, Storen had to pay the league for the franchise. One of his partners was an executive from Stax Records.

And, oh, yes. As general manager of the Sounds, Storen hired Bob Bass, Finley's coach in 1972–73.

**IX**

## MORE PIECES

After every home game of the 1970 season, John McNamara would drive home to Sacramento, some eighty miles from the Coliseum and the telephone in the manager's office. John could attempt to unwind on Interstate 80 and be sufficiently relaxed to cope with more telephone calls after he arrived home. The calls were not from fans, or writers, or players, or neighbors. Guess.

That spring and early summer John was buffeted by the Charlie-Reggie crosswinds. The manager had a potential winner on his hands, but, oh, the accompanying grief. Reggie no longer considered John a friend, and with the A's lagging far behind Minnesota in the West by late May there was reason to believe Charlie wanted to fire McNamara. At one point in July, the Owner was negotiating with Billy Martin to take over the club, except that Martin knew he would not be permitted the control a Billy Martin needs. Before the All Star break, Finley called a press conference to "guarantee that Johnny McNamara will be the manager of this ball club for at least the balance of this year." Not at least. At most.

As the season wound down, McNamara was intent on resigning

to salvage pride. Yet there lingered the possibility—slim, but who knows?—that Charlie might rehire him. So McNamara waited.

> *Dave Duncan* (former A's catcher, on the next-to-last day of the 1970 season): It doesn't matter who manages this ball club. There's only one man who manages this club, Charlie Finley. And we'll never win as long as he manages.

Duncan had shared catching duties that season with Frank Fernandez and Gene Tenace. Dave was twenty-four, an impatient, freckled strongman. He was troubled in the summer of 1970 about baseball and life. In Oakland he shared an apartment with a coach, Charlie Lau. Both were separated from their wives. "Neither of us was making a big bundle of money, so it was a good financial arrangement. Plus I really appreciated the baseball knowledge I gained from being around Charlie Lau. I think I learned an awful lot about the game from him," Dave said.

In his blast at the Owner, Duncan also said, "Everybody's always worried about Charlie Finley—you can't say that, you can't say this, or he'll be mad. Nobody will speak out. But how can they, with their jobs to protect?" Duncan said he hoped Finley would trade him, otherwise he was contemplating quitting. And all of these things he said were being noted by a sportswriter.

> *Finley* (at an Oakland press conference the day after the 1970 season ended and after Duncan's comments were printed): As of two days ago, Johnny McNamara had just as much of a chance of managing this ball club as anyone else. But when the Dave Duncan story broke, that was the end of his chances. . . . I definitely know that overall there was a great harmony on this team this year. We had only two problems on our club of players spouting off—my good friend, Reggie Jackson, and Duncan. . . . No manager can allow one of his players to criticize unfairly, knowing the facts himself, without

getting pinched. John McNamara didn't lose this job. His players took it from him.

As Ron Bergman's "Mustache Gang" recounts that press conference, Charlie spent "a half hour in an all-out attack on Duncan" that included this bit of Finley condemnation: "One day I found out that Duncan was sleeping with coach Charlie Lau. By that, I mean they were rooming together, sharing expenses." Finley said he had ordered the arrangement ended earlier "because, as we all know, in the Army troops don't fraternize with officers." But those orders had been ignored.

McNamara and Lau were fired that day. Duncan stayed around two more seasons before being traded to Cleveland after a salary dispute with Charlie. "I just felt I was being taken for granted," Dave said after the trade.

The A's were 89–73 in 1970. With a happy Jackson and a properly used Blue they might have been much, much better. Well, they were one game better than in 1969, and their attendance had increased—by 123. People, not thousands. The A's outdrew the Giants by nearly forty thousand. In 1971, the Giants had a new third base coach, John McNamara, and the A's a new manager, Dick Williams.

Joe Rudi, finally playing in more than a hundred games, batted .309 in 1970. Gene Tenace was around for thirty-eight games, hit .305. Sal Bando drove in seventy-five runs, had twenty homers. Monday finished at .290 but with only thirty-seven RBIs. Hunter had won eighteen games, Chuck Dobson sixteen. Blue had thrown his late-season no-hitter against the Twins. Fingers was both relieving and starting. The pitching workhorse, however, was Jim Grant, the "Mudcat," at least thirty-five years old and revered by his teammates. Grant knew the game as well as anybody on the club. And the fans dug him. "Mudcat" could sing, worked occasionally at an Oakland nightspot. He was instant p.r., a valuable commodity for many reasons. Before the season ended, he was dealt to Pittsburgh. He returned briefly and ineffectively the following year. Charlie had been able earlier in 1971 to obtain a left-handed reliever, Darold Knowles, from Washington.

Knowles and Fingers, waiting for World Series work.

Arriving from the Senators in the same deal as Knowles was first baseman Mike Epstein, something of a brilliant incorrigible but the answer—for a season and a half—to Finley's first base problems.

It almost all came together, finally, in 1971. At least during the regular season. Blue won twenty-four and Hunter twenty-one of the club's 101 victories. Bando and Jackson had fifty-six home runs and 174 runs batted in between them. Duncan and Tenace shared the catching on a two-thirds, one-third basis and combined for twenty-two homers and sixty-five runs batted in. The bench was not bad—particularly pinch hitter Tommy Davis. The only low note was the performance of Rick Monday. He slumped to a .245 batting average despite reaching his Oakland high of eighteen home runs. Even before the magnificent season had ended (the A's took their division by sixteen games), there were rumors that Monday would be traded. In November he went to the Chicago Cubs for left-handed pitcher Ken Holtzman. Trading bells had finally broken up that young gang of Charlie's. But Holtzman turned out to be the last essential piece of the puzzle. When the A's came to Oakland they did not have a fit southpaw starting pitcher. Only five times in the 1968 season did a left-hander start a game for the A's. In 1972, despite Blue's delayed entrance, southpaws started for Oakland seventy-four times.

Finley had his players, and his manager.

Charlie was ready for a tough-guy manager in 1971 and could not have made a better choice than Richard Hirshfeld Williams, a man to match the Owner-General Manager Mountain. Before spring training began, Williams had met with and mollified Reggie Jackson and Dave Duncan. By opening day of 1971, Williams had decided that Vida Blue could mean a pennant. By the second week of the season, the players knew where they stood: One of them had ripped off a bullhorn from an airplane in Milwaukee, precipitating an immediate lecture on the team bus.

> *Dick Williams:* Gentlemen, some of you think you can be pricks. But I've got news for you: I can be the biggest prick of all. The plane can't leave without the bullhorn, and we're not going to leave until the plane can if we have to sit here all night. I have no small fines. I would suggest to you that you stay in your rooms this entire road trip. And if you want to phone Charlie, I have three numbers where he can be reached.

The bullhorn turned up moments later. Dick Williams, after all, was a man who once fined that great American athlete Carl Yastrzemski for nonhustle. A man who would hop on Yastrzemski would hop on anybody.

He had played nearly everywhere. He had played every position except pitcher and catcher in ball parks from Santa Barbara to Brooklyn. Dick Williams played in Ebbets Field, pre-Finley Kansas City, Baltimore, Cleveland, Boston, Fort Worth, St. Paul, Montreal. He was comfortable anywhere. Especially on dugout benches, where he had spent most of a major league career that ran from 1951 to 1964. An early shoulder injury impaired his ability to throw, turned him from an outfielder into a handyman, the sort of utility player who fills a roster while filling a variety of needs. He would sit and watch and learn and listen. The baseball absorption process. The years of sitting exposed him to good managers and bad. Mostly those years gave him a feeling for what baseball calls "the extra men," because he often felt as extra as they come. The big secret to his work in Oakland was no secret at all: He knew how to use all twenty-five men and made most of them feel needed.

Because he had to strain and grunt and squeeze as a player, the teams he managed tended to take on his character. The word "eke" once was employed by sports headline writers until managing editors demanded more powerful verbs. But Williams' Athletics eked; yes, they did. A friend and coach of Williams, ex-Yankee Irv Noren, described the Oakland teams of 1971–73 as "those raggedy-ass A's." Which meant that nothing came easy, that you win late and narrowly, but that you do in fact win. More often than not with your extra men.

> *John McNamara:* There's only one manager of the Athletics and that's Charlie. A man who takes the job had better learn to live with it. I don't know what Dick does, but he's got to be the greatest politician of all times.
>
> *Ralph Houk* (veteran major league manager): There's nothing mysterious about managing. How many moves can you make? Players fire managers. If they believe in you, you don't have to do anything else.
>
> *Finley:* It doesn't take a genius to run a baseball team. A monkey could stand out there on the field and wave at his pitchers.

Let us suppose that McNamara, Houk, and Finley are all correct. Then let us apply their theorems to Dick Williams.

For most of three years, Dick did learn to live with Charlie. And yes, Mr. McNamara, Dick may be one of the greatest sports politicians of all time because of his understanding of the art of compromise. A's team captain Sal Bando would charge a machine gun nest for Williams. Unarmed. Sal Bando will tell you, "The players respected Dick because he could compromise with Finley. He would do some things that Charlie wanted and some things that he wanted. Dick got away with some things because I think Charlie respected him. For fighting with him. And that's why it hurt Finley so much to see Dick leave. Dick only cared about winning. Not keeping his job. Winning. And Dick brought out the talent in us."

Yes, Mr. Houk, the players—and not infrequently the Owner— believed in Dick Williams.

And yes, Mr. Finley, it does not take a genius to run a baseball team. Your baseball team, perhaps, but not most. Dick did know when to wave at his pitchers. In 1971 he gave his relievers plenty of work. Rollie Fingers made forty relief appearances, Darold Knowles forty-three, Bob Locker forty-seven. By the time the playoffs against Baltimore opened, Dick was waving in frustration. Two of his starters were sore-armed. He could open the best-of-five series with Man of the Year Blue, then throw Hunter, then pray. The A's might have won the opener if Williams' romance with the suicide squeeze had not backfired in the second inning. Instead, Blue lost. As did Hunter the next day. As did emergency starter Diego Segui in the third game. Dick admitted some of his decisions had backfired, and Charlie solemnly shook his manager's hand. And retained him.

The San Francisco Giants would lose the National League playoffs in four games, to Pittsburgh. There would be no Bay Bridge World Series in 1971. But the combined regular season attendance of the two clubs would be some two million: A's, 914,993; Giants, 1,106,043. Lots of people, lots of harbingers. Willie Mays and the Giants would now go downhill. Dick Williams and the A's were about to become the best team in baseball. Williams had taken the Boston Red Sox to their "Impossible

Dream" pennant in 1967. Now he would fulfill a few dreams of Charles O. Finley, including Charlie's Second Base Platoon.

> *Dick Green:* I think Dick Williams just got to the A's at the right time. But he managed the team very well. He got the most out of us. I think so now [in the 1974 season] more than when he was managing. Charlie didn't tell Dick to do as much as he told other managers. Although I'm not saying that Dick managed one hundred percent. He certainly didn't.

Not when it came to the Second Base Platoon, he didn't. The 1972 Western Division championship did not come easily to the Oakland A's. They shuffled through forty-seven players. There was the matter of Blue's holdout-disaffection; there was the improvement of the Dick Allen-buoyed Chicago White Sox; there was the midseason illness of productive Mike Epstein, and in August Reggie Jackson was hurt. During a four-game series in Oakland, Chicago briefly moved into first place in the West, fueling rumors of Williams' imminent dismissal. But Charlie phoned Dick, gave him a raise, extended his contract, provided him with an unknown left-handed pinch hitter named Gonzalo Marquez, adding to Dick's rather decent bench strength. By the end of August, Williams had such left-handed hitters available for quick use as Mike Hegan, Don Mincher, Matty Alou, and Marquez. Potential right-handed pinch hitters were Angel Mangual, George Hendrick, and Duncan or Gene Tenace (whichever wasn't catching that day). There was a plethora of infielders, too, on the bench, people like Ted Kubiak, Dal Maxvill, and Tim Cullen. All three could surely play second base, although Maxvill's long credentials were as a shortstop. All three would play second base, along with Dick Green, the starter at that position. And all four would play there nearly every day in the final weeks of the 1972 season.

History (as it blushes) will show that in 1972 the Oakland
Athletics employed twelve men to play a combined total of 246
games at second base. (A year later the figures were eleven and
266.)

The Second Base Platoon of '72 was an offspring of The Catcher
Platoon of '69, an aborted brainchild of the Owner. During one
fortnight of the 1969 season, the A's had four catchers. Manager
Hank Bauer told a writer that Charlie wanted to pinch hit for a
catcher "every time a catcher was due to bat." Bauer refused.
Finley later would deny making the suggestion. As for the Second
Base Platoon . . .

*Ted Kubiak:* I had heard it was Finley's idea, but I remember
seeing in the paper that Williams said it was his plan. And that was
the first I knew about it—reading the paper. The guys that were
involved in it right away didn't like it. We didn't think it would help
the club because you can't really do what you're capable of doing on
a part-time basis like that. Especially one or two innings a game. I
think it worked, though, because of the ability we each had, and we
had some hot pinch hitters at the time. I think Charlie is an
innovative man. He's got ideas. He's willing to try something new.

*Dick Williams:* Don't give me the credit for this. It was Charlie's
idea. He suggested it, I talked it over with my staff, and we couldn't
see anything wrong in it.

*Dick Green:* I was happy with it as long as we were winning. After
the 1972 season, I told Charlie he was hurting the team if he didn't
play me regularly as long as I did a halfway decent job with the bat.
It stands to reason that having a guy come off the bench to hit or
field isn't as good as having a guy out there getting a feel of the game
right along. It was tough for Kubiak and the others. I don't know
how they ever did such a good job as they did—coming cold off the
bench. But Charlie thought—and still thinks—that he's got twenty-
five men on the team and he wants twenty-five men ready at all

times, that the bench should be ready. I agree with that, but only if the guys coming off the bench get the hits.

They did, in the September stretch drive, and again in the excruciating five-game playoff victory over Detroit. In that fifth game, won by the courage of John Odom, Reggie Jackson, and Vida Blue, plus a Gene Tenace single, Williams did not make a substitution at second base. In the seven-game World Series victory over Cincinnati, Dick concentrated on shuffling pitchers. Eight of them appeared a total of twenty-two times. Rollie Fingers pitched in six of the seven games. Six of the seven were decided by one run. Williams, armed with a brilliant scouting report from old St. Louis Browns pitcher Al Hollingsworth, made an estimated fifty-five trips to the mound to talk to his pitchers. Those raggedy-ass A's, slowly stroking their mustaches, were in no hurry. After the Series, Williams was given another raise.

During one of the Series plane shuttles, Dave Duncan loudly suggested to the Owner: "Charlie, you don't really *know* me." Charlie said sure he did. Duncan meant that Charlie didn't understand him, which was probably correct. Williams, on the other hand, did understand the Duncans and Jacksons, the Epsteins and Blues. They were contemporary; not Williams' contemporaries, simply athletes of the seventies. Dick could *like* a Sal Bando. He could contend with most of the others. He could even dress "mod," grow hair down to his collar, sprout a mustache. Privately, this man from the school of baseball hard knocks might make judgments on the mores of the young men in his clubhouse. Publicly, he was conciliatory. Dick Williams, still in his early forties, had made adjustments, unlike many managers and coaches in professional sports in those years. The A's would, in their words, "bust their asses" for Dick Williams. They viewed him with a combination of fear and respect. He could get nasty when he wished; he also could, and did, put a great deal of money in most of their pockets.

After the final playoff victory over Baltimore in 1973, Joe Rudi—the team's best hitter the previous year but ill and injured much of that season—was adding up the fringe benefits of playing for Dick Williams. With the Series win in '73, the fringe would total more than fifty thousand dollars for each man who had played for Dick three years in Oakland. And Joe said to Dick, "Thank you."

Williams was at least as politic to Finley as to his players. Bando was correct: Dick did some of the things Charlie wanted and some of the things he wanted. He could accept the necessity of using pinch runner Allan Lewis at Charlie's beck and balance that by shuffling the lineup his own way.

> *Ron Bergman* (Oakland *Tribune* baseball writer): Williams had a lot of ego, but he meshed it with Charlie instead of clashing, and that's why it was important for him to quit and not be fired. He could easily have been fired. He could easily have just stopped answering the phone. Stopped putting in all those second basemen. Which he did early in the 1973 season. The night he did it, in Texas, he said, "I might be losing my job right here." I wrote once that Williams had more power than any manager Finley had ever hired, and Finley phoned me and said, "What do you mean by writing that?" He just didn't like that.

He had to have liked Williams' winning. That was the compensation. The 1972 home attendance was the largest in Oakland's history—921,323. (That year's Giants drew 647,744. Willie Mays and his large salary had been deposited with the New York Mets.)

Whatever succumbing he had to do to Charlie, Williams had to be satisfied with the Owner's penchant, and willingness, to spend money to plug gaps in the club. Early in the season, late in the season—Charlie would buy what Dick needed.

The Owner gave the manager handymen Mike Hegan, Curt Blefary, and Larry Brown, plus Epstein and Knowles in 1971. In August of 1972 Charlie handed over Matty Alou, Maxvill, Marquez. The late season arrivals in 1973 were Jesus Alou, Vic Davalillo, Mike Andrews, Rico Carty.

Williams had to repeat in 1973. Anything short of another World Series victory would have been nothing at all. The pieces were shifted gingerly: Tenace, the home run hero of the '72 Series, was now the first baseman; Epstein had been traded to Texas. Ray Fosse would replace the Tenace-Duncan montage as catcher. Aging relief pitcher Bob Locker was sent to the Chicago Cubs for a volatile young center fielder, Bill North, who would eventually win a starting job over at least two other serious candidates.

The team's hard core remained unchanged. Dick and Charlie still had the key ingredient—the good arms. In 1973, Hunter, Blue, and Holtzman each would win at least twenty games. Fingers would save twenty-two and win seven more. Because of injuries, Chicago was not threatening any longer. This year the Kansas City Royals would make the race tight through Labor Day. But the bats of Jackson and Bando and the speed of North and Campaneris would prevail in the West by six games. Oakland ended 1973 with a record of 94–68, one game better than a year earlier. They would need the full five games to beat Baltimore in the playoffs and the full seven to defeat the Mets in the World Series. Oakland was still the best, still raggedy-ass.

CHAPTER **X**

# HOW GREEN
# WAS MY SWEATSHIRT

He has been a surrogate manager for many seasons. Rather, his managers have been surrogate managers for many seasons. "He's part manager," says A's second baseman Dick Green. "Let's say that Dick Williams managed sixty percent and Mr. Finley forty percent."

The most definite contention one can make about Charlie's managerial activities is that he calls most of the shots (i.e., lineup) before the game begins. Once the game has started, the other manager takes over. A few folks claim that Charlie has called the dugout during games with specific orders on pinch running and pinch hitting, but there is no firm evidence for these claims. Veteran Finley-watcher Ron Bergman says, "From what I understand he's never phoned the dugout and said, 'Okay, put this guy in as a runner.' But he does phone down and ask the manager, 'What are you gonna do? What's next? What's the strategy?' He doesn't tell them. He asks."

> *Alvin Dark:* People think Charlie's dumb because he asks so many crazy questions. He's not dumb. He's brilliant. He asks questions because he wants to know, and he's not ashamed to ask.

*Bill Cutler:* Maybe all the owners should do like Charlie—run the team on the phone from Chicago and make the decisions after consulting cabdrivers and the guys in the barbershop.

The reviews of Charlie's performance as a "baseball man" tend to be mixed. As an owner and general manager he is due critical acclaim, for he has, after all, produced a winner. He may not be the foremost authority on rule book and procedural fine print—he didn't know the compensatory precedents in the Dick Williams case—but there always has been someone in his front office to inform and remind him about unconditional waivers and drafts and options. Until 1974 he had no reluctance to pay big money for talent, either future or immediate. He almost always has conferred with his managers before making a deal, but even when operating solo (or in tandem with a cabdriver or barber) Charlie is likely to apprehend the necessary merchandise. In the view of Dick Green, "he's a good front office man who can go out and get the ballplayers you need at the right time. He'll spend anything for that, and there's a lot of owners who don't. I think he knows the game more than eighty-five or ninety percent of the other owners and general managers."

Sportswriter Bergman, who will never be a candidate for president of the Charles O. Finley fan club, is nearly ecstatic when it comes to Finley's flesh-procuring instincts. "He really is a good trader," says Bergman. "Boy, he's never made a bad deal. And he's not afraid to spend the money either. I think he knows players pretty well; he knows who to get and who's good. Obviously he understands a player's ability. He's a good general manager. The Rick Monday–Ken Holtzman trade was brilliant. Same thing with trading Bob Locker for Bill North."

Finley would insist that "baseball people like to make the game sound so complex that nobody but them can run it. It doesn't take a genius to run a ball club." He would suggest "the average fan off the street" could trade with better results than most general managers, that "a park policeman could stand out there and wave pitchers in and out of the ball game."

Ted Bowsfield pitched for Charlie in Kansas City and later became a front office man with the California Angels. He describes the Owner as "like a lot of people in baseball today. They have a tendency to think they can step right into the game and operate it right away. I think that by now Charlie has attained a certain amount of experience. And it's proven that he's gone out and spent good money and got good ballplayers. These guys have got some kind of character and they can play besides."

> *Question:* Does Charlie have an excellent knowledge of the game?
> *Cedric Tallis:* He has a very expensive phone bill. He's a very astute man. He does not know player talent, but he does utilize an extensive system of calling a lot of different people. And he has a good retentive memory. Also, he's been able to swing certain deals because he's thrown a considerable amount of money into the pot to sweeten the kitty. He's been a most astute owner, but I would not say that if I were an owner about to hire a general manager that I would hire Charlie as my general manager. Yet he has done well, and who can laugh at success?

Baltimore executive vice president Frank Cashen has never made a deal with Charlie. "But I know that he's a wheeler-dealer and he'll stay up all night trying to make a deal with you. I don't know anybody else in sports who could have accomplished the things he has by himself."

One of the veteran Athletics says the Owner "has made many good trades because he has the young talent to give up. But he won't trade with everybody. I think he knows he can't bullshit certain club owners and general managers. I don't see him trading with the Dodgers or Mets. And he would never admit he was wrong about any baseball decision."

In late spring of 1974, Calvin Griffith, owner of the Minnesota Twins, said, "Charlie won't make any deals with my club. He's scared of me. He once told me, 'You're one guy I'm not gonna deal with.' He's afraid I might embarrass him. And anytime he trades a ballplayer, it looks like he gets 'em back somehow. Just like we drafted Jim Holt from his organization, and Charlie's been after Holt for two or three years. He's worried he made a mistake letting Holt go, because Jim had a couple good years with us." (In August, 1974, the A's traded Pat Bourque to Minnesota for Jim Holt.) "I don't know," says Griffith, "if Charlie knows the difference between the hit-and-run and run-and-hit or not. But he must have somebody advising him pretty good on the caliber of players. He has good knowledge of what we have in our organization and he knows the value of his players. That knowledge is pretty sound."

Knowing values does not a baseball strategist make. A horse trader, especially one armed with cash, persistence, and a telephone, can buy and sell colts with impressive facility. This does not mean said horse trader also can cover six furlongs in 1:10 with one of his newly purchased steeds. Yet if enough of his stable wins, he might start considering the jockey superfluous. Thus, the assimilation of expertise as perceived by the Owner and General Manager—although not by too many others.

> *An A's veteran:* Charlie has a basic understanding of the game, but he's not knowledgeable about it. He goes too much by statistics and not by value. Daily value. He knows you have to have good players to win, but he doesn't understand what the good players do, what makes them good. He doesn't understand about giving yourself up at the plate, about playing when you're hurt. He thinks he knows a lot about the game because he's been successful. I don't think you can base knowledge on success.

At the beginning of the 1974 season, Oakland designated hitter Deron Johnson picked up right where he left off in the final six weeks of the 1973 season—in a deep, dismal batting slump. Manager Alvin Dark decided to bench Deron one evening against a right-handed pitcher and instead use left-handed-hitting Vic Davalillo; a percentage move to begin with, plus the temporary removal of a struggling player. Shortly before game time, Johnson was back in the batting order and Davalillo on the bench. Dark explained: "I talk with Charlie Finley every day, either before or after the game, or both. I mentioned this thought [using Davalillo] to him. He said, 'I'm not sure I like it but do what you think is proper.' Later he called and said, 'Who's your designated hitter?' I said, 'Davalillo. Don't you like the idea?' He said, 'We've got to get Deron hitting. We can't ignore all the runs he batted in last season. I'd rather see him in there.' So I said, 'You're right.'" (Neither player finished the season with Oakland.)

Dark was different from most previous Finley managers in that he would admit he was following orders vis-à-vis lineup changes and personnel moves. Others would invent excuses for shifts or ascribe these changes to their own ideas and hunches. It is humbling for a fellow to admit that "Charlie wants it this way." Dark was taunted for his openness in early 1974, but he was being straight. You had to respect the man for that—until, in midsummer, he changed courses and would only confess to some of the Owner's dabbling.

The players resent all of Charlie's lineup fingerpaintings. Unless, of course, they are the individual(s) benefiting from his moves. The same goes with the changes of an unimpeded manager. Bitching is as inimical to a clubhouse as towels. The Oakland players bitch more only because there are more frequent changes. For years they have asked for pat lineups, the plea being "Let's play our best people every day." But Charlie's impetuosity gets in the way of this stability. Properly, baseball is a day-to-day game; there is no assurance a player will perform today the same as he did against the same opponent two weeks ago. The Owner, however, makes it a minute-to-minute game, manifesting insecurity, instability, incongruity (shifting Joe Rudi, the league's best defensive left fielder, to first base for a lengthy period in 1974). And doing it over the telephone, without the benefit of seeing what it is you're changing, save for the box score numerology in the morning paper.

"It's kind of tough to know the game when you're in an insurance office," says A's catcher-first baseman Gene Tenace. He said this several months before he was promised "I wouldn't have to catch anymore except in an emergency" and then was started as catcher within forty-eight hours.

> *Vida Blue:* If I had a multimillion dollar operation, I'd want my finger on every little thing, too. But Charlie Finley goes beyond that nine times out of ten. He's totally involved. I can see where he's coming from by wanting to be *part* of the team. But he does so much that you think he wants to be the whole team. And there's no way that's possible. It could be he's a disappointed baseball player. Or maybe just a disappointed bat boy.

A disappointed manager? The Connie Mack of expansion baseball?

Just remember, fans. If Charles O. Finley actually did manage a major league baseball team, that team would have to lose a couple of games every season. And the manager might have to take the blame for some of those losses. Down deep, the Owner and General Manager may want to sit in the dugout and manage. Down deeper, the Owner needs somebody else sitting in the dugout and losing.

---

Bill Veeck owned the Cleveland Indians, St. Louis Browns, and Chicago White Sox, all the while being disowned by the baseball Establishment. After all, he would stand outside the ticket windows or walk through the stands and talk to fans. To fans! He would present the customers with an oddball gift assortment. Giveaways! He was a nut for pyrotechnic displays. Fireworks! Clowns coached, midgets batted, aging relief pitchers reclined on bullpen lawn chairs. A bleeping heretic!

> *Calvin Griffith:* We've had some pretty good promoters in our game, and they've kind of hurt the game. Bill Veeck promoted every way. He would spend two dollars and one cent to get two dollars in the till. And you can't do it. I believe in color and all that, but I tell you, the way I was brought up in this game, your attraction is baseball players. And you've got to have the ballplayers regardless of how many sideshows you have. The people aren't coming to see a mule or something else like that.

Finley was reminiscing in 1971. "I have great admiration for Bill Veeck and I said when I first got into baseball I would try to take his ideas and incorporate them with my own ideas, maybe even improve on them. I think Bill Veeck was good for baseball. I'd like to see him back and compete with him. I think this game needs more Bill Veecks." He was quoted in the *New York Times* two years later: "Veeck and I are supposed to be kooks. We couldn't care less."

Charlie had seen Veeck's Chicago operation, in fact had tried to become a partner. Veeck made the game enjoyable for Charlie. Charlie would try to do the same for others, if he could only force the men who wouldn't listen to Veeck to listen to him. Charlie lacked Veeck's flair, sense of humor, subtlety. But he had more physical energy, more money, and more resolve. Veeck was a fan-businessman, Finley a businessman-fan.

*Finley* (to *Sports Illustrated*, 1965): Baseball has never rolled with the punch, never made the fans feel wanted and appreciated. In any business, you draw a line called success and a line called failure. When your business starts slipping, you may not discover the line has gone down for several years. You have slipped to the point of no return before you find out. Baseball has definitely slipped. No doubt about it. But how far? Let's pray we haven't reached the point of no return. The pathetic, frustrating thing is that all the owners know baseball has slipped, but they don't do anything. In baseball, we could correct the problems overnight.

*Finley* (to *Look*, 1971): *Overnight!* It's stupidity that we don't. Gross stupidity, which is 144 times worse than plain stupidity. And stupidity I can't stand. Laziness and stupidity. My god, when you're in business and you know sales are slipping and you know why your sales are not increasing with population growth and you do nothing about it, that's stupid. I tell you, with a few changes attendance would increase twenty percent the first year.

*Finley* (to *Sports Illustrated*, 1972): We've got to bring action back into this game. Just look at all the rule changes in football, basketball, and hockey over the past twenty-five years. In our game there hasn't been one significant rule change in the last eighty-six years! And I'll say this, if we don't make some substantial changes soon, I'm gonna get out!

Within the year, the American League would adopt the designated hitter rule and in the 1973 season set a new attendance record of 13,433,605—up almost two million from 1972. Somebody was reading and listening. You couldn't miss the voice, the intonation, the sell, the build-up. Color uniforms in 1963, white shoes in 1967, night World Series games in 1971, the designated hitter in 1973. Not yet a three-ball walk, orange baseball, or designated runner. Not yet . . .

*An unidentified A's veteran* (in 1968): We got a fellow from the Yankees a couple years ago, and when the clubhouse man handed him all those crazy uniforms he looked as though they were asking him to go out on the field stark naked. He kept hiding behind things.

"It used to be," the Owner was telling a fellow from *Sports Illustrated* in 1965, "that all cars were black. Now you almost never see a black car. The colors don't make cars run better, but they sure sell better." And, to a *Life* lad in 1968: "No supermarket tries to sell anything in plain packages. Why should baseball be different? Look at hockey uniforms. Look at football uniforms. Now, there are people who object to our white shoes. But imagine playing *tennis* in black shoes." Or, to another *Sports Illustrated* man in 1972: "When I first came out with our green and gold suits and the white shoes, all those owners threw up their hands and cried, 'What is the man doing to our beloved game!' Now just look at the way they're dressing their teams."

It came to pass, and the color was better. In 1963, American League owners patronized Charlie, granted his cry for hues. Kansas City disposed of the traditional home whites and road grays. Kansas City played its baseball games in "wedding gown" white and Kelly green and "Fort Knox" gold and "Pacific Ocean misty" green. On Sunday you wear this. On the road you wear that. In second games of double-headers you change to something else. Mix, match, play. The other clubs suggested the A's resembled a girls' softball team. "I remember when we first came out with those godawful looking yellow things," says Ted Bowsfield. "The Yankees laughed us right off the field. Those uniforms were just horrible at first. But now it's the accepted thing. Everybody's looking for more color."

"The uniforms were kind of a bother," says Chuck Dobson. "We had green sweatshirts, gold sweatshirts, white hats, green hats, gold pants, white pants, green pants, white shirt, gold shirt, green shirt. Sometimes we didn't know what we were supposed to look like."

There was that initial ridicule. Well, let 'em laugh; the embarrassment of the laughter would be more palatable to the Owner than switching back to the whites and grays. A return to "tradition" would have been the admission of a mistake. The Owner does not make mistakes. The others would come around— even if it meant compounding his rebellion by shodding his players in "albino kangaroo" in 1967.

"I remember Jim Nash was pitching on opening day against Cleveland," says Lew Krausse. "Nash had a big, high kick and right away the hitter, Jose Cardenal, called time out and said he couldn't see the ball because of the white shoes."

"But, you know," says Dobson, "we liked the novelty of the white shoes when we first got 'em. We thought we looked good in them, too. We were a bunch of young guys who just liked to be novel. We even voted on wearing white when we had a choice."

Ex-Athletic Deron Johnson recalls, "Over in the National League there used to be some kidding when the A's first started wearing their white shoes. But then we went to red ones when I was playing for Philadelphia. When the Phillies sent me to Oakland, I really didn't give any thought to the color of uniforms or shoes. I just wanted to get the fuck to the A's and play for a winner." Perspective.

"Finley's uniforms," says Cedric Tallis, "created the atmosphere that enabled many of us in this business to maybe be a little more daring in our own uniform selection." Tallis, however, has no truck with another of Charlie's color creations—an orange baseball. He says, "When they get an orange cow, they'll probably have an orange baseball. They'd have to make some careful studies as far as visibility."

*Finley:* The Army dresses our ski troops in white so nobody can see them. In baseball, we fire a white ball out of a white uniform [in many cases, still] under a bright sky. Suddenly we realize that's dangerous and make the players wear helmets. Why not an orange baseball that everybody can see? [He suggested "electric" orange.]

Every so often, he would have his players toss an orange ball around the infield between innings. They flipped it good-naturedly, but they did not want to bat against it. "Hard for the hitter to see," said Gene Tenace. "It'll just screw up the ballplayers," said Deron Johnson.

Derision, laughter. Again.

"I think there's a possibility Charlie's theory of an orange baseball will come to pass," says Baltimore's Cashen.

In the spring of 1974, Sean Downey, Jr., was attempting to piece together a new professional baseball league, the World Baseball Association. He said his league would use orange baseballs. "Instead of saying here comes the old apple," he said, "they'll be saying here comes the old orange."

If Charlie had his druthers, they might be saying here comes the old orange, ball three, walk. The Owner's Innovation of the Year Club was offering as an alternate selection in 1971 a lowering of the requirements for a walk from four balls to three. Charlie anticipated fewer wasteful pitches, more baserunners, more scoring, more pro football-type offense. Thus, an experiment in spring training. Alvin Dark, then managing Cleveland, went along willingly in exhibition games. Alvin would say later—after being rehired by the Owner—that he admired Charlie because "he was always willing to take a chance, and if an idea wasn't his own he'd run with it, anyway."

Not so willing to cooperate with Finley that spring was California Angel general manager Dick Walsh. He claimed there was no official sanction for the three-ball exhibition game, but Charlie convinced the umpire crew that he had league permission.

Walsh phoned Finley, then quickly hung up. "I'm not talking to him anymore," Walsh said later. "He called me a fucking idiot."

Finley would contend he said no such thing to Mr. Walsh. "What I told him was to quit *acting* like a fucking idiot."

There were nineteen walks in each of the two exhibition games against Cleveland, sixteen in the embittered afternoon with the Angels. The games had not been excessively long, but Commissioner Bowie Kuhn decided against further experimentation, even on a minor league level. Too many walks, he said. And Charlie shifted his campaigning from balls to bats. And feet.

> *Fan letter to the* Sporting News: What makes baseball unique is that nine men are required to play on both offense and defense. The American League owners have sold themselves out in an attempt to draw fans. The game will suffer.
> *Joe DiMaggio:* I think it's great. It's a change, and if there's anything baseball needs it's a change.

The designated hitter rule, adopted by American League owners on January 11, 1973, in an 8–4 vote, was the most significant rule change in baseball since Bob Newhart answered that telephone call from a Mr. Doubleday. (Actually, eighty years.) The more commercially successful National League, via president Chub Feeney, tended to scoff at the radicalism of their AL brethren. "It will take something away from the game," said Feeney, suggesting that a man who did nothing but bat was not a complete baseball player. On the other hand, pitchers had a batting average of .145 in 1972—102 points lower than nonpitchers. These batting pitchers struck out 1,705 times, which clearly made them complete ballplayers. The designated hitter, or dh, or desi, would bat in the place of the pitcher in 1973 and, league-wide, average .257. The batting average of the entire

American League rose from .239 in 1972 to .259 in 1973 thanks to the incomplete ballplayers. An average of about one and a half more runs a game were scored in the American League in 1973. The designated hitters themselves may have been bored between times at bat (one of them would listen to the radio in the clubhouse), but their presence did reduce tedium in the stands.

The change, bandied by some baseball men after too many drinks (and in whispers) during World War II, was effective, albeit tardy. It had taken the big league owners four years to ponder the results of a dh test in a minor league (International). Purists move slowly. Too slowly for Charlie, who deserves some credit—not total—for thumping for a dh.

Frank Lane, Finley's first general manager at Kansas City in 1961, says, "I had been for the dh for fifteen years and couldn't get a real vote on the damn thing. Then Charlie came along and helped get the rule. He put the blessing on it, and I have to give him credit for getting the league to accept it."

"I can't sit here and tell you that Finley was the guy who originally dreamed up the dh, but he certainly was one of the people in the forefront of it. A champion of it," says Baltimore's Cashen. "But the dh would have come to pass, anyway."

Leonard Koppett of the *New York Times*, the nation's most studious, yet wry baseball writer, remembers hearing dh talk "in the late fifties, when Ted Williams was getting old. And it became a revived idea. Charlie Finley didn't think it up but he deserves credit for advocating his point of view strongly from a position of power. Others in power didn't."

The Owner's advocacy put him in a curious bind. Before the rule was passed, he had released a potential designated hitter, weak-kneed Orlando Cepeda, who would catch on as the Boston dh in 1973. And a season earlier, Charlie had relieved himself of excellent pinch-hitter Tommy Davis, who would become the

Baltimore dh in 1973 and lead all the specialists in batting (.306, eighty-nine runs batted in). The A's were nearly a month into the first dh season without a dh type, so Charlie had to obtain veteran Deron Johnson from the Philadelphia Phillies. Deron would later say, "I liked the dh rule even before I came to the American League. It's good for baseball." Johnson made it good for Finley, too, in the 1973 season.

> *Calvin Griffith:* You know, just before the time we approved the dh, Charlie almost killed it. He said he didn't want the dh unless he could have a designated pinch runner rule, too.

The American League owners rejected a proposal to permit a designated pinch runner at the same time they approved the dh. The rejection was a blow to Charlie for he had been developing the atmosphere for this new baseball creature since 1967, when he first promoted fleet Allan Lewis to the Kansas City Athletics. Lewis was not a bad minor league hitter and just a fair outfielder. But he—thanks to Charlie's propaganda—became a celebrated runner and spent parts of six seasons with the A's.

Players and managers were bitter about Lewis' presence on a major league roster. "Charlie thought it was a good promotion idea," says team captain Sal Bando. "But from a player's point of view it's a terrible idea. It takes good men out of close ball games. And Allan Lewis couldn't even run that well. He had no knowledge of running the bases. The idea of a designated runner is sound, but not the Allan Lewis way."

Allan Lewis was a mere glint in 1967–73. American League rejection or no, Charlie would, in 1974, creep in with his personal designated runner on the little cat feet of one Herbie Washington.

> *A's press release* (mid-March, 1974): The Oakland A's announce the signing of Herb Washington, the world's fastest human.

Washington holds the world record in the fifty-yard dash of five seconds flat, which he set in 1971, and also holds the world record of 5.8 seconds for sixty yards, which he set in 1972. . . . He spent four years on the Michigan State University track team and two on the football team as a wide receiver. . . . A's Manager Alvin Dark has always known Oakland owner Charles O. Finley's feelings regarding the value of having a pinch runner and agrees with the importance of such a player. As a matter of fact, Dark stated to Finley (a few days ago) that he should go out and try to get the world's fastest human, Herb Washington. . . . Both Finley and Dark feel that Washington will be directly responsible for winning ten games this year.

*Herb Washington* (who had not played baseball since his sophomore year in high school, some eight years before signing with the A's): I wouldn't have been more surprised if the Milwaukee Bucks had called. I'd had very little baseball experience. I never thought that something like this would come about. But if Charlie Finley felt that I could contribute to his team, then okay.

Washington said published reports that he received a bonus of thirty thousand dollars and a season's contract of twenty-five thousand dollars were "reasonably accurate." He would not say he had a "no cut" contract but did say, "if you're really gonna see how effective I'm gonna be, I need at least a year. I'll be around for the World Series."

Maury Wills, retired stealer of five hundred bases, was hired to coach Washington for six days at the A's training camp in Mesa, Arizona. Wills felt that "maybe Herb will win five games for the A's by taking an extra base that no one else could have taken or scoring from third on a sacrifice that no one else could have scored on. Five games is a lot. That's how Finley thinks. He knows how to win. This is just an experiment. It may not work and then he'll drop it. But at least he has the courage to try. No one else does."

Herbie Washington needed more courage than the Owner. In the first few weeks of the season, the pinch-running specialist was making a fool of himself. He was being caught stealing more often than not. And picked off first base. He was an embarrassment to baseball; fans, writers, teammates were laughing at him. He would say later, "I had a crude and shaky start. If I wasn't strong-willed and didn't believe in myself, I would have packed up and left. I knew I wasn't being welcomed into the clubhouse with open arms. Finally at a team meeting I said, 'Hey, there are a lot of things that have been written and said about me by you guys. All I want is some consistency. Don't laugh and joke with me to my face and then say bad things to the press about me. Either you like me or you don't like me. I can accept that.' Things began to loosen up after that meeting. I think they realized that I wasn't going to take any shit from anybody."

But several of the players continued to talk behind his back. Whenever a player was sent to the minors, some Athletic would grumble that it was a shame that an all-round player would have to leave while Herbie was permitted to stay. They called him "Freak," for he was not a baseball player. He did not bat. He did not field. He ran—with more intelligence by late summer, but still not expertly. He admitted he had much to learn about "getting the jump" on pitchers and sliding. Herbie would dive head-first, without any feints, and fielders would be waiting for him at the bag. He would come close to his goal of thirty stolen bases, and he would be partially responsible for three or four Oakland victories. But he would not be totally accepted.

*Billy Martin* (manager of the Texas Rangers): Herb Washington didn't bother me. I wouldn't be surprised if Finley threw a jackass out there.

If the mulish metaphor fits, the Owner has not minded wearing it. In most matters, he is the tenacious, stubborn insurance salesman. After writing a letter about weekend-weeknight World Series games and weekend season openers to then Commissioner Ford Frick in 1963, Charlie oozed the notion in every major interview. To many, the idea seemed to belong to Finley. But not in the view of the baseball Establishment.

The Series and opening day revisions were "suggested way back," says Calvin Griffith. "But Charlie did bring them into focus, brought these things to our attention. Old Charlie most likely would be able to sell Alcatraz back to the government as a prison. I kid him. I say, 'Charlie, you come up with all these ideas that a fellow named Larry McPhail used to talk about when he was playing night games in Cincinnati in the thirties.' "

Baltimore's Cashen calls Finley "just one of the people who backed the weekend-weeknight World Series. A lot of people had talked about it for years. Why, back in the middle sixties some of the daytime weekday Series games weren't selling out. So we started talking about playing at night to help sell tickets as well as exposing our game to a maximum of people."

Kansas City's Tallis takes the middle ground. "I'm sure many people mentioned the Series changes at some time or another, but you have to give Charlie Finley credit for creating the impetus that resulted in the new schedule. He was the first to come out vocally and strongly for the changes. And the changes were very desirable."

National League president Chub Feeney calls Finley "the most vociferous supporter of the idea. But it was not original with him. I don't remember who originated the thought. But it was Bowie Kuhn who got it done. It's not what you'd call a tough idea to come up with."

If you wish to be practical about the Series schedule shift,

*Charlie gave pitcher Vida Blue a day and a Caddy as the young southpaw tormented the league in 1971. But a few months later, the Owner wasn't in a giving mood at all. Blue signed only after the commissioner intervened.*

*Aspiring manager Finley has a glinty-eyed assessment for titular manager Dick Williams during '72 season. Waiting for a mandate in the Oakland dugout are catcher Dave Duncan (hatless) and third baseman-captain Sal Bando (clearly pensive).*

*Dick Williams, manager.*

*...fielder Joe Rudi made ...ic catches in Series ...es in '72 and '73. But at ...y arbitration time in ...Finley said that "just ...Joe" was inadequate ...nsively and really ...t deserve a raise. The ...rator agreed, leaving ...morose.*

Finley figured Rick Monday wou[l]
the A's big hero in Oakland, but R[eggie]
Jackson (taking a big cut, above[) was]
the club's surprise budding supe[r.]
Reg was so good in 1969 that C[harlie]
considered sending him back t[o the]
minors in 1970. The Owner sent in[felder]
Mike Andrews even farther away [in]
Game Two of the '73 Series. Mike [who]
was acutely dejected after makin[g two]
errors in one inning of that game. [A few]
minutes later, Andrews became a[n even]
more tragic figure—declared by a [team]
doctor and Finley as physically [unfit]
to continue playing in the Serie[s. The]
commissioner changed Charlie's [story]
and Andrews emerged as a martyr [who]
later sued Finley.

es Augustus (Catfish)
ter was grabbed off a
olina farm by the
er, fed milk shakes
groomed to become
eague's finest pitcher.
ch, by 1974, he was.
r that season, however,
arbitrator ruled that
lie had breached Jim's
ract—and Hunter
nly took $3.75 million
oin the New York
ees.

ie Washington may be
y's best-known "toy."
ie was a world-class
er turned pinch run-
n Oakland in 1974.
all he did—run. And
with lack of baseball
    Teammates grum-
about Herbie's high
. But Washington
the pay, and Charlie
he bizarre excitement
tolen-base attempt.

Somewhere behind the Oakland dugout, glee concealed under smoked glass, is the Owner and General Manager at World Series time. Everybody around him is waving an A's pennant because he has made sure that everybody around him has been given an A's pennant. His straw-hatted Dixieland combo adds to the aura of utter Finleyana.

Another day, another world's title for the Oakland A's. Charlie wanted six World Series championships in a row, to snap the Yankee record. At least that's what he said for the record. In truth, he wanted an infinite number of world championships in a row.

*Charles Oscar Finley—a winner in 1973. His health was slipping, his manager quitting, his wife not far from estrangement, his most significant insurance client on the brink of departure. But the Owner was continuing to win. He was showing 'em. He had to.*

believe that Kuhn initiated weekend starts to accommodate television. And the change from weekday games to weeknights? "Monday night football on TV showed the kind of audience that was available," says the *New York Times'* Koppett, who wonders if that available audience has truly been a blessing for the status of the World Series. "The impact of weekday Series games may not have been as great in terms of rating numbers, but there was more talk, more interruption—in offices, schools, on the street. In the daytime during the week, the World Series was more of a special thing."

Baseball itself used to be more of a special thing, before professional football built better mousetraps. Why, in 1924, before the heresy of a Finley, Brooklyn shocked ministerial associations by playing a game on a Sunday. Easter Sunday. It was opening day. Maybe Charlie read about that in the library.

In one of his published hard sells for an orange baseball, Charlie demanded, "We need a commissioner who is not afraid, who has enough red blood to stand up for what is right." He has endured three baseball commissioners—Ford Frick, William Eckert, Bowie Kuhn—without discovering enough red blood to satisfy him. (Although Bela Lugosi, on a good shooting day, might not have been sufficiently insatiable for Charlie.) Since the days of Judge Landis, there has been widespread doubt about the independence of the commissioner of baseball. Charlie, who treats current commissioner Bowie Kuhn with the same respect he would show, say, one of his switchboard operators, would be pleased with the appraisal of Kuhn by an A's pitcher, Ken Holtzman.

"In my opinion, Kuhn is a figurehead. A man hired by the owners. He has absolutely no authority whatsoever. As far as I'm concerned, Mr. Finley's squabbles with Bowie Kuhn mean absolutely zilch. If Mr. Finley wants to get a rule changed or something, he's not going to talk to Bowie Kuhn first. He's going to talk to some of the owners—O'Malley, Busch, Hoffberger, Wrigley. What the hell do you have to talk to Kuhn for?" On behalf of Charlie and the entire A's organization, thank you, Ken Holtzman.

Your turn, Sal Bando. "Charlie goes more by what he feels is right and not what's *supposed* to be right. If he feels that challenging the commissioner is the right thing, he goes ahead and does it despite what the Establishment might say. And I think he's right. I think he feels he has the power to back up what he says."

Former A's pitcher Dobson respects Charlie "for bucking the commissioner. He pays that guy. Why should Charlie put up with that?"

On the other hand, Ted Kubiak, A's infielder: "I don't hold much respect for Kuhn, but I can't respect Mr. Finley for the way he talks to the man who's supposed to be *his* boss. He doesn't like anybody cutting *him* down."

Sportswriter Ron Bergman reads Finley's chronic displeasure with the commissioner as Charlie's fear-hatred of losing. "If the rules stand in his way, that's just too bad. He just wants to get what he wants to get. To this day, he says he didn't fire Mike Andrews. Why, Kuhn hates Finley so much he doesn't want to talk to him at all." If the Owner has placed himself above the commissioner, why not try to become the commissioner? Now there would be a surplus of red blood.

> *Frank Cashen:* I think we all sometimes don't do what the commissioner or the league presidents want done. I don't feel that we all have to bow down to the commissioner. But I don't think Charlie would make a good commissioner. I don't think he could learn to live with twenty-four people [the owners]. Charlie is very deep with his own convictions and he believes that his thoughts are right and should predominate. It would be very difficult for him to be an effective commissioner.

*Cedric Tallis:* He's not constitutionally equipped to be the commissioner of baseball. He's too aggressive and competitive to be that objective.

*Calvin Griffith:* Charlie has too many radical ideas. He might even want to have specialized umpires. And no one umpire could continually squat down there behind home plate day in and day out. That's a difficult job.

*Finley* (to United Press International, 1972): Why would I want to be the commissioner? What the hell, I own my team. I've got my own business.

But what is it, really? Selling? Innovating? Promoting? Out-Veecking Veeck? Stitching a baseball in the shape of the profile of Charles O. Finley?

The Establishment remains wary. They do not see him as a great promoter (a belief he fancies) because he does not sell that many seats. They acknowledge that he has people talking baseball but wonder if it's positive chatter. They admit he's put together a helluva ball club but wonder if it can hold up under all those internal pressures. They say he *encourages* innovation but does little original thinking. And they persist in questioning his motives.

*Question:* Hasn't all the publicity he's gotten—whether good or bad—brought attention to the game?
*National League president Chub Feeney:* Or to Finley?

That's what they ask when they answer. That's what they asked in the days when they used to have to answer questions about Bill Veeck.

And then, in 1974, *Sport* magazine asked Bill Veeck about Charlie. Bill Veeck admitted ambivalence. "He at least is willing to try something. But he usually manages to louse up whatever he tries. He just does things without class. But at least he tries things. No one else does. It's a phenomenon to be innovative in baseball."

CHAPTER **XI**

# THE ANDREWS CASE
# AND THE WILLIAMS
# DEPARTURE

On the first Saturday of October, 1973, two young men were standing in front of the Baltimore Hilton Hotel trying to hail a taxicab. Milling around the hotel's entrance were a half dozen youngsters, waiting to get autographs of members of the Oakland Athletics, in town for the American League playoff series with the Orioles. A taxi was not immediately available, so the two men just stood around eyeing the traffic. The kids just stood around eyeing the door to the lobby. Finally, after a wait of about twenty minutes, the two men pounced on a cab. Pat Bourque, a reserve first baseman for the A's, and Mike Andrews, a utility infielder with the club, sped off to dinner. One of the boys watched the two depart and quickly turned his attention back to the hotel, but not before asking another man standing nearby, "Hey, mister, see any ballplayers around?"

On the last Friday of October, 1973, baseball commissioner Bowie K. Kuhn sent the following memorandum—inscribed as "private and confidential"—to Charlie O. Finley.

During the World Series, I brought to your attention various matters which I said I would consider at the conclusion of the Series.

First, the Oakland Club authorized a public address announcement during Game 1, the sole purpose of which was to embarrass the New York Club for its unwillingness to approve an Oakland roster change. Further, the announcement was made in deliberate defiance of instructions by John Johnson of my office that no such announcement be made.

Second, Game 2 was delayed because the field lights were turned on by the Oakland Club though no direction to do so had been received from the umpires. This was in direct violation of both World Series and regular season procedure well known to the Oakland Club.

Third, the Oakland Club submitted to me a letter dated October 14, 1973, and signed by Dr. Harry Walker stating that Mike Andrews was disabled. This letter was also signed by Andrews beneath a sentence reading "I agree to the above." I am satisfied that Andrews had advised you he did not believe he was disabled, but was nonetheless persuaded by you to sign a statement which you know he believed to be false. This statement by Andrews was then urged upon me by the Oakland Club as a reason for replacing Andrews on your World Series squad.

I find that in these instances, the Oakland Club was guilty of calculated and intentional misconduct in callous disregard of the best interests of Baseball.

I further find that you personally were the guiding force behind this misconduct.

Under Major League Rule 50 (a), which may be applicable to the first two of the above offenses, my authority to impose fines is limited to $1,000 per violation. I clearly am not so limited in relation to the third offense, as to which a $5,000 limit applies. Because of the deliberate nature of the misconduct in all three instances, I have determined to impose the maximum permissible fines.

Accordingly, the Oakland Club is hereby directed to remit the sum of $7,000.00, its check to be received here not later than Thursday, November 1, 1973. I also determine that you personally shall be placed on probation until further notice, and warn you that further conduct not in the best interests of Baseball may lead to disciplinary action against you as provided in Article I of the Major League Agreement.

There was no "best regards" or "yours very truly" or "sincerely." Just the signature of Bowie K. Kuhn.

The Owner had to anticipate trouble with Bowie Kuhn over Mike Andrews. He had to figure that he just might not be able to get away with it. And what could happen if he failed? A censure? Or a fine? A little bad publicity, maybe? Surely there was nothing to lose. But if he could pull it off, why, from his point of view, it truly would help the ball club. He could get Manny Trillo, a decent glove, in the lineup and then perhaps lock up this World Series. What difference could it possibly make? Everything was connected with winning, and Oakland had a better chance to win with Manny Trillo on the bench than with Mike Andrews. Sound baseball, that's all. Sound, winning baseball. So try, because if you don't try, you don't know.

And he tried. And he found out. He had totally underestimated the results, the potential titanic embarrassment. Charlie Finley "disabled" Mike Andrews and was drawn and quartered in twenty-two million American homes. On a Wednesday. At night. The precise time he always knew would be in the best interests of baseball.

 *Finley* (in a letter to commissioner of baseball Ford C. Frick, dated November 7, 1963): What are we doing to indicate our appreciation of the working man's support? What are we doing to attract and sustain the interest of today's children for their future support? What are we doing to attract NEW FANS to baseball? I am, of course, speaking exclusively of the present scheduling and televising of the World Series. The answer is nothing—ABSO-LUTELY NOTHING. In essence, we have been saying for years to the working man, "Thanks, friend, we appreciate your support during the season and now that it's time to stage America's Greatest Sports Spectacle, we are going to stage it at the most inconvenient and unreasonable time for you to see it. We are going to start it on a Wednesday afternoon when you are working at the steel mills, coal mines, factories, or offices. You can get the details when you get home from work." We are also saying to today's children, tomor-row's baseball fans, "Boys and girls, we love you too—we are starting the World Series when you too can't see it—you are all back in school." My suggestion is to . . . play the first and second games on Saturday and Sunday afternoons. Travel on Monday. Play the third, fourth, and fifth games at night—Tuesday, Wednesday, and Thursday. . . . This arrangement would make it possible for almost everyone . . . *to see the entire World Series.* . . .

That's the way it was starting in 1971. By the time Game Four of the 1973 World Series came along in Shea Stadium on the night of October 17, the working men and school children of America were conditioned to seeing America's Greatest Sports Spectacle at a convenient, reasonable time.

The 1973 World Series was not Mike Andrews' first. He was Boston's regular second baseman in their 1967 Series loss to St. Louis and batted .308. Two years later he was named to the American League All Star team. He was a boyishly handsome southern Californian, the sort of fellow a teenaged girl would love to have living next door. He seemed aptly typecast for baseball stardom, but it just didn't work out that way. His best season in the major leagues was 1969; two years later Boston traded him to the Chicago White Sox, and by the start of the 1973 season he was no longer considered a front-liner. Kansas City Royal general manager Cedric Tallis said that "all of us knew at the start of 1973 that Mike Andrews could not throw." There was big league gossip about a chronic shoulder problem; the White Sox intended to use Andrews mainly as a designated hitter.

Mike was not happy with the Chicago situation and did not sign a new contract with them in '73, instead playing under the terms of his old contract. Despite a strong first few weeks, he was unproductive at bat (.201) and on July 10, the day after his thirtieth birthday, was given his outright release by Chicago. His major league career apparently was over.

Dick Williams, Andrews' manager in the good years at Boston, had tried at least once to bring Mike to Oakland. But somehow, possibly because of Andrews' high salary (just under fifty thousand dollars), a deal never was made. But then at the end of July, when the A's were foundering and in danger of dropping out of first place in the American League's Western Division, the Owner saw the necessity of making several deals. Within twenty-four hours, Charlie picked up three veterans. On July 31 he bought outfielder Jesus Alou from Houston. On August 1 he purchased Vic Davalillo from Pittsburgh and signed a free agent named Mike Andrews, who was the first of the three to report.

Andrews played in eighteen games for Oakland and ended the regular season with an overall batting average of .200. He saw action in two of the five American League playoff games against Baltimore, was hitless in one official at bat and made a brief appearance on defense—at first base. He did not figure to be any sort of factor in the upcoming World Series.

> *Mike Andrews:* When I came to Oakland, Dick told me he would use me strictly as a pinch hitter or designated hitter. I was very disappointed in the fact I didn't play much as a dh. I thought I'd be used more. So when the Series came along, I saw myself then as

strictly a pinch hitter and bullpen catcher. That's what I figured on. I don't think I'd played an inning of second base for about at least a month before the Series. They were using me strictly as a pinch hitter, and they had Trillo.

Manny Trillo, a spare, silent Venezuelan, was Finley's second baseman of the future, whenever Dick Green decided to retire for real. He was summoned from Tucson early in September, 1973, and singled in a run in his first big league at bat. Another Latin arrived about the same time as Trillo, the itinerant pinch-running favorite of Finley, Allan "The Panamanian Express" Lewis. Williams nearly giggled when he told newsmen, "Oh, yes, and we're bringing up Lewis again." Lewis' value as an all-round baseball player is best evidenced by the fact that he batted only twenty-nine times in the 156 major league games in which he appeared over the portions of half a dozen seasons for the Athletics; in those 156 games, he played on defense (outfield) ten times. Herb Washington's predecessor was clearly there to run. Charlie loved having him around.

Lewis had slipped onto the A's World Series roster in 1972. But because he did not join the '73 club until after September 1, "The Express" would not be eligible for postseason play again. Not unless there was an injury, and only if the opposition agreed.

On September 18, the A's sold a bulky catcher named Jose Morales to the Montreal Expos. Morales had come to Oakland from Tucson in August. Morales would have been eligible for any playoff or Series games, and now the Oakland roster for those big games had an opening. Maybe. There was chatter that Finley had dealt Jose to make room for "The Express." Well, let's wait and see.

The waiting took only two days. Regular center fielder Bill North tripped over first base in Minnesota on September 20 and severely sprained his right ankle. There was pessimism about his availability for the playoffs and Series, a correct diagnosis as it turned out. And Allan Lewis had himself a roster spot.

But wait. There was still the Morales-induced opening. How about Manny Trillo?

The A's and Baltimore agreed that Manny could play for Oakland in the playoffs as long as the Orioles could fill a roster opening of their own. (Trivia fans will recall the use of catcher Sergio Robles for the injured Elrod Hendricks.) Trillo was okay for the playoffs, but was not used in any of the five games. The Series was another matter. Lewis could sub for the injured North, sure, but the National League, standing firmly and properly on Rule 40, denied the A's permission to use Trillo for Morales. Thus the public address announcement at the first Series game about those nasty, nasty Mets stopping Manny Trillo from playing, the announcement that cost Charlie a grand.

Oakland was playing the Mets with twenty-four men, although one of the A's said, "Hell, with Lewis, it's just like having twenty-three."

And then there were twenty-two.

In the sixth inning of Game Two of the 1973 World Series, Angel Mangual batted for A's regular second baseman Dick Green. Ted Kubiak played the position in the seventh inning and was pinch hit for in the eighth. By Mike Andrews. Who remained in the game. At second base, a position he had played in only fifteen games in the 1973 season.

> *Mike Andrews:* When I had to go in at second, I wouldn't say I was really uptight or nervous. I thought I might be because I hadn't played there much. But I'd been taking ground balls at second base in practice just about every day. Although it's not like being in a game.

The score was tied at 6–6 in the twelfth inning. With two out and two runners on, forty-two-year-old Willie Mays grounded a single through the middle to put the Mets ahead. Mays, once the classic center fielder, had botched two plays in the outfield earlier, and later said in the clubhouse, "It's hard to get the feel of the game when you don't play too often."

Now it was Andrews' turn to get the feel of the game. After Mays' single, another base hit loaded the bases for New York. Then John Milner bounced a ground ball toward Mike Andrews. The ball hopped right through Mike's legs, and two runs scored. The next batter grounded to Andrews near second base, and Mike's throw to first was wide—another run scoring. On two plays, Andrews had cost his club three runs and, as it turned out, the ball game, as Oakland ended up with a 10–7 defeat in the longest World Series game (four hours, thirteen minutes) in history.

> *Mike Andrews:* When I did make the errors it was more a case of mistiming than being nervous. I wasn't nervous at all.

The Series was tied at a game apiece, and in the clubhouse the players were packing for their trip to New York.

Andrews' packing was interrupted by a message to go into the trainer's room for a medical examination. He said later that he couldn't understand the summons and hesitated before going in.

A few feet from the trainer's room, where Dr. Harry Walker was probing Andrews' right arm and shoulder, the Owner was talking to Dick Williams in the manager's office. Talking about a roster change the Owner had in mind.

Finley then ascended to his own office and was joined there by Dr. Walker, secretary Roberta Johnson, and administrative assistant John Claiborne. While Andrews was showering and shaving in the clubhouse, Finley was dictating a memorandum saying that Mike's shoulder was in such a state of disrepair that he could not possibly finish out the World Series. The memo took the form of a doctor's report, and the Owner took it down to Williams' office. Andrews was called in and found Finley, Williams, and Claiborne waiting for him. Andrews said later that Finley immediately began a sales pitch—saying that Mike's removal from the roster would benefit the club because a young, healthy Manny Trillo could now be added to the roster. Would Mike sign this medical report and show his team spirit? He would not. Would he go up two flights to Finley's office and talk some more? He would.

> Mike Andrews: The only thing Dick Williams told me was "do what you feel is best for yourself." I assumed that if I didn't sign that piece of paper I wouldn't be back with the A's. I figured I was dead one way or the other, that even if I signed I wouldn't play with Oakland again.

Andrews said Finley did not threaten him. There was just the continual talk, the Finley hard sell, on an athlete suddenly confronted with a bizarre request, an athlete still dazed and down from making two costly errors.

At one point, Andrews interrupted the Finley dissertation to ask if by signing the medical report he would still be an Athletic in 1974. Finley could not give that guarantee. Mike later said that Finley's pitch simply wore him down, and he signed, "I agree to the above." The team bus left without him. Andrews went home to Peabody, Massachusetts, instead of to New York. By noon the next day, the world was informed that Mike Andrews had been "fired" for making two errors. And the games became incidental.

The press charter reached Kennedy in the middle of the night following Game Two. Dick O'Connor of the Palo Alto *Times* and I were assigned to a modest room on the same floor as the A's players in the Americana Hotel. We couldn't understand the reason for an early morning phone call to our room. The caller asked for Mike Andrews. Wrong room. Actually, it was the right room but a substitution had been made. O'Connor and Michelson had been sent in to pinch-sleep for Andrews. During the next four days, we would be getting several phone calls for Andrews. And Bowie Kuhn would be making several phone calls *about* Andrews. There was no way the commissioner or the National League or the Mets or anybody was going to buy the plot to put Manny Trillo on the Oakland roster.

> *Sal Bando:* That's a joke. I've seen some bush things on this club, but this is going too far.
> *Reggie Jackson:* All that nonbaseball stuff takes the little boy out of you.
> *Joe Rudi:* Sure makes it difficult to go in with just twenty-three men.
> *Ted Kubiak:* Nothing really surprises me anymore. This sort of thing happens with this club every year.

Newsmen recorded the players' grousing in the lobby, then followed them to Shea Stadium. A Monday afternoon workout was scheduled—in uniform. In uniforms bearing makeshift black armbands on which had been pinned the number 17. Mike Andrews' number.

> *Dick Green:* I was the one who started putting Mike's number on our sleeves that day. I told Charlie, because I've always been honest with him. But when I told him, he said he knew it already. I did the number thing for a joke. I certainly didn't know it would be treated like it was. I didn't know what the press in New York was like at World Series time. I'm sure Charlie was absolutely embarrassed by

the Andrews thing. He said to me that he got fifty thousand dollars worth of bad publicity out of it—and that it will always be there. So from that comment, I assumed he regretted it. I guess he just didn't think that Mike could do the job and that we needed another ballplayer to take his place. Charlie really doesn't care about individuals *now*. He'll do anything to win, and the Andrews case is an example right there.

"Winning" was the motive. That was the analysis of many of the A's players after they had had a winter to reflect.

On Tuesday Bowie Kuhn said the dismissal of Andrews was a disgrace to the game and to Mike Andrews. Kuhn said Mike should come back and play. Finley said he'd try to find him.

On the bus ride to Shea that afternoon, one of the A's said, "Everybody at the ball park will be shouting, 'We want Andrews.' So let's make a sign that says, 'So do we.'"

And A's first baseman Gene Tenace said, "A guy makes two errors and becomes a household word."

Andrews was not at Shea for Game Three. He was home in Peabody, not quite certain if he wanted to rejoin the ball club. He phoned the A's clubhouse and spoke with Jackson and pitcher Jim Hunter. They said he told them he would come to New York if he could tell his side of the story.

The clubhouse was very busy that night. The players had a meeting to talk about the Andrews case. One said there was no discussion of stunts or boycotts or official complaints. "We all just talked about the way we felt," said one of the pitchers. "Even though Mike wasn't with us too long, we all like him."

Jackson said that Andrews thanked everybody for sticking up for him. "I told him over the phone," said Reggie, "that sometimes all of us have to be men and stand up to Finley on this kind of thing. It's a shame we have to be bothered with this during the

World Series. It cuts a man's brain right down the middle. But what's right is right. We're not trying to beat Charlie on this issue. Hell, I don't need to beat Finley at anything."

> *Jim Hunter:* You've *got* to get involved in this kind of thing. What Charlie did hurt the team. More than that, it hurt baseball. And I don't like anything that hurts the game.

Several of the players thought that Finley might react to their statements by trading them. They said they didn't care. "All I want is peace," said Jackson. "San Diego sounds just fine to me," said Bando. "I think I've already been traded," said pitcher John Odom.

Somebody else truly was going to change clubs.

Shortly before the game, Dick Williams told his players that he was quitting immediately after the Series. Win or lose. He did not say he planned to work for the New York Yankees. Nor did he say the Andrews affair had any direct bearing on his resignation.

Early in 1974, however, Williams told a reporter that the Andrews business was the last straw. "That finished it. It was all off after that. My players were unhappy, to say the least, and I was caught in the middle."

He said he had told Finley in Oakland after the Sunday game, "Charlie, there's just about a ten percent chance of your getting away with a thing like this. You can't do it."

Andrews watched the A's win Game Three on television at the home of a neighbor. He was ready to come back.

> *Mike Andrews:* Finley called me at home. He didn't say that he wanted me to come to New York. All he said was that the commissioner had reinstated me and I *was* to come back.

His first stop in New York was the commissioner's office. Kuhn was trying to determine if Andrews had signed the doctor's memo under duress. He was making a thorough investigation and said he also would talk with "people in the Oakland organization."

From Kuhn's office, Andrews was escorted on foot to the Americana Hotel. Somebody sucked up all the newsmen in the lobby and swept them into a press conference in a hotel ballroom. Mike had an attorney with him as he told "his side."

> *Ken Holtzman:* None of this baseball stuff really seems too important anymore. I was sitting in the dugout before the third game and thinking about the war going on in the Middle East, and what happened to Mike, and just all kinds of human things. And you know, it is just very, very hard for me to care about playing in the World Series.

The chartered bus taking the Athletics to Shea Stadium for Game Four on Wednesday was parked at the side entrance to the Americana. Andrews slipped on early with Dick Williams and took a window seat near the back of the bus. When Mike boarded, the autograph seekers were all inside the lobby besieging the more recognizable Athletics for autographs. Andrews' name was every-where in New York, but he was physically anonymous.

Most of his teammates knew he was back with the club; none had seen him, though, until getting on the bus. Each new arrival would feign surprise, shake hands, ask questions, kid a little bit.

"Shame you had to come back," said relief pitcher Darold Knowles. "We already voted to split up your Series share between the rest of us."

Andrews was wearing the same lightweight suit in which he had left Oakland on Sunday evening. His trunk had by now been sent from the Americana's storage room to the A's clubhouse at Shea.

"They'll have to peel me out of this outfit," he said.

"Stop overdressing," said one of the players.

Vida Blue did a fake double take as he walked toward Andrews, and said, "Hey, man, where's my five?" Mike stuck out his hand, but Vida said he was talking about a football bet. Andrews paid.

The bus rolled now through the claustrophobic late afternoon traffic in midtown Manhattan. Shea was forty-five minutes away, but Mike was in no rush. He knew what was waiting there: more questions, more noise, more crowded confusion.

Catcher Ray Fosse shouted across the bus aisle to him, "Now, when we get on the field for practice, I want you to run out there to center field and fire that pea into me at the plate. Really stretch out that old shoulder, Mike. Show 'em your arm."

Mike smiled. He insisted his shoulder was just fine. He said the only reason he had trouble throwing was because he had been repeatedly told that he should have trouble throwing.

I remember writing "psychosomatic" in my steno notebook. Williams had said it was okay for me to ride along. Hell, by that stage, Dick didn't care too much about anything but ending the Series. Winning it, hopefully. Ending it, for sure. Play it, formally quit, go to work for the Yankees. And maybe, when it was convenient, do something for Mike.

When the bus pulled up to the players' entrance at Shea, Andrews grew perceptibly pale. He was not ready. Jim Hunter and Mike were among the last to get off—Hunter pretending he was going to shield the world-famous utility infielder.

Youngsters at the gate did not recognize Mike, but when the players streamed inside, Hunter told a long line of policemen guarding a corridor, "Here he is, boys. America's hero." And the cops whispered to each other that this must be that Andrews guy. You know, *him.*

In half an hour, Mike was uniformed and on the field. Instantly, he was devoured by media inquiries. He did not want to go into his press conference statement again, he said. He was sorry if they missed it, he said, but he was awfully tired of explaining.

Was that press conference the worst moment he ever had?

"No," he said quickly. "Signing that piece of paper was."

Ken Holtzman was the starting pitcher for Oakland in Game Four and didn't survive the first inning. By the eighth inning, the Mets led 6–1. The scheduled leadoff batter for Oakland in that inning was relief pitcher Horacio Pina. He did not bat.

> *Mike Andrews:* I was catching in the bullpen when Dick called me up to pinch hit. I remember somebody in the dugout saying about Dick, "He'll probably get fired for this." By the time I started to walk up to the plate, I was kind of numb to everything. I was kind of in a daze. It had been a long day.

The attendance at Game Four in Shea was 54,817. As Andrews came out of the dugout with a bat, only 54,810 people stood up to applaud and yell and smile. Charles O. Finley and his party remained seated. Finley did nothing for several seconds. Finally, he twirled his A's pennant over his head and into twenty-two million living rooms.

> *Jon Matlack* (Met pitcher in the eighth inning of Game Four): I was especially pleased to see Andrews come out of the dugout. I think everybody was almost anticipating that he would be the pinch hitter. The place really did go wild. It was quite an ovation—and quite a thing just to be in the ball park, let alone on the mound, when something like that happened. I took particular notice to look over at Mr. Finley, and he was just sorta sitting there and taking it all in. But his facial expression never did change. It was just a very inspiring moment, and I felt very happy for Andrews. I think he got a bad rap, and I was glad to see fifty-odd thousand New York fans showing that they thought so, too.

*Wayne Garrett* (Met third baseman): At a time like that, even though it's the opposing team and you're in the World Series, I was hoping that he would get a base hit. I was. I was just hoping that he'd do good. I could put myself in his place. There are probably a lot of ballplayers that've been right there in his position, and it isn't right. It isn't right what the owners and the management do to ballplayers. They don't deserve it. I think all the fans felt the same as the players. They were all against Finley, I guess. Seemed like everybody was.

*Reggie Jackson:* I wanted the guy to get a hit—just to show up Charlie, you know?

Matlack said he wasn't worried about Andrews. "I had a good lead and I was just gonna throw the ball over the plate and make him hit it—take the chance he might hit one out. But we'd still be in good shape." Matlack challenged him with a fast ball, and Andrews grounded to Wayne Garrett at third. Seven months later Garrett could not even remember that he had handled the ball.

Just a routine out. And Mike Andrews' final major league appearance.

*Mike Andrews:* Did I see Finley in the stands? Well, I knew he was sitting near the dugout someplace. I knew he was there, but I didn't look over there. And even if I had given it thought beforehand, before coming up to pinch hit, I wouldn't have given him the satisfaction of looking, anyhow. No, I didn't look.

After the seventh game of the Series in Oakland, Finley was in the clubhouse congratulating his champions. Including Mike Andrews. "He came by and said something like, 'Thanks, despite everything . . . thanks.' Something very passing. In other words, we won, so let's be happy. He did say thank you," said Mike.

Above Mike's locker in Oakland on October 21, 1973, was the

name Andrews and the number 17 scratched in felt-tip pen on a slash of white adhesive tape. The other Athletics had solid green identification plates adorning their cubicles.

"Doesn't make me feel too permanent," said Andrews.

In the few moments that I kibitzed with Mike that day, I noticed that no one else from the media stopped in front of his locker.

On October 26 Andrews was released by the Oakland Athletics. "I was kinda shocked it took *that* long," he said later.

Charles O. Finley appealed his fine in a hearing before the commissioner on November 16. "It's not the money," the Owner said, "just the principle. I intend to prove I didn't do anything detrimental to baseball." Shortly after the hearing, Kuhn refused to withdraw the fine. The implication of his edict was: One more bad move and Charlie Finley might have his franchise taken away.

Mike Andrews received a one-quarter World Series share, about six thousand dollars. "More than fair," he said. "All the guys on the team were super to me."

Early in 1974 he said that he had been given a clean bill of health in an examination by two Boston orthopedic specialists. He said he sent a copy of their report and a letter asking for a shot at a job to every major league club except the Chicago White Sox and the Oakland A's.

> *Mike Andrews:* Most of them wrote back and said they were set and they were going with the players they had. It was hard for me to conceive that none of them could use me. I know I'm better than some of the people playing in the majors this year. But I guess too much damage had been done because of my contract problems in Chicago and especially because of what happened in the Series. I guess people in baseball figure Andrews had a bad arm and bad publicity, so forget Andrews. Still, in a way I'm kind of mystified,

really. You know, when you get out of baseball, you kind of have to start your life all over again.

In the summer of 1974, Mike Andrews, father of three children, aged eleven, eight, and six, was attempting to get his own franchised tire dealership and was employed by the city of Boston to conduct baseball clinics. He also said he was contemplating a damage suit against Charles O. Finley.

A man who had no official connection with professional sports set in motion in the late summer of 1973 the conversations that would lead to Dick Williams' resignation as manager of the Oakland A's, eventual signing as manager of the New York Yankees, eventual unsigning as manager of the New York Yankees, and brief odyssey into baseball limbo.

Williams was indeed ready to quit; he was, as Reggie Jackson says, "up to here with Charlie." One day during that season, Dick was seated near an employee of Finley who was talking—rather, listening—to the Owner and General Manager over the telephone. The way the employee recalls the scene, he was catching an earful of abuse from Chicago. The invectives were so loud, even Dick could hear. After the conversation ended, Williams asked the other man: "I've never heard that from him before. Does he always talk to you like that?" The other fellow said, "To me and a lot of other people." He said that Williams appeared disgusted.

The few people close to Dick would learn of his eagerness to finish the year and get the hell out. Well, maybe not eagerness. Resignation.

A New York businessman, a close friend of one of Dick's close friends, had come to know Williams through this mutual acquaintance. The businessman had no ties to baseball, although he was a longtime Yankee fan. When he heard that Dick appeared on the brink of leaving the A's, he spoke to a Yankee executive to inquire of the club's interest in hiring a new manager, a fellow like Williams perhaps. The New York club had made a run at the American League East title earlier that year but couldn't hang on. Ralph Houk had been in the Yankee organization forever—as player, coach, manager, general manager, and, finally, manager again. The club had been sold by CBS in 1973, and Houk would finally be leaving. Certainly the Yankees would be interested in a fellow like Dick Williams, but not openly. In fact, the businessman was in effect told that the Yankees could not get involved talking terms to a manager whose contract with another ball club still had two years to run. The fellow was not deterred, however. There is reason to believe that during the final weeks of the 1973 season this gentleman chatted frequently with both Williams and the Yankees. It is unlikely any firm requests or offers were bartered by the fellow; he was merely striking a match on the come. And the come came.

Within an hour after Mike Andrews signed that piece of paper in Oakland following the second game of the World Series, Williams told one of his players, "That's it. I'm quitting." Two evenings later, in the clubhouse at Shea Stadium, he said the same thing to the entire team. There had been rumors earlier in the year that Houston was interested in signing Dick, that the Angels were desirous of his services; but the Yankee connection did not surface until September 30, when Houk quit New York to take the manager's job at Detroit, effective 1974. Half of the press covering the '73 Series was asking the other half of the press if it knew anything about Williams' taking the Yankee job. When word of his resignation speech to the players was leaked, the press added "to become manager of the New York Yankees." But until the Series ended, Dick would not admit anything, would deny he even was leaving Oakland. The Series was not over. First things first.

> *Gene Tenace:* He left for the players. When the Mike Andrews incident took place, we all knew it was wrong. But *we* couldn't quit. Players can't quit. Dick was the only one who could take a stand. He thought he'd lose our respect if he didn't take a stand. It hit him wrong, and at a bad time, during the Series. He took a stand. He quit.

Williams' resignation message to his players was not particularly inspirational. They won that night, lost the next two games at Shea. "What really bothered me," said one of the A's, "was how Dick said he was quitting win or *lose*. I got the feeling he didn't care if we won or lost the Series."

Misinterpretation. Winning is as important to Dick Williams as to the Owner and General Manager. Williams is not short on ego or cool. After the final game of the Series, he made the resignation official. He had managed his team to two consecutive world championships. The last manager to do that had been Ralph Houk (New York Yankees, 1961–62).

Wafting through the foam of Series victory champagne in the Oakland clubhouse after Game Seven came the voices of Dick and Charlie in a touching farewell—on network television.

> *Finley:* Even though you're not going to be with us next year, I want to thank you for the great job that you've done for the three years you've been with me.
>
> *Dick Williams:* Thank you, Charlie, very much, and I'm going to miss not being with you but I've made a decision and I'm going to stay with it.

Within the hour Charlie would tell at least two sportswriters,

"Dick Williams did an outstanding job and I hate to see him go. He still has a two-year contract, you know, but I don't feel I should stand in his way."

After the postgame telecast ended, Williams went upstairs to a crowded press interview room and had nothing but praise for Charles O. Finley. "An exemplary relationship," he said. "I have great regard for Charlie. Not at any time did he tell me to do anything about who to play or who not to play." He said he was leaving Oakland so he could spend more time with his family in Riviera Beach, Florida. He said Riviera Beach was a "thirty minute and twenty-two second drive" from Fort Lauderdale, Florida, spring training site for the New York Yankees. He smiled when he said that. He said he had been thinking of leaving Oakland since midsummer. He said he had told his players before the third Series game because "of stories that we had a lot of dissension. I thought it might help a little to tell the players." He said the Mike Andrews incident "came at an unfortunate time. But Mr. Finley was trying to help the team. Mike and I are very, very close friends. Mr. Finley and I are very, very close friends. The timing was just poor." He said he hated to leave. He said that Charlie and team captain Sal Bando had asked him to reconsider. It was all very friendly, he said. He repeatedly said his resignation from the A's now put him in the status of being unemployed. "Sure," he said, "I know the Yankees have been mentioned, but I have not talked to them, nor they to me. Right now, I'm looking for a job."

He was not asked, and did not say, if he had talked to a New York businessman.

*Reggie Jackson:* Dick Williams taught Reggie Jackson how to be a winner. I'd love to follow him anywhere, but I know I have about as much chance of being traded as Secretariat.

Jackson had been responsible for getting Williams a contract extension on July 4, 1973. After the game in Oakland that evening, Reggie complained about what he considered the coaches' criticisms of certain players. He knocked the coaches, not Williams. The next day Charlie extended the contracts of the coaches *and* Williams. Charlie later said that Dick was so pleased with that show of faith "he said he'd kiss my cheeks at second base."

After that final Series game, Dick was verbally kissing Charlie's cheeks. The manager finished his press conference platitudes, went back down to the clubhouse to shower and dress, and then joined his wife in the Series hospitality room. He did not appear at all weary, at least not as tired as relief pitcher Darold Knowles, on the mound for the final out and the first man ever to pitch in all seven games of a Series. By the following summer, Knowles would be in the doghouse of Williams' replacement, Alvin Dark. But on October 21, 1973, nobody was in anybody's doghouse in the booze-dripping hospitality room. I stumbled over to Williams as he was leaving and told him I thought he "went out with a lot of class." Actually—as everyone knew—Dick's valedictory was a bunch of bullshit. But that's okay. The baseball Establishment does not want its members knocked. Knock, and you may find it tough getting a job. Williams was a pure baseball politician. He played his entire departure with political gobbledygook-dignity. He could have jawed himself into a firing earlier. Any number of courses—criticizing Charlie, disobeying personnel instructions repeatedly—would have brought him dismissal and immediate access to another job. But the idea of dismissal is repugnant to most men, particularly to a prideful man like Dick Williams, canned as a manager four years earlier by the Boston Red Sox. He saw diplomacy as his best escape route from Finley. Surely he must have believed Charlie would not stand in his way. And after the Owner's comments that final day, Dick had to assume he had chosen the single, best getaway. Never, Richard, assume.

Finley got more heat than he deserved for his eventual refusal to permit Williams to manage the Yankees. Charlie's only mistake was telling the world, in the blush of the Series victory that Sunday, that he wouldn't stand in Williams' way. He presumably did not know what else to say. And he definitely did not know—*that* day—that alternatives existed.

Typically, Finley dealt with Williams' pending departure on an impulsive basis. First of all, he truly found it hard to believe that Dick was going to quit. The resignation was beyond Charlie's comprehension—for after all, hadn't he taken care of his manager with raises and contract extensions? Why should Dick abdicate this sinecure? Leaving a champion? Charlie, like everyone, had heard the news earlier that week about Williams' speech in the Shea clubhouse. But he refused to believe it, refused to examine in advance the courses open to him. Because of his recent illness and the reaction to the Andrews incident, Charlie was physically and emotionally spent during Series week, and so the imminence of Dick's departure was just something that had to be put out of mind, not believed, a matter to be dealt with later. But later became too late—from a public relations point of view.

What Charlie could have done after reading the Shea statement was ask fellow baseball executives about his prerogatives. But he must have felt that in the end, Charlie the salesman would prevail; Charlie could talk Dick into staying. And he never got the time to sell. Not that Williams could have been sold, anyway. For love, money, or a *fifty*-year contract extension.

So the man from the network puts a mike in your face and you say what everybody expects you to say: Godspeed, Dick Williams. Nice guy, that Charlie, right?

Two days later, the Owner realized he had prerogatives. Charlie was informed by an executive of at least one other major league club that he was entitled to compensation for Williams. There was precedent: the Washington Senators had title to the contract of Gil Hodges when the New York Mets hired him to manage in 1968. To obtain Hodges, the Mets gave the Nats a quarter of a million dollars and a pitcher, Bill Denehy. Back in 1935 the Boston Red Sox gave Washington the same amount of money so they could hire as manager a fellow named Cronin. So the options were quickly clear for Charlie. On October 23, Finley announced that if the Yankees or any other team wanted Williams, the A's would have to be compensated. Otherwise, Dick was still working for him. He also threatened to charge the Yankees with tampering. In the next few days, Dick would be saying: "I thought everything was all set with Charlie. He said he would not stand in my way. I'm very much surprised at this turn of events. Charlie has never gone back on his word with me. He's an honest man. . . . My resignation is irrevocable. That's one decision that can't change."

American League president Joe Cronin, the original precedent man, was retiring at year's end. You can imagine how delighted Cronin was with this going-away present. He would have to work out an amicable agreement, middleman the Yanks and Charlie. Cronin did not enjoy the challenge of problem-solving. At the league meeting in Houston in December, New York offered Oakland $150,000 and two minor league players for Williams. Finley refused that deal and, as was rumored, an offer of Yankee second baseman Horace Clarke plus cash.

On December 18, Williams signed a managerial contract with the Yankees, who fully expected litigation by Charlie. Good guess. That same day, in federal district court in San Francisco, Williams was enjoined from managing any club except the A's. And on December 20, Cronin voided New York's agreement with Dick. Referring to the post-Series telecast, Cronin said, "A man can't divorce his wife by making such a statement on television. He must go through the judicial process." (That same day the Yankees lost another decision as Cronin upheld Detroit's hiring of Houk as manager sans compensation.)

The Yankees flirted with a countermove against Charlie but found none justified, and thus on January 3, 1974, hired Bill Virdon as manager.

Until the day spring training opened, there was some confusion about the components of Finley's injunction against Williams. At first it was rumored that Williams could manage any team but the Yankees. Then it was thought that Dick could not manage anyone except the A's in 1974. But the court order seemed to effectively prevent Williams from managing at all in both 1974 and 1975 on the basis of breach of contract.

On February 20, within days of spring training, Finley announced the hiring of Alvin Dark as his new manager. Yet a tantalizing mystery lingered: what if Dick Williams showed up on the opening day of spring training to honor his contract commitment with the A's? The new American League president, Lee McPhail (previously general manager of—the Yankees), said, "The fact that Oakland signed a new manager doesn't release Williams from his obligations to Oakland."

Dick would be quoted in the Los Angeles *Times* on February 21 as saying Finley pleaded with him to come back just before Dark was hired. "Finley only wanted me back so he could fire me. He would have been happy to pay me two years' salary just for the personal pleasure of booting me out. That's his way, but I won't give him the satisfaction."

Williams did not attend opening rites at the A's camp in Mesa, Arizona. It would have been much fun.

In that L.A. *Times* story, by Shav Glick, Williams finally gushed his bill of particulars against Charlie. "You can just take so much of Charlie," Dick was quoted. "And I took more than most. The Andrews case did it, but it was only the tip of the iceberg. . . . I was manager of the champions and yet I was the only manager in the majors without an expense account. After the '73 Series he docked me twenty-one hundred dollars from my Series check for expenses, things like taking my coaches to dinner, cabs for TV appearances. . . . Finley likes to have everyone in his employ— and I mean everyone, from the manager to the shoeshine boy—under his thumb. Then he pushes as hard as he can to keep them down. No one could get along with him. . . . One day we had a day off, a rare thing these days. The team was going good, so I gave the fellows the day off. A couple of coaches and I decided to play golf. When I came in after nine holes there was a stack of message notes a mile high from Finley. I called him and he asked me what I was doing. I told him I was playing golf, that the players and I needed a little relaxation. He said he had a lot of things to do and he didn't want any of his employees out playing golf. He didn't have anything important for me to do, he just wanted to bug me. . . . He sat in Chicago and listened to Oakland games on the radio or read about them in the papers. Then he'd call me and tell me what I did wrong. Even when we won he'd be on the phone telling me how we could have won easier or by using different players. He was never satisfied."

(One former Finley manager said Charlie "would chew me out more after a win than when we lost.")

"If he hadn't called by midnight after a night game," Williams' quote in the L.A. *Times* continued, "I knew he'd be ringing by seven in the morning. He was second-guessing every pitching change I made. It didn't matter if I took the pitcher out early or left him in, Finley would disagree."

Williams complained to Glick about being stuck with pinch runner Allan Lewis. "He wasn't even a good base runner. It was like asking me to manage a team with twenty-four players when all the others had twenty-five."

Williams was no longer the politician on February 20, 1974. Glick reported Dick told him Charlie "is continually pumping the players for complaints. Things like, 'Why didn't Williams use you instead of so-and-so the other night?' Or, 'Don't you think you're a better second baseman than so-and-so?' Things like that can cause unrest and start players thinking about things other than winning. He just couldn't keep from meddling in everyone's affairs."

In regard to Dick's resignation, Glick quoted Williams as saying, "I had four separate conversations with Finley, two in private, one on local TV, and one on national TV after the World Series. Each time he said it was OK with him, but when the Yankees signed me, he changed his mind. At least he said he changed it. I wouldn't be surprised if he planned it that way."

Williams was not unemployed on the day Charlie hired Alvin Dark. Dick was working as an administrative assistant (for public relations) to seventy-seven year old Florida billionaire John D. MacArthur. His office was in the Colonnades Beach Hotel, less than a five minute drive from Dick's home on posh Singer Island in Riviera Beach. Well, he had said he was quitting the A's so he could spend more time with his family (three children, one an excellent pitching prospect).

A Miami *Herald* story of March 3 reported that Finley was in Florida talking to Williams' boss about buying the A's. "MacArthur had no intention of ever buying the A's," the story quoted Williams. "He told me he was in the business of renting rooms and if Mr. Finley wanted to stop at the Colonnades Beach, fine." In that same story, Williams talked about the voiding of his contract with the Yankees. "The lawyers for the Yankees were of the opinion that I was all right in signing. After all, Finley wished me well on TV and said he wouldn't stand in my way. But Cronin ran scared after the injunction. And I should know that Finley is the type who will say one thing and do another."

Dick's news potential ebbed by the time the season began. He was now nothing more than an ex-major league manager. For the first time in twenty-eight years, Williams was out of baseball. The way things looked he might have to sit out for two years.

He appeared as a guest "color" commentator on a network baseball telecast of a game in early June between his two old teams, the A's and Red Sox. He did not use the forum to rap Charlie, except to say, "I miss baseball, but not Mr. Finley. I haven't missed Mr. Finley since the day I resigned."

During that trip to Boston he would tell a *Christian Science Monitor* writer, "There is no way I'm going to rip Charlie, who is one of the world's greatest businessmen. Mostly, he's been good for baseball." The writer predicted that Williams might soon be managing the California Angels, a job he landed on June 27 with a contract to run through the 1977 season. He would be paid at least a quarter of a million dollars under the contract terms. And live in the area of his youth—Pasadena, California.

"I'm quite pleased to be back in baseball," Williams said. His first series as Angel manager was in Anaheim against the A's, and Oakland won all four games.

> *Finley:* I'm tired of developing managers and executives for other teams to use. I was perfectly correct in this matter. I don't see that a manager is any different than a ballplayer when it comes to contractual obligations.

Williams' return to Oakland, on Labor Day, 1974, was heralded by the million dollar Finley scoreboard with the repeated message: "WELCOME DICK WILLIAMS TO THE OAKLAND COLI-SEUM—HOME OF THE WORLD CHAMPIONS." The message flashed on and off throughout the game. Nobody would say who had ordered the scoreboard computer operators to program those words. Just as no one would admit who ordered the programming of these words in the top of the ninth inning, two outs before Dick's Angels would lose to the A's: "GOOD NIGHT DICK." Several of the A's called that message "the most bush thing" they had ever seen. "Sure wasn't major league," said Sal Bando.

"You know who ordered that message," said Reggie Jackson. "Next time something like that happens, I'm walking off the field and I don't care how much they fine me."

"Dick Williams is a class guy," said Oakland center fielder Bill North, "and that was a classless thing to do."

Williams, who had been standing in the visitors' dugout in a direct line with the sign while he was being bade a good night, said he didn't see the sign. A cozy man still.

# XII

# ARBITRATION

In 1967, the A's final year in Kansas City, Finley's expenditure for a budget item described as "major league players, managers, coaches, and staff" was, according to a reliable estimate, approximately $443,000. That was for a uniformed group of at least thirty men. Seven years later, after the initial impact of Marvin Miller's arbitration plan, the Owner and General Manager was paying about $425,000 to a combined total of *four* uniformed men: Reggie Jackson, Sal Bando, Jim Hunter, Ken Holtzman. All except Holtzman were being paid at least a hundred thousand dollars to play baseball in 1974. All except Hunter secured their big paychecks through arbitration. What Marvin Miller wrought partially deprived Charles O. Finley of one of his most delightful chores—salary negotiating. There was now a middleman, an arbitrator, between Finley and his athletes. No longer could Finley be the final word, the dominating force. Marvin J. Miller had encroached upon the autonomy of Charles O. Finley; executive privilege was being breached by a creative force from the ranks of organized labor. Miller, before taking over the Players Association

271

in 1966, was assistant to the president of the United Steelworkers of America, an irony that must drive Finley bonkers.

Miller sold the arbitration plan to the Establishment late in 1973. The procedure was simple: any player with at least two years of big league service could tell his owner to stuff it and take his salary case to an arbitrator. The player had his asking price, the owner his offering price. If the two couldn't agree on a compromise salary, the arbitrator would make the final decision. He would grant the player what he asked for or what the owner offered. One figure or the other, but nothing in between. And the arbitrator's decision was binding.

Fourteen arbitrators were selected by Miller and the baseball Establishment. Each arbitrator was given a confidential list of *all* major league salaries to use as a basis of comparison in each case. Third baseman Sal Bando of the Athletics, for example, would be able to learn what third baseman Bill Melton of the Chicago White Sox was being paid and thus ask for equity—from an arbitrator, not from Finley—with a chance of getting it.

"The players now have a dignified status with the clubs," said Miller. "The essential dignity of equals sitting down together just can't be overemphasized."

In 1974, the first year of arbitration proceedings, fifty-four big league players filed for the new deal. Before the sessions actually got started, though, twenty-five of them were able to compromise with their club owners. That left twenty-nine, and nine of them were employees of Charles Oscar Finley. Seven of the nine were men who had given Finley two consecutive world championships. The eighth was a recently acquired utility infielder who didn't figure to stick with the club. The ninth was a veteran utility infielder, Ted Kubiak, who had come up through Finley's farm system and first joined the Athletics in Kansas City in 1967. He is not a big name, but his picture has been delivered to millions of homes: *Sports Illustrated* featured Kubiak on a subscription card. He has been stuffed, with an enclosed check, into many an envelope, unless you want them to bill you later.

*Ted Kubiak:* In 1972 I was with the A's only about half a season and didn't do a damn thing but play second base in that rotation system and hit only .181. Finley sent me a contract for a four grand raise, and that was very fair. I was surprised. My salary for 1973 was thirty-five thousand dollars. I'm with the club all year, I play a month as a regular when Dick Green was hurt and hit .270 [although he ended up at .220], and Finley offers me only a twenty-five hundred dollar raise for 1974. I was mad when I got that first contract from him and I didn't get in touch with him. A week or so later he calls me and asks why I hadn't returned my contract. I told him I didn't like the offer and I wasn't going to sign it. There was no real discussion of the offer, no negotiations or anything. He said, "That's all you're getting. I'm not sending you another contract." I said, "How are we supposed to negotiate? Are we going to have-to go to arbitration?" He said he'd submit my name for arbitration proceedings, and we left it at that and hung up. A few weeks later, he calls again and says, "Ted, I'm giving you three choices: I'm going to release you, I'm going to trade you to Texas, or you can sign the contract I sent you." Well, it kind of shook me up to hear stuff like that. I don't think he meant it, because I feel I know the guy's techniques now. If it was a few years earlier, I would have signed that first contract. So I answer him by saying, "Do I get any time to think it over or do you want an answer right now?" He said I could call him back the next day.

Kubiak was frankly scared. After the 1973 season, he had purchased a new home in the old-line wealthy Oakland suburb of Piedmont and been given a decent job by a major real estate company. Ted and his wife, Janie, were prepared to settle in Oakland after bouncing around with the A's, Seattle, Milwaukee,

St. Louis, Texas. He knew Finley respected his fielding ability but he also realized that Charlie fancied a rookie infielder named Manny Trillo. Kubiak was vulnerable. Finley, he knew, was "capable of doing anything." And Ted had reached the point in his baseball career where he finally felt he belonged. He was enjoying baseball and Oakland. So he phoned Marvin Miller for advice.

> *Ted Kubiak:* Marvin told me that Finley was basically doing the same thing to the other players. So the more I thought about it, the more I knew that Charlie was really just trying to get me to sign. I thought he'd call me again before the arbitration proceedings started. But I didn't talk to him again until I walked into the arbitrator's room. I went in asking for forty-two thousand five hundred dollars—a raise of seventy-five hundred dollars. Finley and I were five grand apart. I think that my request was too much of a raise for the 1973 season alone. But arbitration should tend to equalize your salary based on your entire career.

Los Angeles was supposed to be the arbitration site for players on California's five major league teams. But with nine A's involved, the proceedings were moved to the Sheraton-Palace Hotel in San Francisco in February, 1974. Finley was there, as was Marvin Miller.

> *Ted Kubiak:* Mr. Finley was very friendly, as he usually is, when we walked into the arbitration suite. He can be charming, you know. The basic argument my attorney gave involved the raise I got for 1973 and the fact I'd done more on the club that year than in '72. We presented comparable figures with other major leaguers in my situation, but there aren't many of my type and the only guy we could find was Paul Popovich [then of the Chicago Cubs], who was making more than me for the same length of major league service.

Marvin brought up the fact that the average major league salary was about thirty-six thousand seven hundred dollars, and that was based on an average of four and a half years' service. Here I was with seven years in the majors and a salary of thirty-five thousand dollars. Marvin said seven-year men averaged about fifty-nine thousand, and that included superstars and utility men. But of course I wasn't looking for a twenty-four grand raise. Just the seventy-five hundred dollars to forty-two thousand five hundred dollars. Then comes Finley's turn to put his case to the arbitrator. He gets up in his own inimitable way, pacing slowly back and forth. He stares at me all the time, rips me to shreds, says that I'm not a big league ballplayer, that I can't hit, that I've passed my peak defensively, that if he has to use me as the regular second baseman in 1974, the A's won't win their division. He said he put me on waivers and nobody wanted me—and I don't know if he really did. He said he tried to trade me and nobody wanted me—and I don't believe that. Hearing him say all that made me mad, but I know what the hell he's like. I understand the guy, but I was just hoping the arbitrator could see through him.

After the arguments were over, I felt my case could have gone either way. When we got outside the suite, Finley called me over and gave me a World Series charm for my wife and said, "Don't take what I said in there personally. I've done this to everybody. It's just business." I told him that I understood. Then we started walking down to have lunch, and he said, "Hey, Ted, I've just been thinking about something." He gives a five-minute speech and finally gets it out that he wants to split the difference, that he would give me a five grand raise to forty thousand. [Compromising was permissible until the arbitrator's announced verdict.] Well, shit, we could have settled the whole damn thing two months earlier instead of dickering over twenty-five hundred bucks. But he was playing his goddamn game. Both my attorney and Marvin told me to make my own decision about taking the compromise offer. At that point, I'd gone so damn far I figured I'd go for broke with the arbitrator.

And he lost.

So did Joe Rudi, an outfielder who was the team's best hitter in 1972 but less than effective most of 1973 because of illness and injury. Rudi is a farm boy with tremendous dedication to the game. He taught himself how to field after several years of embarrassment. In both the 1972 and 1973 World Series, Rudi made memorable catches. Charles O. Finley delights in telling how he cooked up the first batch of grits that Joe Rudi ever ate. Going into arbitration, Rudi was reported to be asking for a twelve thousand five hundred dollar raise (to sixty-two thousand five hundred dollars), with Finley's offer at an estimated fifty-five thousand dollars.

> *Joe Rudi:* I'm not really afraid of Finley anymore. There was a time down the line there when I was trying to come up in baseball, and if the owner doesn't like you he can bury you. But once you become established, you're not so worried about him burying you, or putting the screws to you. Finley likes to have all the players bowing down and like that and saying what a great man he is. He likes to be the lord and master of everything, but arbitration has taken some of this power away from him. At my session, he said that I was the worst left fielder in baseball, that I was one of the slowest men in the game, that sure I caught everything but that there were so many balls that fell in for hits that would be caught by normal ballplayers. He said that I had a very weak arm, that Campaneris [A's shortstop] had to go halfway to the outfield to take relay throws. He said that you always put your most mediocre outfielder in left field. I expected him to say those kind of things but it ticked me off that the arbitrator bought his line of bullshit. After it was over Finley said, "I still love you like a son."

When left-handed pitcher Ken Holtzman was traded by the Chicago Cubs to the A's after the 1971 season, he found it much easier "to talk contract." In Oakland he did not have to deal with a middleman, with a general manager like Chicago's John Holland. Not that Holtzman disliked Holland, but he would have preferred talking terms directly with Cub owner Phil Wrigley. "It seemed to me," said Holtzman, "that whatever Holland said in terms of contract was coming from Wrigley, whom I had never met in seven years. Why couldn't I talk to Wrigley personally? At least with the A's you don't have to go through a relay man. I can get Mr. Finley's thoughts right from him."

In two years with Oakland, Holtzman won forty games. More satisfying, however, was the nearly fifty thousand dollars Ken picked up in World Series shares. He does not hesitate to tell you he pitches baseball games for money. Ken Holtzman is a businessman-ballplayer, and not ashamed to admit it. Finley paid him a reported fifty-five thousand dollars in 1973, offered him eighty thousand dollars for 1974. Ken was thinking more in terms of about ninety-three thousand dollars and went into arbitration. He and relief pitchers Rollie Fingers and Darold Knowles hired Washington, D.C. attorney Jerry Kapstein to argue their cases to the arbitrator, and Kapstein beat Finley all three times. Holtzman's case was the first among the nine A's to be heard.

> *Ken Holtzman:* One of the first things Mr. Finley said when he got up to talk—and he looked me right in the eye—was "Kenny, don't take it personally," and he eventually said that I wasn't as good as my record showed. But it didn't bother me, because when he said that, Jerry Kapstein said, "Well, we're going to say things here, Mr. Finley, that *you* might not like, and don't take it personally."

> *Sal Bando* (he was paid sixty thousand dollars in 1973, asked for one hundred thousand dollars for 1974, was offered seventy-five thousand dollars by Finley): After listening to Holtzman, I thought there might be a lot of mudslinging going on. But Charlie started off by praising me to the arbitrator, then tried to show why I wasn't worth a hundred grand. It was really very pleasant, and I think

Charlie thought he could win just by his salesmanship, not facts. I was a little worried going in, because I know he's a good salesman. I don't think I could have won without my attorney with me. Charlie didn't bring a lawyer because he believes in his sales ability.

When the arbitrator made Bando a hundred thousand dollar a year ballplayer, Sal immediately phoned family and friends and didn't stop smiling for two days. Or three.

Here's your final score: Players, 5; Finley, 4.

Bando's raise was not the largest to come out of arbitration. Reggie Jackson played for seventy-five thousand dollars in 1973 and $135,000 in 1974. Finley had offered him one hundred grand even.

Fingers made off with ten thousand dollars more than Finley had offered. Knowles picked up an extra four thousand from the arbitrator.

Kubiak, Rudi, and Tenace were joined in the losers' column by infielder Jack Heidemann, who didn't survive spring training of 1974 with the A's.

On balance, the arbitration results cost Charlie Finley about sixty thousand dollars in salaries he hadn't intended to pay. He did save attorney's fees, though.

One year later, the A's again led the major leagues in player arbitration filings—this time with thirteen. Charlie settled "out of court" with seven of them, including Rudi, and beat the others 4–2. Among the losers were 1974 arbitration winners Bando, Jackson and Holtzman. Ingenue disputant Ray Fosse, who had batted .196 during an injury-pocked 1974 season, wanted an $18,500 raise from the arbitrator. "If he beats me," said Finley, "I'll get out of the game." Fosse didn't beat him.

Fingers won again, as did 1974 loser Ted Kubiak in what seemed a replay. The utility infielder wanted forty-two thousand five hundred dollars; Charlie offered a no-raise thirty-seven thousand five hundred dollars. When the arbitration session ended, Finley offered a compromise increase of two thousand five hundred dollars. As he did a year earlier, Teddy said no. "A matter of justice," he said. After winning, Kubiak said, "Compared to the others, my case is inconsequential. But it sure was nice to beat Charlie."

Finley, courting the press throughout the 1975 proceedings, told us, "There's an old truism that applies to what's going on here: Hogs go to market and pigs get fat. But most of these players aren't being pigs. They aren't being hogs. They're just being gluttons. And the fans aren't going to put up with it much longer."

In his 1975 arbitration with Bando, Finley called his team captain "the worst fielding third baseman in the American League." Charlie was mad because Sal had said the A's front office was "not first class. It's run by and for only one man." Sal took wife Sandy into the arbitration hearing, and this bothered Charlie.

"I hate to be critical of a player in front of his wife," said the Owner. "It makes me uncomfortable."

"The only reason I brought Sandy with me," said Sal, "was to keep my temper under control. I felt like beating the shit out of Charlie for the things he said about me. But not with Sandy there."

# XIII

## THE PRESS

In November, 1973, shortly before baseball's annual winter meeting, Jim Street phoned Finley. Street had covered the A's for the San Jose *Mercury-News* for a couple of seasons. Rarely had Finley been less than cordial with him. On this day, Street had just a few questions, and recalls this conversation:

> *Street:* Will you have a manager soon?
> *Finley:* None of your fucking business.
> *Street:* Have you narrowed down the list of managerial candidates?
> *Finley:* None of your fucking business.
> *Street:* Who do you want from the Yankees in compensation for Dick Williams?
> *Finley:* None of your fucking business.
> *Street:* Any trades pending?
> *Finley:* None of your fucking business.
> *Street:* Are you going to the winter meetings in Houston?
> *Finley:* None of your fucking business.

Street thanked Charles O. Finley and hung up.

When Finley offered me the job of public relations director with the A's in early 1970, I quietly insisted on knowing where he wanted his p.r. man to sit during ball games at the Oakland Coliseum. Previously, the club's p.r. man had been stationed in the scoreboard operator's booth, some distance from the press box. His job was to help develop messages for the computer to feed into the scoreboard, words of glowing wisdom like, "Hit means a run, Sal" or "You can do it, Reg" or "C'mon, Joe." At least three exclamation points followed each message. There is no solid evidence that Finley devised these messages and fed them to the p.r. man for feeding into the computer, but the exclamation marks did smack of brush strokes coming out of a Chicago insurance office. Finley speaks that way persistently; not words, exclamations. Not always shrieks, but usually stern, commanding finalities. Had Picasso been commissioned for a Finley portrait, the Owner and General Manager would have, one can be certain, emerged as an upside-down exclamation point. The dot in gold and the sheath in green, of course. Maybe Warhol will oblige.

I couldn't see myself exclaiming giant, flashing "Beep-Beeps" for Bert Campaneris' base-stealing efforts over six months and eighty-one home games. Perhaps I was being an intellectual snob, but I did believe that a p.r. man should mingle with the press and make the writers feel good about the ball club and perhaps even about Charles O. Finley. So in the first hour of my interview with Finley, I wondered about the possibility of sitting in the press box—were I indeed hired for the public relations directorship. Finley brushed past the question quickly with a "doesn't matter to me, whatever you think is the way to do the job." Three hours later he began a discussion of my duties in the scoreboard booth. But, gee whiz, Mr. Finley, didn't you say earlier that I could sit in the press box during the games so that I could best service the newspapermen? "Wouldn't waste my time with them," he said, knowing full well that I was one of them and might continue to be. "Most of them are a bunch of assholes anyway!!!"

I didn't respond. I just !'d. And the scoreboard glowing inside my eyelids thwarted any hopes of a rally by registering: "You Can't Do It, Herb!!!" For an asshole, I felt pretty good.

Ron Bergman is the best day-to-day baseball writer in the San Francisco Bay area. He has covered the A's for the Oakland *Tribune* since the club's arrival from Kansas City. Bergman is a quick, deft reporter, a stylish, thorough writer and anathema to Charles O. Finley. Bergman does not write what Finley wants to see written about the A's. For instance: In the summer of 1971, when A's pitcher Vida Blue was the most important professional athlete in these United States, Bergman wisely saw fit to report that Blue was having a remarkable effect on betting odds with each outing. Trouble was, from Finley's point of view, Bergman wrote that story the day after Charlie's annual team fiesta at the LaPorte, Indiana, estate of the Owner and General Manager. Finley wondered why Bergman didn't cover the barbecued social event ("to help promote baseball in Oakland") rather than the machinations of those men in Vegas. Bergman didn't bother with a lengthy explanation.

That bit of editorial advice was the least of Bergman's problems with Finley in more than six years on the A's beat. The most of these problems are a few pages away, but indicative of the relationship between the two men is this documented recollection, by Bergman, of a telephone interview he had with Finley in mid-January of 1974. It lacks the brevity and clarity of the Street-Finley chat a few months earlier, but is nonetheless heartwarming.

> *Finley* (in Chicago, returning Bergman's call): This is Finley.
> *Bergman:* Hi, this is Ron Bergman.

*Finley:* What's on your mind?

*Bergman:* Couple of things.

*Finley:* Shoot.

*Bergman:* This is the start of arbitration over player salaries. How many of your players are going into it?

*Finley:* I have no idea.

*Bergman:* You think it's going to be a lot or . . .

*Finley:* I have no idea.

*Bergman:* Or harder?

*Finley:* I have no idea. I have no idea. I have never experienced arbitration before.

*Bergman:* It's having no effect then on how you're dealing with the players?

*Finley:* I have no idea. I don't know how this thing's going to work out.

*Bergman:* Now about hiring a new manager . . .

*Finley:* I have no idea about the manager.

*Bergman:* Uh, when would you like to have one? Can you wait until spring training?

*Finley:* I can wait as long as I want to wait.

*Bergman:* Let's say, just for example, that it's somebody who already has a job in baseball. Like Dave Bristol. He's a coach at Montreal. How long can you . . .

*Finley:* I will not bandy anybody's name around. I will not speak on hypothetical situations.

*Bergman:* Are you holding off naming a manager for 1974 because you still have Dick Williams under contract?

*Finley:* I have plenty of time.

*Bergman:* Is it that you feel you have time or that you just don't have anybody in mind?

*Finley:* I cannot enlighten you at all on anything. You can speculate all you wish. That's your prerogative. I have no facts that I can give you at all. Okay?

*Bergman:* Is that all you want to talk? [Ron is taking notes.]

*Finley:* I mean, if you've got questions, okay. But I can't sit here and wait for you to pick your nose and go to the bathroom, you know.

*Bergman:* I'm just trying to write it down.

*Finley:* Ask the questions, you can write later. I can't sit here, I'm a busy man.

*Bergman:* Is your suit against Dick Williams still in effect?

*Finley:* I don't know, why don't you call the courts? All you've got to do is call the courts over there and find out.

*Bergman:* Okay. I thought maybe you'd know.

*Finley:* Yes, I know, but I have no comments to make on it—other than to say they have until Monday to answer, and they didn't answer so I don't know. Call the court and find out what the hell the story is.

*Bergman:* Okay.

*Finley:* I haven't withdrawn anything.

*Bergman:* You had mentioned last year the possibility of suing the . . .

*Finley:* Now, look, you're a shit stirrer, and if you're going to stir a lot of shit I don't want to talk to you. Okay? If you want to talk on something constructive, fine.

*Bergman:* Name me something constructive.

*Finley:* I don't know anything constructive. Write any goddamn thing you want to. I don't know anything to tell you. As I told you before, you can do all the speculating you want to. But all the hell you are is a shit stirrer, and I haven't got any use for shit stirrers. So you go ahead and write any goddamn thing you want to. Okay?

*Bergman:* Yup.

*Finley:* All right, I'm busy. I've got to get back to work.

*Bergman:* Okay.

Is Ron Bergman, father of two, homeowner, TV late movie freak, cigar smoker, Woody Allen mannerist, indeed a shit stirrer? None of your fucking business.

*Safe Assumption Number One:* Charles O. Finley has no respect for most of the people who write about him and his ball club, although if you are one of those writers the bulk of your time and space is spent on Charlie and *not* the ball club. Every team hits and pitches; every team is not owned and general-managed by Charles O. Finley.

He may, as many do, see sportswriters as a grabby, free-loading, paunchy, cliché-clutching pox on American letters. Hell, there are even sportswriters who hold that view of other sportswriters. Nobody's cattier than a newspaperman, unless it's an actress. You will not find massive camaraderie in any given press box; somebody there always hates somebody else there, often for no other reason than because that somebody else has more circulation, or writes funnier, or writes too soberly, or is too reserved, or makes too much noise. Or is an asshole. One American League team has been covered on the road for several seasons by the same two writers, and only these two. One would think they huddle for warmth. One is wrong. They do not speak; they sit as far away from each other in the press box as possible. And they're both very pleasant guys. Individually. If Charlie owned the team they cover, he would delight in widening the estrangement—first giving one a scoop a week for months and then transferring his exclusive affection to the other guy. Oh, would he relish that situation.

If Finley doesn't respect most sportswriters as artists, he does unquestionably respect their printed space. It is, after all, free—inarguably and wonderfully free—and name me five insurance men who don't own baseball teams who can telephone San Francisco *Examiner* sports columnist Prescott Sullivan and get their names in the paper almost anytime they wish. Go ahead, name them. You lose.

Charlie knows, better than the sportswriters, that no, he doesn't have power over them, but yes, he does. He can't get LaPorte barbecue stories out of most of them, but he can insinuate Finley into whatever situation Finley desires. They will listen and they will write. Something, any old time he likes. If they're friendly, they fill space. If they're unfriendly, they fill space. You can ignore the lawn picnics, but by god you can't ignore Finley.

*Safe Assumption Number Two:* Outside of Chicago, Charles O. Finley is his own circulation. As far as he is concerned, he is the only reader of the newspapers in the Bay area that cover his ball club day-to-day. Bergman and Street and the others are writing for his eyes only, but please don't tell Bergman and Street and the others.

The Bay area papers enter the A's offices on the mezzanine level of the Oakland Coliseum, are read by eyes with voices that reach by telephone to the insurance office on Michigan Avenue. The only important reader, thus served, can act. I suspect that the only reason Finley has never spoken harshly with me in my six plus seasons of covering his team is that the A's office does not subscribe to the newspapers for which I write. That borders on executive clemency, I suppose, but as far as Finley is concerned I am a tree falling in an uninhabited forest, unrequited ink.

Chicago is different, for that is Charlie's turf. People read newspapers there. People Charlie knows and does business with and, presumably, covets. Finley must thank his gods daily that Bergman does not work for the Chicago *Tribune*, lest he be an Owner and General Manager without honor in his own land. Well, Bergman probably never will work for any of the three Chicago dailies, but Dave Nightingale does.

Writing about Finley's cardiac problems, Nightingale quoted Bob Elson (fired as an A's radio announcer by Charlie) as doubting the illness. "Impossible," Nightingale said Elson said. "He doesn't have a heart."

Dave Nightingale succeeded the idol of my youth, John P.

Carmichael, as lead sports columnist on the Chicago *Daily News* and has gradually become one of the idols of my unyouth. He clinched that niche by outrushing Bobby Riggs to the net moments after Riggs clipped Margaret Court. Riggs' handshake was over-shadowed by the figure of a man in an embarrassingly gaudy quilted sports jacket. Dave Nightingale, who with his opaque eyes has always reminded me of Little Orphan Annie, was making his debut on nationwide TV and clearly flaunting it. David knows baseball and newspapering. And Finley.

He wriggled his way into the Finley retinue during the 1972 American League playoffs in Detroit and managed to sup with Charlie and twenty-four others. Nightingale described the evening acidly in a column distributed nationally by The Daily News Syndicate. Finley caught up with the piece in Cincinnati and, as Nightingale quotes him, "didn't particularly care for it."

A few days later, Nightingale was speaking to Mrs. Charles O. Finley as the two of them, and 173 others, were about to board an Oakland-Cincinnati jet flight chartered for the World Series.

> *Dave Nightingale:* I was in midsentence when a hand on my shoulder spun me around. I looked up in time to see Finley's open right hand headed toward my kisser. I tried to duck, but the fingers smacked me across the mouth. No blood. Nothing like that. Sorry to say, but it didn't even smart. Finley screamed, "Don't you ever do that again, goddamnit. Don't you ever talk to her again." Later, he said to me, "I really didn't hit you, Dave. I just poked two fingers under your eyes. Like this." Early the next morning, outside of a hotel in Cincinnati, Finley told me, "I have never hated a Chicago sportswriter as much as I hate you. When I get through with you, I will have destroyed you, and I'll stay with it until I do. I will personally plow you under, you s.o.b., and don't forget it."

More than one year later, Nightingale had not been plowed

under. When you look like Little Orphan Annie, you survive. With your looks and your Chicago circulation.

The next recorded instance of the old finger-under-the-eye poke trick was about thirteen months later, in the Astroworld Hotel in Houston. This time, young, kind, industrious Jim Street of the San Jose *Mercury-News* was the pokee, and was he ever surprised. Two days earlier he and Bergman had interviewed Finley in the Owner and General Manager's hotel suite. As they left, says Street, Finley told them to feel free to call on him any time they needed something. So they came back needing something in a couple of days.

They knocked, and had to wait a few moments for an answer, which finally came at a side door to the Finley suite on the Astroworld's eighth floor.

A voice asked who was there and was informed that Street and Bergman were there. "We'd like to talk to you, but we can come back later if you want," Bergman told the door. The voice on the other side, Finley's, said to wait. Five minutes later, another door to the suite opened and, as Street recalls it, there stood Finley in a raincoat and boots.

> *Jim Street:* He had sort of a blank look in his eyes, and I can't remember if either Bergman or I said anything. Finally, Charlie turned to Bergman and said, "*You*, get out of here." So Bergman backed up down the hall. Then Charlie turned toward me, staring, and walked toward me. I started backing up. I thought he was kidding or something. Then he threw both hands at me, and his right caught my nose and lip as I leaned back. I didn't even know he hit me, but I kind of grabbed his arms. I can't remember him saying anything until then, except that he was a sick man and we had no reason waking him up like that. It was about two o'clock in the afternoon. He saw I was bleeding and invited both Bergman and me in the room—apologizing as we went to the bathroom to get some

washcloths, which he wet and put on my face. The three of us then sat around a table for an interview. And Charlie kept asking me how I was. He also asked that I not say anything in the paper, because, as he put it, "We have enough problems already." Meaning the A's problems with the Yankees over Dick Williams. The interview lasted about ninety minutes, and then Finley asked to speak to me alone. Bergman [not overtly stirring any shit that day] left the room. Again, Charlie asked me to keep this thing quiet. I didn't know exactly what else to do at the time, so I agreed. It took Charlie about a month to talk to me again—even on the phone—and when he finally did he inquired about my wounds.

There is no confirmation of the rampant gossip that Finley attempted to sell group accident and health coverage to Nightingale and Street.

*Safe Assumption Number Three:* It pays to be friendly with at least one important sportswriter—one important Chicago sportswriter. Charlie's friend is David Condon, of The Chicago *Tribune*, the same David Condon who, at Finley's behest, ran onto the field at White Sox Park in drag to embrace an Oakland infielder, much as a busty young lady was doing that season elsewhere in the majors. The word was that Condon did it on a dare-bet from Finley. Certainly made a good story.

Charlie had a no-win public relations decision to make when he came to Oakland in 1968: He could try to outromance San Francisco Giants owner Horace Stoneham in dealing with the press of the Bay area, or he could pluck pocket lint for the sportswriters. Finley chose the latter course. He decided not to pay the travel, hotel, and food expenses for local baseball writers. If one of the Bay area newspapers wished to cover the A's on the road, the coverage would be at the paper's own expense. Sports editors were pissed, but Charlie wouldn't budge.

It's unlikely he even took into account Stoneham's love-thy-scribe policy in putting down freeloading writers. The competition didn't matter; the expense did.

Finley could have outspent Stoneham, sure, when it came to dallying with the press. But Horace had a decade's head start and a charmer of a publicity man in craggy, baseball-wise Garry Schumacher. He handled the writers for Stoneham, handled them with great charm and much booze and insightful Brooklynese. The Giants had a lock on the media when Charlie arrived, and if Finley had tried to become too lavish and obsequious with the writers (a ludicrous thought to begin with) he would have been accused of trying to copy Stoneham, or horn in on Horace.

So Charlie said no free trips, and was partially ignored by the two leading circulation newspapers in the area, the San Francisco *Chronicle* and San Francisco *Examiner*. Especially by the *Chronicle*, with its relatively titanic morning readership. From time to time the *Examiner* did decide to send a man on the road with the A's, but not the *Chronicle*, save for an infrequent jaunt by a columnist. Very infrequent.

*Chronicle* management ultimately concluded that it would be unfair to the solicitous Giants to cover the road games of the unsolicitous A's. Even though the A's had the audacity to win two consecutive world championships, their travels were still ignored by the *Chronicle*, although out-of-town World Series games were staffed in A's title years by that distinguished journal.

Often, the *Chronicle* will cover the A's travels by rewriting the Oakland *Tribune*'s Bergman the next day. The *Tribune* and the San Jose *Mercury-News* were the only Bay area papers to cover all of the A's games from 1968 through 1973. In 1974, the San Jose combine scratched its traveling A's writer, which left Mr. Finley with only his old friend Bergman, the shit stirrer.

"Charlie has tried numerous times to get me fired or taken off the beat," says the fidgety, fearless little Bergman. "He would talk to my sports editor [George Ross] or my publisher [the late William F. Knowland] about me. Ross told me that Finley threatened to move the ball club if I wasn't taken off the beat."

But Bergman survived, despite the fact that Knowland was a member of the board of the Oakland-Alameda County Coliseum Commission and a prime mover in getting the ball park built. Knowland, and the rest of Oakland's Establishment, wanted a tenant in that stadium to join the football Oakland Raiders, and Finley became the key eighty-one-games-a-year occupier. The *Tribune* wouldn't want Charlie ruffled, but Knowland didn't like to be pushed either. There was difficulty—even for a Charlie Finley—in telling a former minority leader of the United States Senate whom to remove from an assignment. Can't blame Charlie for trying, though, and he is persistent. The *Tribune* refused to dislodge Bergman but at the same time found other ways to appease Finley. Two columns critical of the Owner and General Manager—written during the Mike Andrews interlude—were pulled out of the *Tribune* after the first edition. One was written by their own lead columnist, the other by a rather popular national columnist named Jim Murray. And Bergman suggested in one of his pieces out of Shea Stadium that "Hitler had a better press in New York than Charles O. Finley." That line died with the other two columns. Bergman suggests he wasn't comparing Hitler and Finley as human beings, however, which is fair seeing that the Gestapo didn't wear white shoes.

In all of his years on the A's beat, says Bergman, Finley has praised him—once. Ron turned out a long feature on one of Charlie's pets, pinch-running specialist Allan Lewis, and Finley said he liked it very much. Quite possibly Finley tells others of his admiration for Bergman and swears them to secrecy, but one tends

to doubt that. Charlie's dislike for Bergman simply is too rooted to
be tainted by affection at this late date. The Owner's first beef
with the quick man from the Oakland *Tribune* came in July of the
Athletics' first season in the West.

> *Ron Bergman:* It didn't take long. Reggie Jackson was playing
> with a sprained thumb and injured himself more seriously by trying
> to remove the bandage and cutting his hand in the process. The next
> day, a Sunday, Jackson's name wasn't on the lineup card. Before the
> game, I asked one of the team doctors about Reggie's condition. I
> was told that he wouldn't play for two or three days. Then I
> watched the doctor [Harry Walker, of Mike Andrews' examination
> fame] walk into the owner's box and sit down with Finley. Five
> minutes later the game was starting and there was Reggie running
> out to play right field. I remembered what the doctor had told me,
> but in those days I wasn't hip to anything.

After the game, Ron made his usual stop in the clubhouse and
found Jackson fuming. Ron says Reggie told him, "This is going to
cost that man a whole lot of money next year. I'm not working in
one of his Birmingham steel mills."

> *Ron Bergman:* But I still wasn't sure what was going on. Finally,
> one of the players took me aside and told me that Charlie had
> phoned the dugout and ordered Reggie to play. That's why Reggie
> was so pissed off. At that time, my paper was trying its damnedest to
> maintain good relations with Charlie, and I was under orders not to
> play up this kind of stuff. But I thought it was important, and I put
> the Reggie thing at the bottom of my story—reporting that the
> owner had phoned the dugout.

And that, until shortly before the next game at the Oakland
Coliseum, was that. Bergman was rummaging about the press box
early that evening when the phone rang.

*Ron Bergman:* Finley was calling about the story and asked me to come to his office. I told him I wouldn't do it. I told him that I don't go on anybody's carpet but my boss's. And it so happened that my boss, George Ross, was also in the press box that night. And George told Finley that he wasn't going down to his office either, that if Charlie wanted to talk to him he should come up to the press box. So a few minutes later, here comes Charlie storming through the press box door. I saw him coming, and when I saw the way he looked, I said to myself, I don't know what this guy is going to do, but I'm going to get as close to him as I can. And if he wants to take a swing at me, he won't be able to do it. And Charlie just said to me, "You lying little fucker, you, how can you print that shit? It's a lie. I never phoned the dugout." I really got shook, so I asked around the clubhouse again. And again, the story was confirmed—the call had come down. It wasn't until the end of the season that I found out it wasn't Charlie who had called the dugout that day, but that it was Dr. Walker, that Charlie had made Dr. Walker call.

Over the years, Finley must have thought that Bergman had him tapped. Charlie's phone calls had a habit of turning up in Ron's stories.

In the 1973 season, veteran outfielder Jay Johnstone was hitting a ton at the A's farm club in Tucson and was summoned to the big club for possible designated hitter duties. Johnstone joined the team in Kansas City and received a 7:45 P.M. long distance call in the dugout from Finley, inquiring about Jay's contract, the fit of his shoes, and the state of his health. As Bergman detailed it later, Johnstone told the Owner that everything was just fine, the shoes were nifty, there were no contract problems. After a few minutes of this amiable chatting, there was a roar in the background that seemed to puzzle Charlie.

"What's that noise?" he asked Johnstone.

The outfielder said, "Well, Mr. Finley, uh, the game's going on."

Finley told Johnstone he thought the games in Kansas City began at 8:00 P.M., and the Owner hung up.

Bergman told the story in *The Sporting News*, baseball's quasi-house organ, in the form of a short "note" item and didn't think anything of it.

> *Ron Bergman:* Next time I phoned Charlie, I got a lot of yup/nope from him, and I knew something was wrong, so I asked him. He just exploded over that Johnstone phone call thing. He said I was trying to humiliate him. He said, "Who told you about that story? Who told you?" I said, "Who do you think told me?" And Charlie said, "If that's true, I'm gonna farm his ass to the minors." And very soon afterward, Mr. Johnstone was in the minors. He was hitting only .130 or something anyway.

There have been moments, albeit rare, when Bergman has ignored and chosen not to publish a self-damaging Finley outburst. Ron recognizes the man's impulsive nature and tries to sift the importance of whims and temper, although Bergman has concluded that on his beat "Finley makes the games incidental. After the 1973 Series was over, for example, I had to go back and read about the games to see what happened."

Bergman knows that a few readers are more interested in what Reggie Jackson does at the plate than what Finley says over the phone. Most of the time. The little man from the *Tribune* can impose a sense of selectivity, as at a Finley press conference in early 1972, when Charlie was immersed in that vitriolic contract battle with Vida Blue and the pitcher's attorney, Robert Gerst. While chatting with newsmen about the negotiations, Finley called Gerst a "hook-nosed notary." A few moments after describing the Jewish attorney in that fashion, Finley approached Bergman and asked Ron not to use that statement in his story. "He said it just slipped," says Bergman. "But then he forgot to tell the Associated Press guy not to put that phrase in the story, and it made the national wire."

Bergman's running partner for the first four Oakland seasons was John Lindblom of the San Jose *Mercury-News*, now a facile columnist for that organization. John didn't have very many confrontations with Charlie. Well, hardly ever.

> *John Lindblom:* More than once he called me a son of a bitch. And he vented his wrath on me in 1970 at his farm in LaPorte during an event at which he was supposed to be the proper host. This was after he notified the A's press corps of his intent to send the slumping Jackson to the minor leagues if Reggie didn't start producing at the plate. After learning who it was that informed the disconsolate Reggie of his threat, Finley singled me out while I was speaking with a couple of players and their wives. In a loud monotone, he said, "You're a goddamn blabbermouth. You know that, don't you?" My explanation that I was merely performing the duties of my assignment seemed to go unnoticed. My embarrassment over the incident was not abated by Charlie's admission a few minutes later that I had done exactly what he himself hoped I would do.

Somebody had to tell Reggie, huh?

Twice, the office of the commissioner of baseball has become involved with a Finley press matter. The first occasion was Charlie's first year in baseball, back in Kansas City in 1961. The veteran Ernie Mehl of the Kansas City *Star*, writing about the firing of A's manager Joe Gordon, said that Charlie interfered with Gordon's decision-making processes constantly. There was a suggestion that Joe once handed the umpires a lineup card with the imprinted phrase "Approved by C.O.F." And C.O.F. didn't like Mehl's work at all, so on August 20, 1961, Charlie staged an "Ernie Mehl Appreciation Day" at the ball park and presented the writer, in absentia of course, with a "Poison Pen Award." A truck bearing a large poster of a poison pen was driven around Kansas City's Municipal Stadium and halted at home plate as the public address system blared the strains of "Who's Afraid of the Big, Bad Wolf?" Four days later, Commissioner Ford Frick apologized personally and in the name of the game to Ernie Mehl. The next intercession of the commissioner's office into the public relations activities of the Owner came eleven years later, and wouldn't you know it: Bergman was involved. Finley had tossed Ron off the team's charter flights. No, not in midair, though one might presume that possibility occurred to Finley; or if it hasn't, it will.

Nominally, a baseball team's traveling secretary makes travel and hotel reservations for members of the press who accompany the club on the road. If it's a charter flight, the writer's newspaper will be billed later for a share of the expenses; on a commercial flight there's a firm fare. The point is, there's no trouble for the traveling secretary to add one more body to a flight or one name to a list of fifteen or more hotel reservations. This service to the press is a simple, rather traditional courtesy in baseball, and Bergman was extended this hallowed dispensation by the A's from the moment he began covering the club. Suddenly, midway through the 1972 season, he was told to make his own travel arrangements. The source of the order was Charles O. Finley, and Ron's travel travails percolated tiny but noisy ripples in the baseball world.

In order to reintroduce himself to his wife, a patient woman named Sally, Bergman took a short vacation during the '72 season and, lemminglike, listened to radio broadcasts of Athletics games. That year's air team was Monte Moore, Jim Woods, and Jimmy Piersall, whose collective work was once labeled by an impertinent fellow as "Radio Free Oakland."

Bergman listened one evening as the triumvirate intoned the name of Charles O. Finley eight times in one inning. As Ron recalls the broadcast, one of the announcers saluted Charlie's grand appearance at a banquet; a second announcer suggested that many gatherings would be overwhelmed to have Finley as a guest speaker; a third air voice pointed out that Charlie would love to make all of these appearances if only he weren't so busy running his three great sports franchises and, of course, expending his energies to provide all of this great baseball for Oakland. That particular evening happened to be Bergman's weekly deadline time for his A's piece in *The Sporting News*, so he wrote, as a note, that there were times it appeared the Oakland announcers were in a contest "to see who can make the most complimentary remarks about Owner Charles O. Finley."

Word about the item reached Finley while he was dining in a Chicago key club with physician friends. He was, in Victorian terms, not amused.

> *Ron Bergman:* He phoned me in Dallas, and told me that I had ridiculed his announcers. He said that he never told them what to say. I said I thought they were good announcers and that they'd be better if they didn't mention his name eight times every inning. And then he told me that I was on my own on the road, that the team would no longer make reservations for me. I phoned the hotel at our next stop, the Leamington in Minneapolis, and found out that he had phoned them personally and cancelled my reservation.

Subsequent reports in *The Sporting News, Sports Illustrated*, and many daily newspapers painted Ron in heroic terms. Finley had to be suffering from the penultimate displeasure of seeing himself upstaged in the media by, for chrissakes, *that* little shit stirrer. Charlie had trimmed himself into turbulence in the friendly skies of Bergman. Ron phoned the commissioner's office for succor, comparing the deed to barring a writer from the clubhouse. He spoke with Bowie Kuhn aides Joe Reichler and Monte Irvin and suggested that Charlie's act could set a precedent for censorship.

Reichler, Kuhn's legate to the Oakland Papacy, sought a compromise and soon phoned Bergman with the suggestion that Ron call Charlie—not to apologize but simply to say that he was sorry the incident happened and that often items a writer thought were "cute" tended to emerge differently in print. Bergman says he was indeed sorry about what took place but had no intention of apologizing to the Owner.

"I called Charlie and told him these things," says Bergman. "And he screamed and said that he wanted an apology. I told him that I wouldn't apologize, and we hung up."

Back in Oakland, Finley and Bergman met for their slice of summitry in a tunnel leading to the field. The Owner asked the writer if he wished to get back on the charter flights. Ron said yes, and did.

A few months later, *Sports Illustrated* quoted Finley as saying that the Bergman affair was "probably beneath my dignity."

At the end of Finley's first Oakland season, the Owner fired manager Bob Kennedy. Oakland *Tribune* sports editor George Ross wrote that the Owner owed the A's fans an explanation for canning the only winning skipper Charlie had ever employed to that date (1968). And Charlie telephoned George to say, "I don't owe anybody an explanation about anything. I'm running a private business."

CHAPTER **XIV**

# FOOD, MUSIC,
# AND A MULE

Under what I consider an archaic facet of baseball "law," sportswriters are put in charge of making press arrangements for league championship playoff series and the World Series. The job falls to the chairman of the local chapter of the Baseball Writers Association of America, who also is covering the games. He is supposed to coordinate credentials, seating, feeding, and a variety of other services with the public relations department of the baseball team playing for the pennant and world's championship. For that job, he is paid a maximum of fifteen hundred dollars by the club (five hundred for the playoffs, a grand for the Series). The money is nice but really inadequate for the time and headaches involved. It seems professionally preposterous for one writer to boss around other writers by telling them where to sit and where to type. Better, as with the National Football League, that a group of baseball public relations men handle this entire chore. But the Writers Association has crunch with the game's Establishment, so the procedure lingers.

In Oakland in 1972 and 1973, yours truly was the anointed press arrangements czar. In dealing with Charlie Finley, I found the task to be great fun but just one of those things. In 1972 we tangled over the matter of his beloved Dixieland band, a crisis I'll elaborate on later. The following season the cause célèbre involved box lunches. Repeat: box lunches. Until a few days before the thrilling postseason events, Charles O. Finley had decided not to serve box lunches to the media, a rather grim prospect in view of the fact all of the Oakland games began at lunchtime.

From what I could determine, Finley was pissed at me for overordering $2.50 box lunches in 1972. In estimating the number of press in attendance at the playoffs and series that year, I figured that ninety-five percent of the people who had applied for credentials were coming. Of course they didn't, and the A's were—perhaps literally—forced to eat the cost of all those extra box lunches. At that time I was not aware of Finley's food fetishism, although had I been I still would have accidentally overestimated the box lunch order.

In 1972, the box lunch contained three pieces of chicken, a roll, a pat of butter, two—or it could have been three—cherry tomatoes and two oatmeal cookies. The lunch was the same at each game.

But in 1973 I was advised by Finley's hands that there would be no box lunches. No food in the press box, save for Cokes and coffee. I reacted with sturdy sanctimony. He couldn't do that to me—I liked his box lunches.

I asked a fellow at the American League to order Finley to give the press lunches and was told that Finley didn't have to feed us if he didn't want to. I asked a fellow at the commissioner's office to order the American League to order Finley to give us our goddamn box lunches and was told that it was a league matter, the commissioner's office couldn't interfere. But, I was informed, someone in the commissioner's office would negotiate with Finley on the matter of box lunches at the World Series as that went beyond being merely a league matter.

Both the league and the commissioner's office provide hospitality funds to clubs involved in postseason play but can't demand that the club buy so many pounds of cracked crab or so many fifths of Chivas Regal. And Finley held to his box lunch embargo as I prepared a memo to the press explaining that the owner of the A's chose not to feed us in our little working stalls.

He may have wanted me to beg; I'm not sure. But as the playoff games neared, I'd reached the point of having more fun complaining about the lack of lunches than begging he serve them. Finally, he budged. He phoned to ask if I thought it might be a good idea to serve some sort of food in the press box. I told him it was a helluva notion. What, he asked, did I think of a box lunch containing three pieces of chicken ("a breast, a thigh, and a drumstick"), a roll, a pat of butter, two—or it could have been three—cherry tomatoes and two oatmeal cookies?

"Everybody liked the oatmeal cookies last year," he said.

I asked if a friend had given him fifty thousand free oatmeal cookies, and he became rather indignant. "I wouldn't do a thing like that," he said. I told him I knew he wouldn't.

Was that type of lunch okay with me?

Sure.

How many should he order?

I told him.

Was I sure that was how many he should order?

I told him that this year I had more experience in estimating press attendance.

Okay, but could I guarantee there would be no glaring surplus?

I told him I'd eat the extras myself if necessary.

"You got your box lunches," he said.

"Thanks for your cooperation," I said.

And the hundreds of writers and broadcasters at three playoff and four World Series games in Oakland in 1973 each ate twenty-one pieces of chicken (seven breasts, seven thighs, seven drumsticks), seven rolls smeared with seven pats of butter, fourteen—or it could have been twenty-one—cherry tomatoes and fourteen oatmeal cookies. Plus an unrestricted amount of Cokes and coffee.

*Finley* (to a *Parade* writer): I can cook anything.

*Tom Corwin:* Finley has the largest appetite of any man I've ever seen. I've never seen anybody eat like he does. We were having a staff meeting in the office at Oakland one winter—1968 or 1969—and it got to be dinnertime. He was there working with six or seven of us. He said we should order some chicken so we wouldn't have to stop working, so he ordered about seven buckets of Colonel Sanders. One bucket per person. Well, I can't eat a whole bucket of chicken by myself. That's like fifteen pieces. But he insisted on ordering one bucket per person, even though I kept saying that two or three of us could share one. Because we'd been working all day, I ate maybe five or six pieces. I was hungry. When we were all finished, there was maybe just under one full bucket left. And Finley had the largest stack of bones in front of him that you can *imagine*. He must have eaten two buckets by himself.

*Jim Bank:* The way he orders at a restaurant is he'll take a menu, see, and order for everybody. He won't say bring us some ribs or bring us this kind of food or that. He'll just say, "Bring me the top line. Bring me this column." And you eat it. If it's sitting there, he tells you to eat it. Or he'll eat it. He's a big eater.

*Munson Campbell:* There was a restaurant in New York that was always his favorite—on Fifty-second and Third Avenue—called The King of the Sea. That was his lair. He would pompously parade in and with that monotonic walrus voice of his say something like: I'm

Charlie Finley and I'm ready to eat. As soon as he got to a table, the first thing he would do—and this was in the evening at dinner—was take off his coat, loosen his tie, roll up his sleeves, and start this Henry the Eighth-type attack on the food. There would just be oysters by the dozen, clams by the dozen. He would order for everybody and *insist* that they eat it.

The 1972 World Series between the Oakland A's and Cincinnati Reds will best be remembered by baseball fans for Gene Tenace's four home runs, Joe Rudi's wall-hanging catch, the untoward number of one-run games (six) and Dick Williams' fifty thousand trips to the mound to confer with his pitchers. Quite a Series, particularly if you were not dancing the Great Dixieland Band Stomp, as was yours truly. The Stomp, which I often looked upon more as the Shuffle, was a petty little struggle initially involving Charles O. Finley, his staff, and myself. Before the song was ended, the malady lingered on to encompass several hundred members of the sporting press and, quite predictably, the office of the Commissioner of All of Baseball. This musical mishmash lacked the basic sustenance and excitement of the Great Box Lunch Affair of the 1973 World Series, but it was, to say the least, noisier.

Although I was in charge of Oakland press arrangements for the 1972 Series, Finley's staff, overworked but durable, packaged the facilities but needed quasi-official approval from me. Naturally, Charlie told the staff what to do and how to do it. One of the logistical arrangements placed the working press room adjacent to the hospitality room, both in the bowels of the Oakland Coliseum Complex. This meant that hundreds of typewriters would be clacking within putting range of hundreds of eaters and drinkers—separated only by draped partitions. The layout certainly seemed convenient. A writer could pop down to the press room from his press box seat and immediately begin working, after first dipping into the hospitality room wassail bowl. It would all work out. Sure it would.

About two weeks before Series time, an A's staff member told me that Charlie wanted The Swingers playing in the hospitality room after every game. The Swingers was a marvelous Dixieland combo employed by Finley to strum through the stands during games. The Swingers was essentially the same combo that in 1970 played at A's games under the name McNamara's Band. Fetching, because John McNamara managed Oakland that season. The band stayed after McNamara was canned. Of all the Finley promotions and gimmicks, these Dixieland fellows—solid professionals—have been among the most popular. They do good work. The trouble was, there in October of 1972, their good work might intrude upon the intended good work of hundreds of journalists. Editorial offices in newspapers are not the quietest places in the world, but neither are reporters acclimated to the eardrum-piercing strains of "Muskrat Ramble."

I suggested to the Finley staff member with whom I was working that The Swingers be excluded from the hospitality room. I did not think the request was unfair, and as it turned out I was not alone in that belief.

The staff member checked with the Owner and told me The Swingers came with the deal. I next whined about the music to Charlie's secretary in Oakland, Miss Carolyn Coffin, who I felt might make more headway. She listened courteously and said she would see what she could do. She could do nothing—immediately. Then we forged a compromise. The Swingers would indeed play, but would not begin the music until approximately one hour after the game ended. That was the best I could do, short of asking Bowie Kuhn to intercede before the fact. As some wise fellow once told me, "events will occur." Patience, patience.

The first Oakland game in the 1972 World Series was washed out moments before play was to begin. The press surged downstairs to the clubhouses to grab some kind of rainy day story. (For instance, because the A's led the Series two games to none would their "momentum" now be interrupted? Or, what did Dick Williams think of Cincinnati manager Sparky Anderson's crew cut? That sort of thing.) This kind of story is much more difficult to pound out than a game story. There are no heroes or goats or key plays. Just rain.

As I recall, I discussed with Joe Rudi the Freudian aspects of his memorable catch in Game Two. For years I had referred to Rudi as "The Modesto Miracle" (he comes from a small farm town near Modesto, California), and now that he had justified my persistent use of that preposterous nickname I was going to write the story to death. After finishing my clubhouse chat with Rudi, I drifted to the press-hospitality room area—where The Swingers were blaring "South Rampart Street Parade." I looked at my watch to make certain the one-hour grace period hadn't expired. No, it hadn't. The game had "ended"—been officially postponed—only twenty minutes ago. I figured the band must not have gotten the word, or misunderstood, or something. But before I spoke with any of the musicians, I thought I'd check next door in the working press room to make sure the noise level of the music would be as provocative as I had presumed. Yes, it was. At least a dozen writers asked if I could put a stop to the music. So I went back into the hospitality room and talked to the leader of The Swingers. Between numbers, of course. He said nobody had said anything to him about anything. And then I spotted Charlie at a table.

"Sorry to bother you, Charlie, but if you recall our agreement, the band isn't supposed to start playing for another half hour or so. Guess nobody told them."

Charlie said he had given orders for immediate music. "There's no game," he said. "So there's nothing to write about." A rainout did not apply to our agreement. He would not stop the music. I tried to explain that writers still had to file stories, that probably these rainy day stories would take more concentration—and thus require a more pacific atmosphere—than actual game stories. The Owner was adamant about there being nothing to write. And I walked away, feeling that if I pursued my beef any further Charlie might have sent The Swingers into the motel rooms of every writer at four in the morning. I returned to the working press room, now being inundated with the living stereo sounds of "Is It True What They Say about Dixie?" Certainly it was true. I told the writers that the Owner refused to silence his combo, then I went back into the hospitality room and drank heavily. Where was "The Modesto Miracle" when I needed him?

The Baseball Writers Association of America meets to elect officers at World Series time. The election meeting of 1972 was the morning after the rainout and was well attended. The only major topic discussed at the meeting—after elections had been cleared away—was the issue of The Swingers. Never before had so many heard so loudly from so few. I was asked for an explanation, and outlined with great charm and dignity the events leading up to the previous evening. It all seemed so petty, but the noise had been damned annoying to the guys trying to do their work. When I finished soliloquizing, other writers took the floor and demanded some sort of action to silence The Swingers. Bill Gleason, a columnist for the Chicago *Sun-Times*, was vehement in his damnation of the musical interlude. He suggested that National Football League commissioner Pete Rozelle would never permit this sort of disturbance to happen in the Super Bowl press facilities. Gleason was mad, very mad. And quite right, too.

Joe Reichler, the baseball commissioner's right hand for public relations matters, stepped in to suggest that organized baseball was as organized as organized football. He didn't want to hear anymore of this condemnatory attitude toward the grand old game.

"Then get rid of that fucking band," yelled some writer.

"Yah, muzzle the bastards," said another.

Several resolutions were introduced, in more parliamentary terms, of course, and a compromise measure was passed with unanimity urging the commissioner to order Charles O. Finley to knock off the music. Not just for the first hour after game's end. But period.

And Joe Reichler promised he'd see to it.

An event had occurred.

I smiled all afternoon. I kept hearing Bowie Kuhn telling Charlie Finley, "It's not that we all don't love Dixieland, Charlie, but . . ." and I smiled all afternoon.

A half hour before game time, I got a call in the press box from Joe Reichler. He wanted me to meet him in front of the A's dugout. He said Charlie wanted to talk to me about the band. He said that he had worked things out with Charlie and that I should listen courteously to everything Charlie had to say and show my appreciation for what Charlie was about to do.

Down on the field, the Owner was talking to Dick Young, the feisty columnist of the New York *Daily News*. Finley interrupted his chat with Dick to greet me, shake my hand, tell me what a helluva job he thought I was doing. My thanks were effusive. Young turned to leave, but Charlie asked him to listen to what he was about to say.

The Owner told us he had tried his best to make the Series hospitality room a gala place for us. He said he thought we all enjoyed having his mule, Charlie O., walking among the buffet tables and greeting the revelers. He said he thought we all were delighted with the fine spread of beef and seafood. He said he assumed we all would be pleased by having The Swingers stroll in our midst but that he didn't realize the noise of the music would be irksome to some.

"Now I have given this business of the music a lot of thought," he said. "And I have come up with an idea. What do you think about my removing The Swingers completely from the hospitality room? What do you think about that, Dick?"

Young, who also may have been briefed by Reichler, said he thoroughly enjoyed the music but felt that Charlie might be correct.

"Is that gonna be okay with you, Herb?" Charlie inquired.

I told him I thought we could manage just fine without The Swingers.

"Okay then," Charlie said, and there were warm handshakes all around. "But remember this," said the Owner, "I'm not getting rid of my fucking mule."

"If that mule goes, Charlie, so do I," I said.

We damn near kissed.

Garry Schumacher, retired as public relations director of the San Francisco Giants, glanced out of the press box in the Oakland Coliseum and spotted, down along the left field line, a small child riding on the back of a mule. With a half century of baseball wisdom and lore fed by his basic Brooklynese, the old fellow twinkled as he told the rest of us, "Dat's gotta be da best p.r. gimmick dey got goin' heah. Dat mule. Dat's a good ting dat mule."

"People love Charlie O.," Finley told a writer in 1965. "He is a genuine Missouri mule donated to the A's by Governor Warren Hearnes of Missouri after the greatest mule search in history. Everybody's got to see this mule." He once called Charlie O. "the smartest mule that ever lived." One must treat one's namesake with reverence. One must give one's namesake a good life. Charlie O. has been very good to Charlie O., who has been very good for Charlie O., who has found in this animal a loyalty above reproach. The mule didn't put the Owner on the map but it certainly made him more recognizable. Thank you, Governor Hearnes.

In the Kansas City days, the Owner used to take the mule on road trips. He once rode Charlie O. through the lobby of the Americana Hotel in New York. During the World Series of 1972 and 1973, the mule grazed outside the Series headquarters in Oakland. A handsome sorrel. Fourteen hundred pounds. Just over sixteen hands high. "Outside of the Army mules, I'd say he's a big mule," says Stanley Cosca, an Oakland stable owner. In 1974, Charlie O. was nearly eleven years old, and Cosca figured the mule's life expectancy at thirty-five, equal to a 140-year-old person.

Finley was paying at least one hundred dollars a month to board Charlie O. at Cosca's Skyline Ranch in Oakland in 1974. In Kansas City the mule had lived at the Benjamin Stable in the southeast part of town. When the club moved West in 1968, the mule came along. His stall was the only one in Cosca's stable equipped with AM-FM stereo. Cosca said he kept the set tuned to KFOG, a nice, dreamy, middle-of-the-road music station. "Very soothing," says Cosca. "He likes it." Twice a day, at about 6:00 A.M. and 4:00 P.M., Charlie O. was eating eight to ten pounds of a special formula feed Cosca called "all in one," produced by the Newt Robinson farm in Stockton, California. "Charlie O. thrives on it," Cosca said. It was a mix of alfalfa, hay, minerals, and molasses "all chopped up." According to Cosca, the mule's food bill ran to about thirty-five dollars monthly. Water was kept on the opposite side of the mule's stall so he couldn't get to both the food and water at the same time, Cosca said.

Every day, Cosca's lovely twenty-one year old daughter Alexis would drive up to the ranch in her truck and draw a nicker or two from Charlie O. She would ride him daily in the Oakland Hills. "A mule's a lot stronger and more powerful than a horse," she said. "Charlie O.'s gait is smoother than a horse but he's not as fast. He's one in a million. Mules are generally very ornery, and they can get a person with their temperament, but he's not like that at all. He's never kicked anybody."

On weekends and holidays and other special occasions, Charlie O. came to the ball park to strut around and give kids rides. "It's a big thrill for the kids to be able to sit on Charlie," said Cosca. "And the parents get a tremendous kick out of seeing their kids on him. We give rides to all the kids we can in the half hour we have before the game."

In the 1965 season in Kansas City, Finley one day was giving a writer a tour of the ball park when a young boy came over to the Owner and told him he'd come two hundred miles to see the mule. But on that day Charlie O. was being eclipsed by another animal. It was Rabbit Day. Finley was giving away 250 rabbits to illustrate to fans how fast his outfielders were, or something. The boy told Finley he didn't care about rabbits, he wanted to see the mule. The Owner was persuaded by the lad's persistence and walked outside the stadium to get Charlie O. out of his trailer. Finley led the mule through a gate just beyond center field. The boy would get his ride now, huh? Well, no. Finley and the mule nearly bumped into A's center fielder Jim Landis. The second base umpire began running toward the outfield waving his arms and yelling at the Owner, "Get the hell off the field." The game had already begun.

> *Question:* Does the mule recognize the Owner?
> *Stanley Cosca:* I feel he recognizes him to this extent: When Charlie goes up to pet the mule, he'll kind of reach for him and the

mule will stand there and accept it. That's pretty good. That means he'll take to Finley pretty good. But in all honesty, Mr. Finley just doesn't have all that much time to spend with the mule.

*Alexis Cosca:* A mule isn't as affectionate an animal as a dog is. They don't recognize people. Sure, the mule recognizes my dad and me but only because we feed him. He'd recognize whoever fed him.

Alexis says the mule might bring somewhere between seven hundred and fifteen hundred dollars in a sale. There would be no trouble, she says, for someone to get a good day's work out of Charlie O. No retraining would be necessary. "You could still use him for packing or whatever you want, just because he has the disposition that he does. He can do anything, and probably better than the mules that they do use," Alexis said.

In 1973 Charlie O. suffered from a minor malady that caused the hair in his tail to fall out. Cosca ordered a custom-made tail at a cost of fifty-five dollars. Finley, he says, paid the bill without any questions. "Mr. Finley has always been very fair, very open when it comes to any bills for the mule," says Stanley Cosca.

# XV

## OUT AT HOME

The contrast was painfully marked. "Sugar in the Morning," a Finley favorite, was hummed, strummed, whistled, sung, shouted in October, 1972. How sweet it was indeed after waiting twelve years, after spending two and a half million in player bonuses, after mashing managers like so many soda crackers. The formula was right: S was the sum of S and S. There atop the dugout in Cincinnati are Charlie and Shirley Finley and Dick and Norma Williams. They are weaving and waving, kissing and hugging, crying and glowing. They had showed 'em. In the clubhouse of the new world's champions of baseball a newsman is asking the Owner how he feels and the Owner, living a fantasy, juiced on pure pleasure and God knows what else, pauses, grins orgasmically, sings hoarsely "Sugar in the Morning, Sugar in the. . . ." That was 1972. The next October they showed 'em again, without sweetness and hugging and strumming. Too much reality in the Oakland Coliseum after the 1973 World Series.

Dick Williams was quitting. The press wasn't forgetting the indignity of the Mike Andrews case. Shirley had a reported eye ailment and hid any feelings behind dark glasses. Charlie was in ghastly bad shape, still recuperating from his reported heart attack of the summer, trailed by doctors, tranquilized, as pale as somebody else's white home uniform. S and S weren't adding up. It just wasn't the same, and would never be again.

> *Roz Corwin:* Everyone in Gary wanted the A's to win in 1972. Not for the team or just because it was the Series, but for him, for Charles. Because he had worked so hard and this was his one goal.
> *Frances Helmerick McBride:* At our first class reunion—our twenty-fifth in 1961—he had us out to the farm and he made the statement that if and when his baseball team ever went to a World Series, anybody in the class who wanted to could be his guest.

Joe and Mavis Goffiney went. "We were in Cincinnati for the first two games, and we saw Charlie in the hotel bar. He said, 'C'mon along back to Oakland, you'll have the time of your life. All expenses paid. Nothing to worry about. I'll take care of everything.' Which he did," says Joe Goffiney. "About eight or ten of us went back to Oakland and there were a lot of others from Gary in Oakland when we got there. Friends of his from LaPorte, too." The Goffineys were in New York for the 1973 Series with the Finley party. Joe had gall bladder problems there and told Finley he would have to go back home to Hobart, Indiana, instead of returning to Oakland for the final game. "In his generosity, he said, 'Now, Joe, you can come back to Oakland with us and I'll get the best doctors in the country and put you in the hospital. We'll see that everything is all right.' I said, 'Charlie, you're going to worry about me and your team is in the Series?' And you know he does everything himself."

> *An A's player:* His life is constant business, business, business. I think he even made a big thing of his family being officers and stockholders of the club purely for business reasons. I mean, why

bring in outsiders? I think he *uses* his family, by trying to promote a family image, by having his wife travel with him. I know he doesn't trust anybody, and I sometimes wonder if he even trusts his family. Oh, maybe to an extent he does, but he still likes to rule them. I remember that one of his sons had to come to one of our players during a Series to ask for an autographed ball because his father wouldn't let him have one. So you wonder. I think he doesn't want to give his children everything. He wants to make them work for it. But at the same time, there are things that should come easier for these kids. They've got an advantage, and he doesn't let them use that advantage. And he could take more time off to be with his family. He includes them in his life in business ways, not in terms of love so much.

Three weeks after the player made those observations, in late March, 1974, Shirley McCartney Finley filed for divorce. As someone who'd known them for years said, "I'm not surprised it happened. I'm just surprised it took this long to happen."

Shirley sought possession of the farm in LaPorte, bringing an end to Charlie's annual steak-lobster barbecues there for the ball club. "It was always nice," said former A's pitcher Chuck Dobson. "But it was just a big put-on for his influential friends. We'd have a beautiful dinner while his cronies sat around and rubbed shoulders with all the jocks. Big beautiful house, big beautiful yard, big beautiful steaks, big beautiful bottles of liquor, big beautiful children running around."

Seven Finley children. Shirley was once quoted as calling the family "the Finley Nine." Charlie would call them "my board of directors." At the time of the divorce filing, three sons were still living at home—Martin, 18; Luke, 17; David, 15. Paul, 21, was a student at Arizona State University. Son Charlie, Jr., 30, was married and lived just down the road from the farm. The eldest daughter, Sharon, was married to a LaPorte orthodontist. She had given Charlie his first grandson. The other daughter, Kathleen, a one-time campus beauty queen at the University of Colorado, was working in the cosmetics field.

Charles, Jr., had once worked for his father in the Chicago insurance office. A friend of the young man said, "Charlie told him, 'Just watch me work. Do what I do.' After a while, young Charlie asked for something to do. He either quit or was fired."

> *A Finley employee:* Charlie worships his daughters. I've heard him talk to them on the phone. I think he cares very much about his family and they care very, very much about him, but you can see the special gleam in his eye when it comes to his daughters. During one of the Series, I saw him ordering around his sons, just like he treats everybody. But he talks really, really sweet to the daughters.
>
> *Finley:* Our two daughters are redheads with brown eyes, and when they were babies my wife would always dress them in green and gold. I just think that's the most beautiful color combination there is.

Charlie would often talk about Shirley in reverential terms. "That gal can do anything," he told writer Robin Orr, to whom he admitted, "I don't spend as much time [on the farm] as I'd like. My wife will tell you I'm like a bad penny—liable to show up anytime."

"He spent very little time at home," said Ron Mihelic. "All the kids grew up more or less with their mother and the maid, Mildred. But the times he was home, the kids had to toe the line."

Insurance and sports insatiably devoured his time. In 1961 he had headed the national TB Seal drive with great results, a monument to his own recovery from the disease. ("The next year I had to remind him to send a check," says an employee.) His baseball yearbooks reported that he was a "32nd Degree Mason, active in his church, and a sought-after speaker all over the country." There was no time for hobbies, long vacations, or any form of what some people call relaxation. ("The only time he reads anything is when he's looking for his name in the paper," says an employee.)

Shirley was serving her community, especially as a fund raiser. The Salvation Army got itself a new building in LaPorte with Shirley's help. She spent time with the local Literary Guild, hospital auxiliary, Presbyterian church. Artists met in her home. She herself turned out landscape paintings and was an efficient interior designer. "She's got a kind of charisma, just like him," said A's player Ted Kubiak. "She's got a kind of glow about her. She seems like a forceful woman, just through her appearance. I mean her eyes and everything."

> *Ron Mihelic:* My dad got along very well with Charlie until the blowup. Two days after it happened, my dad moved off the farm.

Neither Ron nor John Mihelic will talk about "the blowup," which occurred in mid-March of 1974 on the LaPorte farm. The San Francisco *Chronicle* referred to the incident as a "postmidnight marital battle."

"To the very end, I looked on him as a friend," said John Mihelic. "Even when this business happened. I just happened to walk in on what transpired and couldn't walk out. Since that night, I haven't seen or heard from him."

Mildred Day, the Finley's long-time maid, also moved from the farm after "that night," after "the blowup." She was at her Gary home when I phoned. "All I can say is nice things about him," she said. "He was always good to me for twenty years. So all I can tell you is that he's a nice man. He was a travelin' man, always away on business somewhere. I just quit 'cause I won't be in the middle."

Charlie moved to a posh lakeside apartment building in Chicago. Brother Fred, still working in Finley's insurance office mailroom, had a home across the state line in Munster, Indiana, and the ailing parents, Oscar and Burmah, resided in a house Charlie had bought for them in LaPorte, only minutes from the farm.

Shirley Finley comes to the door of the eighteen-room "farmhouse" to answer the bell in July, 1974. I explain the book project, and she asks if Mr. Finley has authorized it. I tell her no, and she says she would have to ask his approval before she would agree to be interviewed. The ice-blue eyes are neither frightened nor angry. Merely tired. I ask for instructions on backing out of the driveway, and she tells me with charm and courtesy.

Her attorney, John Newby, Sr., of LaPorte, later says, "It wouldn't be wise for her to talk because it's a sticky little deal."

Patrolman K. E. Layton of the LaPorte County Police Department is a pleasant, talkative young man. In response to my questions, he says there have been several calls for police to come to the Finley farm in the past few years. "Always the same thing," he says. "Him and her." Family dispute stuff, he says. "Somebody would just call us and tell us to come and then hang up. Seemed to be a different voice every time. Everything was always over by the time we got there." Nobody, he says, ever preferred charges against anybody. He says he was one of the investigating officers on that March night. He says he's not surprised at the civil action that followed.

Shirley's suit cited an irretrievable breakdown of the Finley's thirty-two-year marriage, recent grounds for divorce in Indiana. She immediately got a restraining order to prevent the Owner and General Manager from "molesting or disturbing" her. She had attended all the arbitration sessions with Charlie in San Francisco in February, been present at the Alvin Dark managerial unveiling in Oakland later that same month. But now her baseball career was over.

She asked for custody of the three youngest sons and weekly support payments of $1,250. Charlie countered with an offer of one hundred dollars a week; she raised the ante to $1,750. Ultimately, she would be granted provisional support of $1,250 plus preliminary attorney's fees of fifteen thousand dollars. At one point in the summer-long proceedings in a Valparaiso, Indiana, court, Charlie was cited for contempt for failure to pay overdue support money and the attorney's fees. A few days after the citation, he paid.

In testimony, Charlie paints a bleak personal financial picture. The extent of his liquid assets, he says, is his share of a twenty-five thousand dollar joint checking account with Shirley in Jack Morfee's bank in Gary. He talks about a three hundred thousand dollar personal loan, says he has a loan with Harris Trust of Chicago for two and a half million dollars, with stock as collateral. If forced to sell the stock, he says, he would get "twenty-five cents on the dollar." He says his corporation owns twenty-five different types of stocks and that Shirley holds thirty percent of the Charles O. Finley company. His current business profits, he says, are running half a million dollars behind expectations. He says he had to borrow money in 1973 to pay his income taxes.

Then bigger bleak: "I could easily suffer a loss of between three and five million dollars" if forced to liquidate his stocks.

He tells Judge Alfred J. Pivarnik that Shirley is secretly putting aside money from their joint checking account. "I don't care what the amount is," he says. "It's the principle."

He complains about Shirley's telephone bills, says they're running between four hundred and six hundred dollars a month. His statement of properties (three farms in LaPorte County, two lots in Birmingham) reveals Charles O. Finley owns forty trees that cost him fifteen thousand dollars, including planting. Shirley asks for ten thousand dollars to take her four youngest sons on a European vacation. Shirley says she has no source of income but concedes that she maintains a small vegetable garden.

The Owner tells the judge he is opposed to divorce. Shirley tells a writer her suit "is just one of those things. A phase that's passing through the country."

There seems no rush by Shirley to obtain a final decree. The preliminaries could go on in perpetuity. In the summer of 1974, northern Indiana newspapers were filled with the financial folderol of the Finleys. The Gary *Post-Tribune* reported that Charlie "remains in reasonably good spirits in spite of potential financial woes brought out in Porter Circuit Court. During a lunch break between court sessions, Finley picked up the tab for everyone at his table in the local restaurant and invited all the same people to be his guests at a baseball game."

Old friend Roz Corwin was genuinely upset by the split. "It just hurts me to think that two such gracious people could be getting a divorce," she said. Joe and Mavis Goffiney hadn't seen or spoken to the Finleys in several months. "Didn't want to bother him," Joe said.

Nearly all of the people who had known Charlie in the old days in Gary refused to talk about the divorce matter. They spoke of the Owner with measured affection, or not at all. "They were all good friends," said John Mihelic. "A friend doesn't like to talk about a friend's bad points."

And on Gary's main street one old friend said, "Everybody in this town has a sense of loyalty to Charlie because he's a success. They believe all the good things they read in the paper. I've seen a lot of workers from the mill walk past the door of his insurance office in the National Bank Building—and you know he's never there—and they'll say to each other, 'What a great man he is.' And they don't even know him."


By 1974 Charlie had finally antagonized most of his veteran athletes. The A's now had their twelfth manager in fourteen years (ten different men—Bauer and Dark twice), their new pinch runner, those lesser rings and a burden to repeat as champions. Fans were calling them crybabies, true in some cases. But Joe Rudi is not a crybaby.

> *Joe Rudi:* In this last year, Mr. Finley has become a less kind person toward the players, and I've found my feelings changing toward him. Not just because I lost in arbitration either. I've spent ten years in his organization, and all that time he kept saying how badly he wanted a winner, right? So we won in '72, and he was excited and stuff. Then in '73 we came back and won it, and it was like he expected it. Like he's taking it for granted now. He told me over the phone that he was mad at the players 'cause we didn't stand behind him in the Mike Andrews case. He still believes he was right. So you kind of come to the realization over the years that he doesn't care about you as an individual. You're just a piece of meat out there. You're just an employee. You do your job, and as soon as you slip a little bit, you're gone. He doesn't care about you personally. I've seen so many guys come and go on this club. I used to think that I'll just be a nice guy and keep my mouth shut and then he won't be trying to get me. But then you see guys like Vida and Reggie and Sal rip him in the papers, and they're still here, making one helluva lot of money. It doesn't make any difference what you say to the man or what you say about him. Not now it doesn't, 'cause these guys are at the top of their career. But he'll get 'em down the line. If he still has this club four or five years from now and any of us are slipping, he's

liable to bury us. He treated this ball club better when it was a loser than he does now. Now he demands more of us and less of himself.

The Owner said that his poor health necessitated selling the A's in 1974. He placed the value at fifteen million dollars. A source says he later asked seventeen and a half million. Eventually the Owner said his doctors had given him a clean bill of health and by late summer spoke no more about selling.

"It's part of my happiness," he told the *Saturday Evening Post* in 1964. "And you don't go around selling happiness."

"If he didn't have the A's, he'd just shrivel up and fold away," said Rudi.

"The game of baseball keeps him going," said John Odom. "I think if he got out of baseball, he'd probably get down on himself and just go down period. He needs baseball. I think it gives him something to care about."

The *New York Times'* Leonard Koppett suggested in June, 1974, that Charlie not only intended to stay in baseball but was preparing to move out of Oakland in "the strikingly similar pattern" that preceded his departure from Kansas City. And Koppett cited attendance and television problems he said Finley had inflicted upon himself "to prove that this area [Oakland] can't or won't support baseball." Seattle and New Orleans seemed attractive to the Owner, wrote Koppett.

"The A's are not moving anywhere," Charlie told a friendly sportswriter. "They are in Oakland to stay. . . . Reports such as these [and there were others besides Koppett's] are grossly unfair to baseball fans and to myself. If they print enough of this sort of thing, people will become confused and not know what to believe."

Patterns.

The year Charlie Finley moved his club to Oakland, 1968, Paul

O'Neil wrote in *Life*: "Finley has been the most consistent of men; he has run his team the Finley way from the first, has continuously visited his enchantment with the unusual upon managers, fans, and other owners, and has never for a moment—despite paroxysms of ingratitude from press, public, and peers—abandoned his guiding principle: That everyone else is wrong, and Charles O. Finley is right, right, right. Circumstances now prompt two intriguing suggestions. Maybe they are. Maybe he is."

And that was before he won, and became righter. One columnist has suggested that Charlie's rightness, his pioneering, will eventually put him in the Hall of Fame. "Because he has been so good for baseball."

> *A Finley insurance client:* For a guy who has so much, he doesn't have very much. He's a very unfortunate man. He's unable to express fondness, regard, love, affection, or respect for anybody without relating it to something tangible. To money. He must be an extremely lonely man.

# EPILOGUE

Because of Charlie, despite Charlie, thanks to Charlie, no thanks to Charlie, the A's won it all anyway in 1974. Again. As Reggie Jackson had said in Mesa in March.

The specter of the Owner and General Manager was constant. Manager Alvin Dark, never without a Bible, freely admitted who was calling the shots. Pitching coach Wes Stock increased his visits to the mound because Charlie told him to get the hell out there more. Trainer Joe Romo scurried onto the field to examine every hangnail because Charlie told him to get the hell out there more.

Player grumbling was unceasing, as usual. Oakland teammates fought, as usual. In early June, Jackson and Billy North attempted to destroy each other in the clubhouse in Detroit. Charlie told Reggie he should have known better, and Jackson sulked the balance of the season after a .400 start. The major victim of the fight was catcher Ray Fosse, who tried to break it up and damned near broke his neck. His absence necessitated moving the remarkable left field glove of Joe Rudi to first base and first baseman Gene Tenace behind the plate. Neither was pleased, until Charlie flew in for a lengthy summit meeting in August and decided to reshuffle the best men back to their best positions. He would change his mind midway through the World Series.

323

Jim Hunter won twenty-five games; Rollie Fingers threw seventy-six times; Sal Bando hit rarely but always productively; Tenace constantly seemed to be either walking or homering; Rudi was a model of efficient consistency; Vida Blue suffered from lack of runs. The A's generally did not hit well in 1974. To win they needed the best pitching staff in the American League, which is what they got (a 2.95 staff earned run average).

A teenager of raw, rippling talent, Claudell Washington, was the sole significant addition to the club, although Charlie did reach out in August for that fellow he was always trying to get back from Minnesota, Jim Holt. The deal looked irrelevant as Holt went almost zero for September. In Game Four of the Series, however, Holt plunked a two-run pinch single, the game-winning hit.

Neither Allan Lewis, nor Frank Fernandez, nor Chuck Dobson was around for Oakland's 90–72 season in 1974. Lewis, "The Panamanian Express," had lost his legs to Herbie Washington, coached a bit in Birmingham, and then drifted back to Panama. Herbie closed with twenty-eight stolen bases. Charlie had said his legs would win ten games. Dark said he could count eight. Bando said "maybe" there were three. Bando also said Dark should not use Herbie in the playoffs or Series. The sprinter was used, though. He did not steal a base and was embarrassingly picked off first in Game Two while thousands of Dodger Stadium fans hooted at Charlie, who tapped the little wooden stick of his A's pennant against a railing.

Catcher Fernandez apparently caught the first ferry back to Staten Island after being released in the spring. An A's official said Frank's "arm has gone bad. He literally can't throw down to second base."

Dobson pitched well in Mexico, signed with the California Angels, and on the final day of the season pitched a five-hit 3–2 victory. Against Oakland.

About that same time the California Golden Seals unveiled their new uniforms, now tinted "Pacific Blue and California Gold." Charlie's Kelly Green was no more. "We wanted to establish a total Bay area identity," said Seals' president Munson Campbell, still running a caretaker operation for the National Hockey League.

Not one member of the Bay area press was invited aboard the A's charter flight for the American League playoffs and World Series (no, not even Ron Bergman), although the airborne retinue did include the reigning Miss California, a lustrous golden girl named Luci. She was at Charlie's side throughout the postseason fortnight and thus stirred reports of a romance, which must have flattered Charlie no end—and must have been well worth the expense of carting around Luci. Most of the Finley children were on the same trips, as were a few of the old Gary hands. Only Shirley was missing.

Mike Andrews turned up, albeit by proxy. On the eve of the Series opening in Los Angeles, an attorney for the 1973 October martyr filed a two and a half million dollar libel-slander suit against the Owner and Dr. Harry Walker. The damage suit charged that Andrews "has been held up to public scorn, contempt, ridicule and disgrace" and alleged that Dr. Walker made a false diagnosis of the condition of Mike's shoulder.

Early in 1975, Andrews signed to play in Japan. That was a few weeks after Oakland's best pitcher, Jim Hunter, had signed to play with the New York Yankees.

Hunter to the Yankees? It was as if Betsy Ross had been hired as a seamstress by the U.S.S.R. And it was also Finley's greatest gaffe. "Catfish" Hunter, because of Charlie's nominal tactics of parsimony and delay, became the most celebrated emancipated athlete in baseball history. The Dred Scott case got less ink.

The whole yarn started to unravel rather absurdly in the few days between the end of Oakland's 1974 playoff victory in Baltimore and the opening of the World Series in Los Angeles. Hunter had won twenty-five regular season games, the final playoff victory and, later, the Cy Young Award as the American League's premier thrower. He was tossing estimably in the first season of a two-year, one hundred grand per year contract—a contract that called for a deferred payment into a non-taxable annuity of fifty thousand dollars midway through the 1974 season. Nobody knew "Catfish" had Charlie on the hook until Hunter unintentionally spread the word that Finley's payment was late.

Hunter mentioned the situation to a playoff visitor, former A's teammate Mike Hershberger. And Mike casually told the story to Jerome Holtzman of the Chicago *Sun-Times*. And Holtzman casually told the world. The story was simple: On the eve of the World Series, Oakland's best pitcher was attempting to become a free agent on the charge that his employer was guilty of breach of contract. Hunter confirmed the story, and a wag suggested Jim would be signed by the Dodgers in time to start the Series against the A's.

Alert sports attorney Jerry Kapstein seized the day, held court in the Dodger press box and received almost more coverage than the game. Kapstein said Hunter had a good case. Hunter wanted Finley to pay the deferred fifty thousand dollars to anyone of his choosing, and chose a North Carolina insurance company. By selecting a "thing" and not a person as recipient, Hunter was depriving Finley of tax write-off benefits—perhaps about twenty-seven thousand five hundred dollars. Charlie fought furiously, but tardily, to protect this potential write-off.

At one point, at a meeting chaired by American League president Lee McPhail, Charlie offered to pay Jim. But it was too late. Kapstein and Hunter's down-home attorney, the deliciously named J. Carlton Cherry Esquire of Ahoskie, North Carolina, steered the case into arbitration. Finley testified that he would have paid the money much earlier but he and his tax accountant just never could seem to make contact. Finley testified that he was going to pay the money but was having trouble getting Shirley to sign the proper papers. Finley testified that he didn't think Hunter wanted the money right away, that he figured Jim preferred that the payment be deferred until after retirement—the sort of deal Charlie had with Reggie Jackson.

Hunter's case was clear-cut: He had a contract, the contract wasn't fulfilled.

Veteran arbitrator Peter Seitz decided for "Catfish." Not simply that the pitcher be paid, with interest—but that Jim Hunter was a free agent.

Finley—and many baseball people—never anticipated that verdict. Hunter could make a deal with any club he wished, and all except the San Francisco Giants wooed him. The teams would send representatives to Ahoskie. Over grits and red gravy they would dangle millions in front of Hunter and J. Carlton Cherry Esquire. Kansas City and San Diego talked big, big money. As did the Yankees. Finley dispatched Alvin Dark to Ahoskie.

"He'll sign anyplace but New York," said A's captain Sal Bando. "On our trips into New York, 'Cat' has never been too happy. He's a country boy, and I think he'd really be uncomfortable in New York. Unless they offer him an awful lot of money. 'Cat' is like a lot of us—not greedy, just money-conscious."

On New Year's Eve, 1974, James Augustus Hunter signed a contract worth approximately $3.75 million with the Yankees. According to reports, he received a one million dollar bonus, an annual salary of one hundred and fifty thousand dollars for five years, a one million dollar life insurance policy, a twenty-five thousand dollar insurance policy on each of his two children, two hundred thousand dollars in attorneys' fees, a ten-year retirement plan at fifty grand a year, and, presumably, a lifetime supply of filet for his eight zillion hunting dogs.

Babe Ruth had never done so well.

Naturally, Finley went to court in hopes of demolishing Seitz' ruling. Charlie was somber, downright funereal at the Alameda County Courthouse in Oakland in early January, 1975. Dark suit. Dark glasses. Nothing to say to the press.

The judge told Charlie's attorney he had done an excellent job, that Charlie should be pleased. "Quality work," said the judge. But, because of precedent, there was no way a California Superior Court judge could overrule the findings of an arbitrator unless the arbitrator acted in a "grossly irrational manner."

"This," said Finley's attorney, "is like hanging a man for a parking violation." There would be an appeal, but by the time it would be heard the 1975 season would be over.

Leonard Koppett of the *New York Times*, pocket calculator in hand, if not pocket, decided the major reason Finley delayed making the deferred payment to Hunter was not the tax deduction. If, theorized Leonard, Finley could have gotten Hunter to wait for the money until after retirement, Charlie could have made at least one hundred thousand dollars in interest on Hunter's money.

"Maybe," hoped Sal Bando, "John Odom can win fifteen games for us." That's without a pocket calculator.

Busy off-field times at that 1974 Series: Miss California, Andrews, Hunter. Plus a clubhouse brawl between pitchers Rollie Fingers and John Odom.

"Getting ourselves in shape for the Series," chuckled Charlie. Fingers needed five stitches in his head; Odom limped on a twisted, swollen ankle. And of course Odom won one Series game, while Fingers picked up a win and two saves and a new car as the week's MVP.

In the five games, four of which ended in scores of 3–2, the still-raggedy-ass A's pecked out a mere thirty hits and only sixteen runs. Pitching, defense (particularly Dick Green), and opportunism did it for Oakland. Dark managed with wisdom and courage and was rehired to "run" the club—two days after the Series ended.

Charlie managed a bit, too, during the playoffs and Series. Fosse's starting status against Baltimore was in doubt until Finley descended upon Oakland from the skies before playoff Game One and gave clearance. And of course Ray banged two big home runs in the postseason.

There was a giggly report that Charlie would present the A's lineup card to the umpires before Series Game Three in Oakland. "Rumors like that," said the Owner, "make us seem more ridiculous than we are." (What he did do before Game Three, however, was telephone President Ford asking him to throw out the first ball in the next night or two. The call was placed on a phone dangling near Charlie's seat behind the A's dugout. That made it nice for the TV audience. Earlier, Charlie had phoned former president Richard M. Nixon with the same invitation. Both men took rain checks, Charlie reported.)

Charlie did change the lineup, though, a few minutes before Game Four, a busy twilight in Oakland for the Owner. He had seen a news story quoting Dodger outfielder Billy Buckner as saying only three Athletics could make the L.A. club (Reggie, Sal, Rudi). Charlie copied the quotes on note paper, called a team meeting and paced up and down in front of the clubhouse cubicles reading aloud. He wore a black-and-white checkered fedora he said was a gift from Alabama football coach Paul Bryant, but the style was more Knute Rockne.

"Took him only thirty seconds to read that little story," said pitcher Paul Lindblad, "but he must have walked half a mile."

One wonders if he glanced at Gene Tenace during that Demosthenic stroll. He had benched Tenace, moved Rudi to first base, plopped Claudell Washington in left field. "All you can do," said Rudi, "is learn to accept what's gonna happen. This is nothing new around here."

(What was new was the nature of the press box food at this Series. Ham-and-cheese sandwiches had replaced the breast, thigh, and drumstick. Still oatmeal cookies, however.)

Tenace was less stoic than Rudi. Gene said Dark told him, "Charlie said it was his turn to make out the lineup card." Tenace said, "I just can't take this stuff anymore" and told the press he'd like to be traded "anywhere, San Diego, anyplace." The chances of Tenace's expendability increased within the week as Charlie obtained the excellent Billy Williams from the Chicago Cubs, recipients of Andrews' caddy, one Manny Trillo.

But Finley could have started himself and the Pointer Sisters in those final two games of the 1974 World Series and still won. Of course Claudell got a couple of hits, but it was Rudi's home run in the seventh inning of Game Five that finally did in the Dodgers. Charlie could have used the revenue from another Series game or two, for the regular season had not been commercially successful for him.

Attendance was down nearly 165,000 (to 836,712). Yet across the waters the situation was funereal. The Giants, in what was their worst San Francisco season by every measurement, were off some 315,000 (to a disgraceful 519,991). Now there were stories that Horace Stoneham and not Charlie Finley would leave the Bay area. Charlie said he offered Horace three million dollars to move the Giants; Stoneham said he couldn't remember such an offer. Another report had the A's moving to Seattle in 1976 to fulfill an

American League commitment. Or to the new Superdome in New Orleans, where former Kansas City Royal executive Cedric Tallis had been hired to lasso a baseball team. Charlie insisted, "I really don't want to sell the A's and I don't want to move. . . ."

Oakland Coliseum president Bob Nahas called the franchise shift rumors "consistent irritation" and cited our old friend the injunctive relief clause.

Again—or still—the games were almost incidental.

A few weeks before the end of the regular 1974 season, Charlie made a rare appearance before a group of Bay area writers and broadcasters and, exuding charm, handled all their questions. Toward the end of the afternoon, I turned on the tape recorder and asked him, "If you were to leave the game tomorrow, how would you want to be remembered?"

Epitaph time.

*Finley:* How would I want to be remembered? That thought, uh, has never entered my mind. I'm just like any athlete. If I left the game of baseball, physically or otherwise, I'd like to go out as a winner. Does that answer your question?

I said, "It's your answer, so I guess it does."
It will, for now, have to do.